Pursuing Equal Opportunities
The Theory and Practice of Egalitarian Justice

Pursuing Equal Opportunities: The Theory and Practice of Egalitarian Justice offers original and innovative contributions to the debate about equality of opportunity. Pursuing equality is an important challenge for any modern democratic society but this challenge faces two sets of difficulties: the theoretical question of what sort of equality to pursue and for whom, and the practical question concerning which legal and political institutions are the most appropriate vehicles for implementing egalitarian social policy and thus realizing egalitarian justice.

Part I sets out a theory of equality of opportunity that presents equal opportunities as a normative device for the regulation of competition for scarce resources. Parts II, III, and IV shift the focus to the consideration of the practical application by courts or legislatures or public policy makers of policies for addressing, respectively, racial, class, or gender injustices in Canada and the United States. The author examines in depth standardized tests in universities and colleges, affirmative action, workfare, universal health care, comparable worth, and the economic consequences of divorce.

Pursuing Equal Opportunities is unique in combining political and legal theory and cutting-edge socio-legal research, as well as in offering an overview of the concept of equality of opportunity and its history and application. As such, it will be of particular interest to professionals and graduate students in social and political philosophy, political science, law, sociology, and education.

Lesley A. Jacobs is Associate Professor and Director of the Law & Society Program at York University, Toronto.

Cambridge Studies in Philosophy and Public Policy

General editor: Douglas MacLean, *University of Maryland, Baltimore County*

Pursuing Equal Opportunities

The Theory and Practice of Egalitarian Justice

LESLEY A. JACOBS

York University

CAMBRIDGE
UNIVERSITY PRESS

PUBLISHED BY THE PRESS SYNDICATE OF THE UNIVERSITY OF CAMBRIDGE
The Pitt Building, Trumpington Street, Cambridge, United Kingdom

CAMBRIDGE UNIVERSITY PRESS
The Edinburgh Building, Cambridge CB2 2RU, UK
40 West 20th Street, New York, NY 10011-4211, USA
477 Williamstown Road, Port Melbourne, VIC 3207, Australia
Ruiz de Alarcón 13, 28014 Madrid, Spain
Dock House, The Waterfront, Cape Town 8001, South Africa

http://www.cambridge.org

First published 2004

Printed in the United States of America

Typeface Palatino 10/13 pt.   *System* LaTeX 2_ε [TB]

A catalog record for this book is available from the British Library.

Library of Congress Cataloging in Publication Data
Jacobs, Lesley A.
Pursuing equal opportunities : the theory and practice of egalitarian justice /
Lesley A. Jacobs.
p.   cm. – (Cambridge studies in philosophy and public policy)
Includes bibliographical references and index.
ISBN 0-521-82320-X – ISBN 0-521-53021-0 (pb.)
1. Equality.   2. Equality – United States.   3. Social justice.   4. Social justice –
United States.   I. Title.   II. Series.
JC575.J33   2004
320'.01'1–dc21   2003043504

ISBN 0 521 82320 x hardback
ISBN 0 521 53021 0 paperback

For Brenda, Aaron, Grace, Oliver, and now Noah

Contents

Contents

Contents

Acknowledgements

This book has been a project of mine for a number of years, and the arguments and analysis I finally offer here have evolved and unfolded in ways I didn't anticipate at the outset. This evolution in my thinking is a reflection of the valuable feedback I have received from many different sources. I am immensely grateful to several universities and their faculty for valuable support. York University in Toronto provided me with two years of paid leave that allowed me to concentrate on the overall research for the book. Harvard Law School awarded me a Liberal Arts Fellowship in 1997–98, during which I became immersed in debates about race and the law and wrote the papers that laid the basis for Chapters 3 to 5. Christopher Edley in particular was a valuable resource from whom I learnt so much. The Centre for Socio-Legal Studies at Oxford University provided me with a Visiting Fellowship for Trinity Term, 1994. There, I first developed the framework that underlies Chapters 8 and 9. I am especially grateful to Mavis Maclean for some insightful conversations and comments. The Social Sciences and Humanities Research Council of Canada provided much appreciated research funds.

I have presented drafts of parts of this book in a wide range of forums. I am grateful to audiences and commentators at a number of universities: the University of British Columbia, the University of Alberta, the University of Toronto Law School, York University, Oxford University, Harvard Law School, the University of Western Ontario, and the University of Buffalo Law School. I have also presented material at numerous academic conferences, including the Law and Society Association Meetings in Snowmass and Glasgow, the Canadian Law and Society Association meeting in Ottawa, and the Canadian Political Science Association meeting in Charlottetown. I have also benefitted immensely from participation and presentations in some smaller scholarly networks, especially the Toronto chapter of CSPT, Will Kymlicka's network on citizenship, and the Regional Socio-Legal Conference.

Numerous individuals have provided me with helpful written comments on particular chapters at some stage or other. At the risk of forgetting someone, the following is a list of individuals whom I recall providing especially helpful advice and criticism: Justine Burley, Joe Carens, Jerry Cohen, David Donaldson, Ronald Dworkin, Avigail Eisenberg, Margaret Moore, Brian Nakata, Eric Rakowski, Alex Smith, Richard Vernon, and Andrew Williams. My greatest debt in this regard is to the three reviewers for Cambridge University Press. Cambridge editor Terence Moore and the Cambridge Studies in Philosophy and Public Policy Series editor Professor Douglas Maclean solicited excellent reports. The three reviewers (including my friend Matthew Clayton) each wrote exemplary constructive assessments of the book as a whole that were invaluable in my putting together the final manuscript.

Although the chapters in the book all appear in their current form for the first time in print, some sections of the chapters were originally parts of journal articles or chapters in books. Chapter 3 draws on 'Equal Opportunity, Natural Inequalities, and Racial Disadvantage: The Bell Curve and Its Critics,' *Philosophy of the Social Sciences, Vol. 29, No. 1* (March 1999), pp. 120–44. Chapter 5 draws on 'Integration, Diversity, and Affirmative Action,' *Law and Society Review, Vol. 32, No. 3* (1998), pp. 725–46. Chapter 6 draws on 'What Are the Normative Foundations of Workfare?' in Patricia Evans, Lesley Jacobs, Alain Noel, and Elisabeth Reynolds, *Workfare: Does It Work? Is It Fair?* (Montreal: Renouf/ Institute for Research on Public Policy, 1995). Chapter 7 draws on 'Can an Egalitarian Justify Universal Access to Health Care?,' *Social Theory and Practice, Vol. 22* (1996), 315–48. Chapter 8 draws on 'Equal Opportunity and Gender Disadvantage,' *The Canadian Journal of Law and Jurisprudence, Vol. 7* (1994), pp. 61–72, and 'Equity and Opportunity' in Francois Gingras, editor, *Gender and Politics in Contemporary Canada* (Toronto: Oxford University Press, 1995).

My greatest debt, as always, is to my family. My partner, Brenda, continues to endure my scholarly pursuits patiently. Our four children, Aaron (11), Grace (9), Oliver (6), and Noah (3) keep me grounded. They provide me with a sense of what is genuinely important in life, and indeed ultimately are the reason why I care so much that the future is more just than the past.

PART I

Retrieving Equality of Opportunity

Chapter 1

Introduction

Pursuing equality is, for many of us, among the most noble and important endeavours of a modern government and society. This endeavour faces, however, a series of theoretical and practical challenges. The theoretical challenges reflect deep philosophical disagreements about what sort of equality should be pursued, and for whom. The practical challenges revolve around questions about which legal and political institutions are the most appropriate vehicles for realizing egalitarian justice, and how to implement effectively egalitarian social policy.

These challenges provide the general parameters for this book. It is my view that the theoretical and practical challenges of pursuing equality are closely inter-related and that neither the theoretical nor the practical challenges can be met without an eye toward the other. This means that it is unhelpful for philosophers to construct elaborate, abstract theories of egalitarian justice without some account of how to address the practical problems of realizing and implementing equality. Likewise, analysis of law and public policy cannot ignore recent sophisticated philosophical discussions around what is equality. The main arguments in this book are a combination of contemporary political philosophy and law and society scholarship. These arguments offer a response to the theoretical challenge of what sort of equality should be pursued, and partially meet the practical challenge of pursuing equality by considering a series of sites where either the courts or legislatures and public policymakers are struggling with the implications of pursuing equality.

The theoretical framework for the book is laid out in the next two chapters. I make a case there for why the concern of egalitarian justice should be with a particular version or model of equality of opportunity. In broad terms, my efforts are intended to retrieve the concept of equality of opportunity from the hands of its critics and show that the most serious philosophical criticisms of that concept are misconceived.[1] This retrieval of equality of opportunity is part of a broader trend to re-assess and elaborate that ideal of egalitarian justice, and the framework I advance is designed to make two important contributions to that retrieval.

In Chapter 2, I elaborate on a distinctive theory of equality of opportunity (called the three-dimensional model of equal opportunities as a regulative ideal) that shows clearly why pursuing equal opportunities involves a concern not just with formal inequalities but also with substantive ones. Equality of opportunity is, I suggest, an ideal for the normative regulation of competitions that distribute valuable opportunities in society. It is possible to distinguish three dimensions of fairness that might guide this regulation. *Procedural fairness* reflects a concern with the basic rules of procedure that guide a competition, including the determination of the winners. *Background fairness* reflects a concern that there be a level playing field for all competitors. *Stakes fairness* focuses on the prizes or what is at stake in the competition. The traditional view of equality of opportunity is one-dimensional, concentrating only on procedural fairness. The two-dimensional view stresses not only procedural fairness but also background fairness. For egalitarians, it constitutes a major advance over the traditional view because it is sensitive to the extent to which the distribution of opportunities is influenced by background socio-economic considerations. The two-dimensional view now dominates perceptions of equality of opportunity. My three-dimensional model of equal opportunities as a regulative ideal is innovative because it adds the dimension of stakes fairness.

Chapter 3 examines the belief that there exist natural inequalities and the pivotal role that belief has in the influential egalitarian charge that equality of opportunity is a fraudulent ideal because it magnifies natural inequalities and in effect amounts to an equal opportunity to become unequal. I reject the belief in natural inequalities and argue instead that all inequalities are a function of social design. This move saves equality of opportunity from the charge that it is a fraudulent ideal and highlights the important role of a normative ideal to regulate the design of inequalities in social institutions and practices.

With this theoretical framework in place, the six chapters that follow provide assessments of particular practices of egalitarian justice

---

[1] This notion of retrieval follows the well-known example of C.B. Macpherson, *Democratic Theory: Essays in Retrieval* (Oxford: Oxford University Press, 1973).

in law and social policy in Canada and the United States. Until the middle of the twentieth century, the pursuit of equality was predominantly the pursuit of political equality – that is to say, equality in the rights of political decision-making and their exercise. The emphasis was on voting rights, political representation, party systems, electoral boundaries, and so on. The domain for pursuing equality since then has dramatically increased. No longer is the emphasis exclusively on political equality. The egalitarian circle has been expanded to include most aspects of modern society. Although the pursuit of political equality for all citizens remains elusive and controversial, the emphasis in this book is instead on the practical challenges of pursuing equality in what I shall call *civil society*.[2] From the perspective of using legal institutions and social policy to pursue equality, civil society is "where the action is."[3]

Civil society is for many a familiar but elusive idea. Let us imagine that in modern societies it is possible to identify three overlapping but nonetheless distinct spheres of life for its members – the state, the private sphere, and civil society.[4] The state is the forum of formal political decision making and the enactment of laws enforced by the threat of coercive force. The state includes familiar institutions such as the legislature, the courts, the civil service and bureaucracy, the military, and so on. The private sphere, on the other hand, demarcates those dimensions

---

[2] I have discussed this elsewhere, e.g. in Lesley Jacobs, *The Democratic Vision of Politics* (Upper Saddle River, NJ: Prentice-Hall, 1997).

[3] I borrow this phrase, slightly out of context, from two influential papers in the fields of political philosophy and law and society, respectively: G.A. Cohen, 'Where the Action Is: The Site of Distributive Justice,' *Philosophy & Public Affairs*, Vol. 26 (Winter 1997), and David Trubek, 'Where the Action Is: Critical Legal Studies and Empiricism,' *Stanford Law Review, Vol. 34* (1984).

[4] Charles Taylor, 'Invoking Civil Society' in *Philosophical Arguments* (Cambridge, MA: Harvard University Press, 1995), esp. pp. 218–24. My focus on civil society should be distinguished from John Rawls' concern with what he calls the "basic structure" of society in his theory of justice as fairness. Although the precise scope of the basic structure is controversial, Rawls maintains generally that it includes the main political, social, and economic institutions that affect the life chances of a society's citizens. See *A Theory of Justice* (Cambridge MA: Harvard University Press, 1971), p. 7, and *Political Liberalism* (New York: Columbia University Press, 1993), pp. 257–89. Difficulties with Rawls' idea of the basic structure have been pressed recently by Cohen, 'Where the Action Is,' pp. 3–30, as well as Susan Moller Okin, *Justice, Gender, and the Family* (New York, Basic Books, 1989), pp. 89–97, and 'Political Liberalism, Justice, and Gender,' *Ethics, Vol. 105* (1995), esp. pp. 23–24. The parameters of civil society, by contrast, are a function of the space between the private and state spheres that can be the subject of a regulative ideal like equality of opportunity.

of a person's life that are in some sense outside the reach of the state. The boundaries of the private sphere are rarely well defined and generally reflect to some degree, with considerable irony, political decisions. Matters of religious conscience and intimate sexual relations between consenting adults are examples of beliefs and behaviour that for many, intuitively, should be viewed as within the domain of the private sphere. As the French philosopher Philippe Montaigne pointed out more than 500 years ago, it seems infeasible for the state to use coercive force to affect these things. Civil society is the domain for much of our daily social life and interaction. Moreover, it acts as a bridge between the state and the private sphere. The most familiar institutions of civil society include economic markets, profit-oriented firms, families, unions, hospitals, universities, schools, charities, neighbourhoods, churches and religious associations. Unlike in the private sphere, state interference with, and legal regulation of, institutions in civil society is an accepted fact of life. The debate centres on the precise extent and character of that interference and regulation, not on its legitimacy *toto caelo*.

The image of civil society that informs this book is one marked by remarkable diversity, plurality, and heterogeneity in the function and make-up of the institutions and practices that constitute civil society. These institutions and practices serve many complex and inter-related purposes ranging from meeting the material needs of individuals to providing the cultural resources that give people's lives meaning and substance. Moreover, the institutions of civil society are rarely closed to the influence of happenings in civil societies elsewhere, and are often structured in a cosmopolitan and globalized fashion. The Roman Catholic Church is a prime example of this feature of civil society. Similarly, the major languages found in one civil society often overlap with those of other civil societies. Clearly, too, economic markets for goods often extend from one civil society to another. It is also noteworthy that civil society is not static in its structure. The institutions and practices of civil society have rather a constantly evolving character.

These features of civil society constrain how we approach the normative regulation of civil society. Although philosophers have sometimes sought to identify a single norm that underlies all institutions of civil society,[5] the complex and constantly evolving structure of civil society

---

[5] See, e.g., Elizabeth Anderson, *Value in Ethics and Economics* (Cambridge, MA: Harvard University Press, 1993), p. 147, and Jeff Spinner, *The Boundaries of Citizenship* (Baltimore: John Hopkins University Press, 1994), p. 44.

suggests to me that this is a misconceived project. The approach I take in this book is to think about the normative regulation of civil society in a less comprehensive fashion, concentrating on specific institutions and practices. The task of equality of opportunity is, I note in the next chapter, the normative regulation of competitive procedures in civil society that distribute scarce resources or goods. At stake in these procedures are what I describe as *competitive opportunities*. Labor markets, university admissions schemes, and divorce courts all are examples of competitions for the distribution of competitive opportunities. Although in modern civil societies, competitive forums prevail and therefore the scope for the application of equality of opportunity is considerable, I leave open in this book what might be the regulative ideal for the distribution of non-competitive opportunities. The broad egalitarian vision of civil society I offer is one where there is great heterogeneity in the competitions that award the benefits and burdens of social life, but these competitions are constrained by the three-dimensional requirements of procedural fairness, background fairness, and stakes fairness.

For many of us, civil society provides the setting where we are most confronted by the inequalities that exist around us. For those living in industrial democracies, glaring political inequalities in terms of, for example, voting rights are rarely apparent, even when they exist. In our everyday lives, however, it is hard not to be confronted by the stark inequalities that result from, and are sometimes constitutive of, the institutions and practices of civil society. My examination of the practice of egalitarian justice is organized around considerations of race, class, and gender. Race, class, and gender are widely recognized by social scientists as among the most important sites for inequalities in civil society. And significantly this is reflected in the legacy of legislatures, courts, and other institutions making public policy in the United States and Canada.

What exactly do race, class, and gender signify? Following much recent scholarly work, my treatment of race, class, and gender is informed by deep-rooted scepticism that they signify 'natural' categories for differentiating between persons. Rather, their significance is as a mode of social differentiation and stratification between persons. Hence, they can be said to denote social realities, not biological or scientific realities.[6] Since race, class, and gender are modes of social differentiation, this means that they identify something *relational* between persons, not

---

[6] For this contrast, see Michael Omni, 'Racial Identity and the State,' *Law and Inequality*, Vol. 15 (1997), p. 7.

something *intrinsic* to persons.[7] In other words, race, class, and gender are a reflection of different social relations between persons and do not have their basis in factual claims about human nature or dubious biological theories. Three important points flow from this analysis. The first is that classifications based on race, class, or gender are not universal across civil societies; they are by necessity social inventions, and like civil society in general have an evolving character. The second point is that race, class, and gender rely on points of comparison or comparative standards, especially between minorities and the majority. As Martha Minnow puts it, "'Difference' is only meaningful as a comparison . . . Legal treatment of difference tends to take for granted an assumed point of comparison: Women are compared to the unstated norm of men, 'minority' races to whites, handicapped persons to the able-bodied, and 'minority' religions to 'majorities'."[8] The third point is that in the institutions and practices of civil society, these comparative standards inform the rules and regulations for competitions awarding many of the important benefits and burdens of social life. As I explain in more depth in Chapter 3, inequalities are by social design, and although perhaps not always deliberate, the role in that design of comparative standards involving vulnerable minorities often raises concerns about procedural, background, and stakes fairness that are at the core of the three-dimensional model of equal opportunities as a regulative ideal.[9]

Part of what is distinctive about writing about the practice of egalitarian justice in the early years of the twenty-first century is that the past fifty years or so have been marked by a series of experiments by courts and legislatures in the United States and Canada that attempt to address race, class, and gender inequalities in civil society. These experiments provide the context for my discussion of specific issues regarding

---

[7] This distinction comes from Martha Minow, 'Justice Engendered,' *Harvard Law Review* (1987), reprinted in Robert E. Goodin & Philip Pettit, *Contemporary Political Philosophy: An Anthology* (Oxford: Basil Blackwell, 1997), p. 512.

[8] *Ibid.*, p. 505.

[9] Clearly, race, gender, and class are not the only relevant modes of social differentiation here. Other modes include sexual orientation, ethnicity, religion, and disablement. Nor are these other modes necessarily more peripheral to pursuing egalitarian justice. As I have argued elsewhere, for instance, disablement is an absolutely crucial testing ground for any adequate theory of equality. See Lesley A. Jacobs, *Rights and Deprivation* (Oxford: Oxford University Press, 1993), p. 173. I place the main emphasis on race, class, and gender in order to keep the argument focussed.

8

inequalities in civil society. Chapters 4 and 5 examine two issues that are at the centre of the efforts to use the law to combat racial inequalities in the United States – (1) the reliance on standardized test scores for making admission decisions regarding universities and colleges, and (2) affirmative action for visible minorities. I show there that consideration of the three dimensions of procedural fairness, background fairness, and stakes fairness offers new insight into these issues and concerns revolving around race and civil society in general. Chapters 6 and 7 shift the focus to social policies widely associated with addressing class inequalities, public assistance for the poor, and universal access to health care. Here the emphasis is more on the Canadian context. The general project, again, is the applicability of the three-dimensional model of equality of opportunity as a regulative ideal. Chapters 8 and 9 consider two sets of policies concerned with gender inequalities, affirmative action, and pay equity in the workplace and post-divorce economic settlements in family law. Those chapters show how an equal-opportunities perspective provides a seamless analysis of the role of gender in the institutions and practices of civil society that draws on informed discussions in political philosophy, social policy, and feminist commentary.

Although my examination of the practice of egalitarian justice in this book is limited to a number of selected issues in law and social policy, it provides a general account of the role of a theory of equality of opportunity in the normative regulation of civil society. The three-dimensional model of equal opportunities as a regulative ideal is designed to function as an independent moral critic of the competitive practices and institutions of civil society. The underlying beliefs are that the pursuit of an egalitarian society involves taking one step at a time and that pursuing equal opportunities is not an all-or-nothing endeavour. The image is an ever-expanding egalitarian circle where the normative standard of equal opportunities governs a constantly expanding set of competitions in civil society. An important aspect of the evolving character of civil society is precisely that these changes are often in response to normative regulation and political governance. The normative regulation of one competition in accordance with the requirements of egalitarian justice opens the door to the regulation of another, as the diverse institutions and practices respond to changes in other parts of civil society as well as elsewhere, until one imagines the successful pursuit of equal opportunities for all.

Chapter 2

Equal Opportunities as a Regulative Ideal

2.1 INTRODUCTION

What kind of equality should we be concerned with pursuing? How do we judge whether our institutions or practices in society are more or less egalitarian? In this chapter, I propose a theory of equality of opportunity designed to answer these two questions. Equality of opportunity in its general form is probably the most familiar account of egalitarian justice. At the core of equality of opportunity, in my view, is the concept that in competitive procedures designed for the allocation of scarce resources and the distribution of the benefits and burdens of social life, those procedures should be governed by criteria that are relevant to the particular goods at stake in the competition and not by irrelevant considerations such as race, religion, class, gender, disability, sexual orientation, ethnicity, or other factors that may hinder some of the competitors' opportunities at success. This concept of equality of opportunity is a very broad and general idea that needs to be interpreted in order for its practical import to be clear. Models of equality of opportunity are particular interpretations of that concept. They can vary both with regard to the key elements of equality of opportunity and what can be said to be its implications. The first three chapters of this book are designed to advance and defend one particular interpretation of this broad concept of equality of opportunity (which I refer to as the three-dimensional model of equal opportunities as a regulative ideal). The rest of the book builds on this theoretical framework by utilizing it in analyses of legal and social policy issues organized around race, class, and gender in civil society.

Among philosophers working on theories of egalitarian justice and those calling for legal reforms and progressive social policy development, the view that the goal of an egalitarian society is equality of opportunity has been marginalized and often explicitly rejected during the past thirty years. This is despite the continued widespread popularity of the concept of equality of opportunity among the citizens of most democratic countries. What's wrong with equality of opportunity? Two very powerful criticisms of equality of opportunity are especially influential among egalitarians. The first criticism is that equality of opportunity amounts only to an ideal of formal equality; it is said to be empty of a commitment to substantive or genuine equality. Equality of opportunity as a principle of law and legislation has generally targetted discriminatory practices and worked on the assumption that, apart from discrimination, there is presumptive equality between persons. The problem is that there exist genuine substantive inequalities between persons along, among other things, the lines of race, class, and gender, and equality of opportunity in practice seems to be blind to these very real inequalities.[1] The second criticism holds that equality of opportunity is flawed because, as Thomas Nagel charges for instance, it "allows too much influence to the morally irrelevant [natural] contingencies of birth and talent."[2] By allowing this influence of nature in the allocation of scarce resources and the benefits and burdens of social life, equality of opportunity is accused of building upon and magnifying natural inequalities.

In this chapter and the next, I shall show why neither of these two criticisms provides compelling grounds for egalitarians to reject pursuing equality of opportunity, at least as I represent that pursuit. In this chapter, I provide a model of equality of opportunity that is not merely formal but also addresses substantive inequalities. Such a theory is consistent with the core idea of the broad concept of equality of opportunity noted earlier, and involves refinements and insights found in recent work on egalitarian justice. In the next chapter, I address the criticism that equality of opportunity builds upon and magnifies natural inequalities by situating that criticism within the controversy about race and IQ. My intention there is to show that the hidden premise of this criticism of the concept of equality of opportunity – that there exist natural inequalities – is deeply problematic, and in fact all inequalities are best viewed as social.

[1] See, for instance, Catharine MacKinnon, 'Francis Biddle's Sister,' in *Feminism Unmodified* (Cambridge, MA: Harvard University Press), pp. 106–107.
[2] Thomas Nagel, 'Rawls on Justice' in Norman Daniels, editor, *Reading Rawls, New Edition* (Stanford: Stanford University Press, 1989), p. 4.

My argument here is a contribution to the retrieval of equality of opportunity as a serious account of egalitarian justice.[3] Among philosophers, the revived interest in equality of opportunity has arisen principally in response to the concern that the pursuit of equality marginalizes the importance of individual responsibility. Defenders of egalitarian justice have been concerned lately to show how different theories of distributional equality are capable of making room for the common-sense moral judgment that a person's share of society's scarce resources should be partly a function of the choices he or she makes.[4] Some influential egalitarians, in particular Richard Arneson and John Roemer, have advanced theories of equality of opportunity principally because they incorporate at the baseline some notion of individual responsibility. Arneson comments, for example, "An opportunity standard of distribution leaves room for final outcomes to be properly determined by individual choices for which individuals are responsible."[5] In a similar vein, Roemer claims, "What society owes its members, under an equal-opportunity policy, is equal access; but the individual is responsible for turning that access into actual advantage by the application of effort."[6] Although I share with most other egalitarians the view that individual responsibility should have an important place in any account of fair shares of the benefits and burdens of social life, I am sceptical of approaches – egalitarian or otherwise – that treat the idea of individual responsibility as simple and straightforward, either in theory or practice. And therefore in turn

---

[3] See, especially, Richard Arneson, 'Equality and Equal Opportunity for Welfare,' *Philosophical Studies, Vol. 56* (1989), pp. 77–93; G.A. Cohen, 'On the Currency of Egalitarian Justice,' *Ethics, Vol. 99* (1989), pp. 906–44; Richard Arneson, 'Liberalism, Distributive Subjectivism, and Equal Opportunity of Welfare,' *Philosophy & Public Affairs, Vol. 19* (1990), pp. 158–94; Richard Arneson, 'A Defense of Equal Opportunity for Welfare,' *Philosophical Studies, Vol. 62* (1991), pp. 187–95; John E. Roemer, *Egalitarian Perspectives* (Cambridge, MA: Harvard University Press, 1996); John E. Roemer, *Equality of Opportunity* (Cambridge, MA: Harvard University Press, 1998); Hillel Steiner, 'Choice and Circumstance' in Andrew Mason, editor, *Ideals of Equality* (Oxford: Blackwell, 1998); and Jonathan Wolff, 'Fairness, Respect, and the Egalitarian Ethos,' *Philosophy & Public Affairs, Vol. 27* (1998), p. 101.

[4] The seminal statement is Ronald Dworkin, 'What Is Equality? Part 2: Equality of Resources,' *Philosophy & Public Affairs, Vol. 10* (1981), pp. 283–345. This paper has been reprinted in Ronald Dworkin, *Sovereign Virtue* (Cambridge MA: Harvard University Press, 2000), ch. 2.

[5] Arneson, 'Liberalism, Distributive Subjectivism, and Equal Opportunity for Welfare,' p. 175.

[6] Roemer, *Equality of Opportunity*, p. 24.

I am sceptical of defenses of equality of opportunity that rely on its alleged link to responsibility. The alternative view I present in this book is that the egalitarian case for retrieving equality of opportunity stems from its distinctive potential to regulate the inequalities that prevail in the diverse institutions and practices of civil society.

2.2 AN OUTLINE OF THE THREE-DIMENSIONAL MODEL

The three-dimensional model of equal opportunities as a regulative ideal focusses on the fair use of competitive procedures as a means for achieving an egalitarian distribution of some scarce resources or goods. Competitive procedures mean that, as in most games, there are winners and losers. Winners enjoy the resources or goods at stake; losers either do not enjoy them at all or only in much more limited ways than winners. As I explain in more depth later in this chapter, the claim that equality of opportunity is principally a regulative ideal for competition means that some goods and resources – for example, health care and elementary and secondary education – should not be allocated through procedures that conform to the model of equality of opportunity I advance here. Although the competitive dimension of equality of opportunity is sometimes downplayed, it seems to me that the distinctive virtue of the concept of equality of opportunity is pre- cisely its application to competitive mechanisms for distribution. And while a non-competitive model of equality of opportunity is not entirely unimaginable, equal-opportunity models of fair competition present it in its strongest and most plausible light, at least as a form of egalitarian justice.[7]

There are three closely related features of equality of opportunity that stand out when its competitive dimension is highlighted. The first is that it involves thinking about egalitarian justice mainly in terms of procedures and regulations.[8] What matters – the demands of

---

[7] See, e.g., David Lloyd-Thomas, 'Competitive Equality of Opportunity,' *Mind,* Vol. 86 (1977) pp. 288–404; and S.J.D. Green, 'Competitive Equality of Opportu- nity: A Defense,' *Ethics, Vol. 100* (1989), pp. 5–32.
[8] It is also noteworthy that not all contests are competitions. Some contests are unregulated, whereas all competitions involve regulations. An example of this contrast is between a free fight and a boxing match. The latter, but not the former, is a competition governed by the so-called Marquis of Queensberry Rules, whereas the latter is governed by no rules at all. See J.P. Day, 'Fairness and Fortune,' *Ratio,* Vol. 19 (1977), pp. 77–78.

justice – are expressed mainly in the form of rules and procedures. The second feature is that equality of opportunity does not have a preconceived winner or outcome. The appropriate analogy is focussing in a description of a game such as football on the rules; nobody claims that those rules capture the whole idea of the game, but they do capture one aspect of it. And the significance of those rules is that when a particular game is played, the winner is a function of those rules. The upshot is that the rules of a competition under competitive equality of opportunity are the most important focus of any model of it as a theory of egalitarian justice. The third feature is that equality of opportunity is principally a normative standard for regulating certain types of competition.

How should rules and procedures be structured in a competitive model of equality of opportunity? Two broad approaches can be distinguished.[9] One approach is *prospect-regarding* in the sense that equality of opportunity is said to hold between two persons when each has the same likelihood or probability of realizing the opportunity. A lottery in which everyone has the same number of tickets is an example of a competition that conforms to this standard of equality of opportunity. Another approach treats competition under conditions of equality of opportunity in terms of a *level playing field*. The main idea here is that equality of opportunity requires everyone to enter competitions at roughly the same starting position. The model of equal opportunities I propose assumes the level playing field approach.

That model identifies three dimensions of the normative regulation of competition required by equality of opportunity.[10] These three dimensions (which I defined in Chapter 1 as *procedural fairness, background fairness*, and *stakes fairness*) can be illustrated by considering the example of a boxing match. Boxing matches characteristically are regulated by certain familiar rules – the so-called Marquis of Queensberry Rules.

---

[9] The distinction drawn here is similar to, but not identical with, the distinction between *prospect-regarding* and *means-regarding* equality of opportunity in Douglas Rae, Douglas Yates, Jennifer Hochschild, Joseph Morone, and Carol Fessler, *Equalities* (Cambridge, MA: Harvard University Press, 1981), pp. 81–82.

[10] The ideas of procedural fairness and background fairness reflect the profound influence of John Rawls' description of fair equality of opportunity in *A Theory of Justice* (Cambridge, MA: Harvard University Press, 1971), pp. 73–76, and Brian Barry's discussion of procedural justice in *Political Argument, Reissue* (Brighton, UK: Harvester/Wheatsheaf, 1990), esp. pp. 102–106. See also James S. Fishkin, *Justice, Equal Opportunity, and the Family* (New Haven: Yale University Press, 1983), ch. 3.

Some of these rules reflect *procedural fairness* such as, for instance, not punching one's opponent below the waist, no head butting, no swinging after the bell goes to end the round, and so on. Likewise, fair matches do not begin with an agreed-upon winner; instead, the winner is determined by rules such as who wins by a knock-out or who scores the most points in the case of a decision fight. Considerations of procedural fairness in this sense are presumably quite familiar. But boxing matches typically respect another dimension of fairness as well. In competitions such as the Olympics, boxers are classified according to their body weight, and fight other boxers in the same class. Underlying this practice is the intuition that there is something fundamentally unfair about a match between a 125-pound featherweight boxer and a 200-pound heavyweight. Assuming that the heavyweight boxer wins a match between the two, that outcome is said to be unfair even if the boxer did not violate the rules of procedural fairness such as hitting the featherweight boxer after the bell ended the round. *Background fairness* reflects the concern that boxers enter a match on roughly equal terms with respect to body weight. Background fairness is met, in other words, when there is a level playing field for all competitors. The third dimension of fairness concerns the prizes or what is at stake in the boxing match. In, for instance, professional boxing, the stake is prize money. The practice is to have the winner receive say 75 percent of the money (say, $750,000) and the loser 25 percent ($250,000). The justification typically is that this is fairer than a winner-take-all prize of $1,000,000. The dimension of fairness drawn upon here is what I mean by *stakes fairness*.

This three-dimensional model of equal opportunities is an innovative advance on how the concept of equality of opportunity has been viewed in treatments of egalitarian justice. The traditional view of equality of opportunity is *one*-dimensional. This view focuses on procedural fairness. In the 1960s, a number of influential liberal political philosophers – most notably, John Rawls and Brian Barry – introduced a two-dimensional view of equality of opportunity. This *two*-dimensional view stressed not only procedural fairness but also background fairness. It constitutes a major advance over the one-dimensional view because it is sensitive to the extent to which the distribution of opportunities is partly a function of background socio-economic differences between individuals. The two-dimensional view can have significant redistributive implications because in order to ensure background fairness, it is often necessary to redistribute some of society's scarce resources. The two-dimensional view continues to dominate perceptions of equality of opportunity. My *three*-dimensional model of equal opportunities is radical, I suggest, because it adds the dimension of stakes fairness.[11]

What standards underlie these three dimensions of fairness? Although I shall elaborate with considerably more precision what I mean by background fairness and stakes fairness later in the chapter (Sections 2.4 and 2.5), let me give here a thumbnail sketch of the standards that underlie these three distinct dimensions of fairness. The standards of procedural fairness are generally specific to the particular competition. What counts as procedurally fair is often linked to what is at stake in the competition. In many competitions, the basic requirements of procedural fairness are not deeply contested. Those requirements often reflect a general consensus, and have developed over time. Sometimes, of course, the rules or regulations governing a competition are found to be unfair and to violate procedural fairness. The clearest breaches of procedural fairness involve the exclusion of certain classes of persons from the competition. There are well-known historical examples of this in professions such as law, medicine, and teaching.[12]

Stakes fairness reflects a concern with the distribution of benefits and burdens within a competition. The issue here is with whether it is fair to have, for instance, a winner-take-all scheme. Imagine, say, divorce settlements that were structured in this way. Most of us would object that this is unfair because it is wrong to have the stakes so high; while it may be acceptable to have the winner receive more benefits, it is unfair that the loser receive nothing. Similarly, in Chapter 5, I consider the labour market in this light. Often, employment in the competitive labour market is perceived in this way; those who get jobs receive wages and other sorts of fringe benefits. One way to view a range of government programmes from unemployment insurance to workfare is as mechanisms to promote stakes fairness rather than attaching all the benefits to the winners in the competitive labour market. My general point is that the ideal of equal opportunities as a regulative ideal is designed not as a justification for the privileges and inequalities that are often a characteristic

---

[11] This distinction between one-, two-, and three-dimensional views of equality of opportunity mimics the three-fold distinction between views of power by Steven Lukes in *Power: A Radical View* (London: Macmillan, 1974).

[12] See, e.g., the discussion of the exclusion of women from the legal profession in Canada by Constance Backhouse, *Petticoats & Prejudice: Women and Law in Nineteenth Century Canada* (Toronto: Osgoode Society, 1991), ch. 10.

result of unregulated competitions, but as a normative standard of procedural and stakes fairness for critiquing those structural privileges and inequalities.

Background fairness is now probably the most familiar site for equal opportunity concerns about fair competition. This dimension of fairness fixates on the initial starting positions or backgrounds of those potentially involved in a competition. The underlying insight is, of course, that the structure of these positions will affect who competes and how they will fare in the competition. From the perspective of competitive equality of opportunity, because pre-existing inequalities infect the fairness of competitive processes, there is a need to regulate these processes with a sensitivity to remedies for these inequalities.

These preliminary observations about the nature of stakes and background fairness suggest how the three-dimensional model of equal opportunities as a regulative ideal meets the objection that all models of equality of opportunity conform to a formal or empty egalitarian standard. That objection certainly holds against one-dimensional models that respect only procedural fairness, but it seems misconceived when applied to two-dimensional models that recognize background fairness, and especially a three-dimensional model that adds stakes fairness too. Both types of models support the claim that in existing societies, a substantial amount of redistribution of wealth and other resources is necessary to ensure genuine equal opportunity for all.

Consider Bernard Williams's well-known use of the hypothetical warrior society to show the potential emptiness of equality of opportunity.[13] Imagine a society that attaches great prestige to membership in a warrior class that as a condition of membership requires the demonstration of great physical strength. Until recently, this class was recruited exclusively from the wealthiest families. But in response to the demands of equality of opportunity, recruitment has been expanded to all segments of the society. This change has had little effect, however, and virtually all warriors continue to come from the wealthiest families because only they are well-nourished enough to exhibit superior physical strength; the rest are so undernourished that their physical strength suffers. The point of the example is that although there is now in

---

[13] Bernard Williams, 'The Idea of Equality' (1962), reprinted in Robert E. Goodin & Philip Pettit, editors, *Contemporary Political Philosophy: An Anthology* (Oxford: Blackwells, 1997), p. 473. This example is also discussed at length in Fishkin, *Justice, Equal Opportunity, and the Family.*

the hypothetical warrior society the appearance of procedural fairness, equality of opportunity is a mere facade of egalitarianism. The inference Williams makes is, "that the supposed equality of opportunity is quite empty – indeed, one may say that it does not really exist – unless it is made more effective than this."[14] The idea of background fairness addresses the warrior society example without necessarily making equality of opportunity more 'effective' in the sense that more people from poorer families become warriors. What, in my view, is unfair in the warrior society is not that the membership in the warrior class did not reflect the broader diversity of the entire society, but rather that in the competition for membership, there was not a level playing field; the starting positions of those from poorer families were far behind those from the wealthiest families.[15] Within the three-dimensional model of equal opportunities as a regulative ideal, the alternative to the hypothetical warrior society is one where, in John Rawls's words, "those who are at the same level of talent and ability, and have the same willingness to use them, should have the same prospects of success regardless of their initial place in the social system, that is, irrespective of the income class into which they are born."[16]

The objection that equality of opportunity is overly formal could be connected instead to the preoccupation with legal barriers in most models of equal opportunity. This emphasis on law in theories of equality of opportunity reveals an assumption that legal obstacles and barriers are the main source of inequalities. But (so it is argued) that assumption is problematic, for many inequalities in society seem to have a basis in the socio-economic structure or culture, not in the law. The main difficulty I have with this line of criticism is that it invokes a very narrow and over-simplistic positivist idea of law. That idea of law is contrary to a wide range of competing conceptions of law extending from Ronald Dworkin's influential view that "law is a matter of rights tenable in court"[17] to Roberto Unger's claim that "legal rules

---

[14] Williams, 'The Idea of Equality,' p. 473.
[15] Here I am disagreeing with Barry's characterization of background fairness as relying on a preconceived notion of the "right result" of a competition. See Barry, *Political Argument*, p. 103.
[16] Rawls, *A Theory of Justice*, p. 73. I gloss over what precisely Rawls means here and whether it is consistent with what he says elsewhere. See in particular Thomas Pogge, *Realizing Rawls* (Ithaca: Cornell University Press, 1989), pp. 161–73.
[17] Ronald Dworkin, *Law's Empire* (Cambridge, MA: Harvard University Press, 1986), p. 401.

and doctrines define the basic institutional arrangements of society"[18] to Allan Hutchinson's post-modernist position that "law is irredeemably indeterminate."[19] Without a consensus on what law is, it seems hard to press a devastating case against any model of equality of opportunity because it recognizes the importance of law.

What really interests me about law in this book is not the extent to which it is the source of inequalities but how it can be used to remedy unequal opportunities in civil society. Law is the main tool the state uses to regulate competitions in civil society. The substantial issues discussed in the seven chapters to follow all revolve around legal change brought about through either adjudication by the courts or by legislation and public policy. While the analysis in those chapters is not always optimistic, there is a general assumption – substantiated by some of the cases and examples I examine – that legal change can enhance equality in civil society. My application of the three-dimensional model of equal opportunities can then be said to assume the transformative potential of law.[20]

Thus far, my description of the three-dimensional model of equal opportunity as a regulative ideal has made no reference to either merit or meritocracy. This may be surprising, for often equality of opportunity is equated with a system of meritocracy, where the positions an individual assumes in society and the goods he or she enjoys are a function solely of his or her merit. Rawls, for instance, comments that a meritocracy "follows the principle of careers open to talents and uses equality of opportunity as a way of releasing men's [sic] energies in the pursuit of economic prosperity and political dominion ... Equality of opportunity means an equal chance to leave the less fortunate behind in the personal

---

[18] Roberto Mangabeira Unger, *The Critical Legal Studies Movement* (Cambridge, MA: Harvard University Press, 1983), p. 21.

[19] Allan C. Hutchinson, *Waiting for Coraf: A Critique of Law and Rights* (Toronto: University of Toronto Press, 1995), p. 56.

[20] See also Drucilla Cornell, *The Imaginary Domain* (New York: Routledge, 1995), p. 236, and Catharine MacKinnon, *Feminism Unmodified* (Cambridge, MA: Harvard University Press, 1987), p. 116. Although I subscribe to the view that law has a transformative potential, I also concur with legal critics such as Duncan Kennedy who emphasize the limits of the potential of law in bringing about social change, in particular, because of its lack of concentration of decision-making power. See, e.g., Kennedy's statement in *A Critique of Adjudication* (Cambridge, MA: Harvard University Press, 1998): 'The diffusion of law-making power reduces the power of ideologically organized majorities, whether liberal or conservative, to bring about significant change in any subject-matter area heavily governed by law,' p. 2.

quest for influence and social position."[21] In a similar line of reasoning, Iris Marion Young says "Today equal opportunity has come to mean only that no one is barred from entering the competition for a relatively few privileged positions . . . Assuming a division between scarce highly rewarded positions and more plentiful less desirable positions as given, the merit principle asserts that this division of labor is just when no group received privileged positions by birth or right."[22] Likewise, Will Kymlicka explains, "In a society that has equality of opportunity, unequal income is fair, because success is 'merited,' it goes to those who 'deserve' it."[23]

It is my view that this close association between equality of opportunity and meritocracy stems from a failure to appreciate fully that equality of opportunity is a normative ideal for regulating fairly competitions of all different types. A meritocracy is a particular type of competition, one that relies heavily on the idea of merit.[24] But not all competitions are versions of meritocracy; some are organized around standards that make no appeal to merit. Equality of opportunity, at least as it is represented in the three-dimensional model, provides a normative standard for governing this range of competitions. Rather than being an integral part of meritocracy, equality of opportunity provides an independent standard of justice for assessing and criticizing it. Chapter 4 shows the force of this distinction between equality of opportunity and meritocracy. The context for the discussion there is the current initiative that civil rights groups in the United States have taken in launching complaints against some of the uses of test scores on standardized tests such as SAT and LSAT by universities and other institutions of higher education when making admissions and scholarship decisions. Even though the uses of these test scores have a negative impact on the admission of some racial minorities and women, relying on test scores is typically defended by some sort of reference to merit. At present, the basis for any civil rights complaint remains unclear, even though there have been a number of cases already decided. Using the three-dimensional model of equal opportunity as a normative ideal for regulating the competition

---

[21] Rawls, *A Theory of Justice*, pp. 106–107.

[22] Iris Marion Young, *Justice and the Politics of Difference* (Princeton: Princeton University Press, 1990), pp. 214–15.

[23] Will Kymlicka, *Contemporary Political Philosophy* (Oxford: Oxford University Press, 1990), p. 56.

[24] Merit itself, as I explain in Chapter 4, is largely a standard that reflects what maximizes the interests of the greatest number in society.

for university admissions and scholarships based on merit, I show why civil rights should sometimes function to trump or curtail reliance on standardized test scores, and how this function is implicit in the leading cases already decided in this area of civil rights litigation.

A similar point can be made about the relationship between equality of opportunity and market institutions. Markets should not be confused with a meritocracy or any other such pure merit-based competition. Market pricing mechanisms often result in allocations tracking who is lucky, not who has merit. Historically, some of the strongest proponents of some version or other of equality of opportunity linked their arguments to the endorsement of a market-based economy. More recently, there have been very sophisticated attempts to place market pricing mechanisms at the centre of theories of egalitarian justice.[25] In abstract formulations of egalitarian justice, the important question is whether markets function to define what is an equal share or are merely valuable instruments for realizing equal shares.[26]

The approach to markets I take in this book has a different focus. My concern is mainly with existing markets as forums for competitions for certain goods and resources. What I ask is what are the implications of the three-dimensional model of equal opportunities as a normative regulative ideal for these markets? Chapter 6 and 8 examine labour markets. My interest is in the normative foundations for certain social policy initiatives and interventions in labour markets; Chapter 6 looks at workfare, Chapter 8 at gender-based affirmative action and pay equity. I show how these controversial policies flow readily from the model of equal opportunities as a regulative ideal on labour markets – in particular, the concerns with stakes and background fairness.

2.3 EQUAL OPPORTUNITIES FOR WHAT?

It is significant that in my formulation of a model of equality of opportunity, the emphasis is on *equal opportunities*, not equal opportunity. This shift parallels one now widely accepted among liberal political

---

[25] The most influential is Dworkin, 'What Is Equality? Part 2: Equality of Resources,' pp. 283–345.
[26] See my discussion in Lesley Jacobs, *Rights and Deprivation* (Oxford: Oxford University Press, 1993), pp. 92–98.

philosophers with regard to liberty or freedom.[27] In the 1950s and 1960s, it was frequently argued by liberals that individuals have an equal right to liberty or should enjoy equal liberty.[28] In important refinements to the theoretical foundations of liberalism, however, several prominent liberals, most notably John Rawls and Ronald Dworkin, argued that the idea of a general right to liberty or equal liberty rests on a misconception.[29] What really matters is not liberty *per se* but rather certain basic liberties such as freedom of expression, religious freedom, freedom of conscience, freedom of association, and freedom of sexual orientation. Rather than advancing equal rights to liberty, the shift has been towards defending equal rights to certain basic liberties. I am calling for a similar shift from advancing models of equality of opportunity towards models of equal opportunities.

The reasoning for making this shift is very simple. Critical reflection on the concept of equality of opportunity has long taught that it is a mistake to regulate *all* aspects of social life by that normative standard. The English socialist R.H. Tawney, writing in the 1930s, for instance, says,

Equality of opportunity implies the establishment of conditions which favour [for the mass of mankind] the expansion . . . of both . . . the opportunity to assert themselves in the contests of the market-place, and to reap the reward of successful rivalry, [and] also qualities which, though no less admirable, do not find their perfection in a competitive struggle . . . Rightly interpreted, it means, not only that what are commonly regarded as the prizes of life should be open to all, but that none should be subjected to arbitrary penalties; not only that exceptional men [sic] should be free to exercise their exceptional powers, but that common men [sic] should be free to make the most of their common humanity.[30]

What Tawney is suggesting is that in its best light, equality of opportunity presupposes that some of the benefits and burdens of social life

---

[27] The observation that there is a parallel is made by Peter Westen, 'The Concept of Equal Opportunity,' *Ethics*, Vol. 95 (1985), p. 849.

[28] I have explained and defended this development in modern political philosophy with considerable care in *An Introduction to Modern Political Philosophy: The Democratic Vision of Politics* (Upper Saddle River, NJ: Prentice-Hall, 1997), ch. 5.

[29] See, especially, John Rawls, 'The Basic Liberties and Their Priority' in *Political Liberalism* (New York: Columbia University Press, 1993) and Ronald Dworkin, 'What Rights Do We Have?' in *Taking Rights Seriously, New Impression* (Cambridge, MA: Harvard University Press, 1978).

[30] R.H. Tawney, *Equality, New Edition* (London: George Allen & Unwin, 1964), p. 108.

not be subject to competition and therefore not be regulated by that ideal. Michael Walzer made a similar point later, saying, "equality of opportunity is a standard for the distribution of some jobs, not all jobs . . . The existence of such jobs opens the way to a kind of success for which people don't need to qualify–indeed, can't qualify – and so sets limits on the authority of the qualified. There are areas of social and economic life where their writ doesn't run. The precise boundaries of these areas will always be problematic, but their reality isn't at all."[31] Underlying the distinction both Walzer and Tawney make is the observation that opportunity is not something homogeneous and simple; there are rather a diversity of types of opportunities. A defensible model of equality of opportunity must, I propose, acknowledge this diversity in types of opportunities and identify those types that should be regulated by the ideal of equality of opportunity.

This proposition illuminates the theory and practice of pursuing equality of opportunity in at least two important respects. First, it provides insight into why the concept of equality of opportunity is a powerful analytical tool for thinking critically about inequalities in the institutions and practices of civil society. Civil society is characterized by extensive diversity and plurality in the opportunities it offers. There appears to be no essentializing or defining feature of the institutions and practices that make up civil society. Therefore, when egalitarians envision a regulative ideal for civil society, it must be an ideal that is sensitive to this pluralism and diversity in opportunities. The shift from equal opportunity to equal opportunities meets this demand. In civil society, pursuing equality means focussing on particular institutions and practices and the opportunities they engender. Although the chapters to follow provide a coherent and systematic application of the three-dimensional model of equal opportunities as a regulative ideal, it is significant that each chapter focusses on a particular competition and the implications of the equal opportunities model for that competition. The narrow and concrete discussions I offer in each of these chapters are a prescription for how to pursue egalitarian justice in civil society: focus on particular individualized competitions and the opportunities at stake in them. Indeed, one key factor that should be regulated is the effects of outcomes in one competition on another competition – for instance, the effects of a father's failures in the labour market on his child's

---

[31] Michael Walzer, *Spheres of Justice: A Defence of Pluralism and Equality* (New York: Basic Books, 1983), pp. 163–64.

prospects for post-secondary education. (Part of the main point here is captured by the very idea of stakes fairness.) The focus on individualized competitions captures effectively the belief that the pursuit of an egalitarian society involves taking one step at a time and that pursuing equality is not an all-or-nothing endeavour. The image I have in mind for the pursuit of equality is that of an ever-expanding circle where the normative standard of equal opportunities governs a constantly expanding set of competitions in civil society. Each extension of the three-dimensional model requires attending to the particular details and features of the individual competitions and involves at some level pioneering developments.

The second important issue this shift from equal opportunity to equal opportunities raises is whether some opportunities are outside the regulatory ambit of the concept of equality of opportunity. What might be the principled basis for drawing such a distinction between opportunities? The distinction I draw is between competitive versus non-competitive opportunities. Competitive opportunities are those that should be allocated through competition, whereas non-competitive opportunities should be allocated through other processes. The relevant point is that the three-dimensional model is designed *only* to regulate competitive opportunities. How do you identify non-competitive opportunities? My extended effort to answer this question comes in Chapter 7, where I discuss the allocation of access to health care. Like most others in developed Western democracies, I believe that all citizens, regardless of their socio-economic class, race, or gender, should be assured access to a certain set of basic or 'medically necessary' health care services and products. This is what is ordinarily described as universal access to health care. Most macro-level health care policy making, even in the United States, assumes a commitment to universal access to health care. Modern theorists of egalitarian justice have generally assumed that this commitment readily flows from their accounts of egalitarian justice. And recently there have been some important attempts to extend developments in general theories of egalitarian justice to health care. But I show that these attempts, when they assume either an equality of opportunity approach or some other approach that emphasizes competition, have generally failed to explain or ground universal access to health care. My intention in Chapter 7 is not to question the commitment to universal access to health care but rather to show clearly the limits in application of any model of equality of opportunity, including my own. Access to a basic level of health care is a type of non-competitive opportunity and therefore should not be allocated on a competitive basis with winners and losers, regardless of whether that competition is subject to a regulative ideal such as equality of opportunity. The lesson is for defenders of equal opportunity to recognize the limited scope of application of that egalitarian ideal; Tawney pressed this point more than a half century ago, and I am merely repeating it because it still seems to be under-appreciated.

Drawing the line for the application of equality of opportunity between competitive and non-competitive opportunities in civil society has considerable explanatory potential in other policy areas too. In Chapters 8 and 9, which discuss gender, I focus on two policy areas–labour market interventions and the economic consequences of divorce. What unites my analysis of gender there is the claim that injustices within the family affect significantly the opportunities women face in the labour market and after divorce. Measures such as affirmative action and pay equity that intervene in the labour market can be understood as policy responses to injustices within the family. Likewise, major developments in family law around the economic settlement after divorce with regard to property division and child support payments can be seen as a response to growing sensitivity to the injustices that exist within families. What is noteworthy here is that I don't advocate any policy initiatives that directly intervene with families to make them more just; the policies I concentrate on simply limit the effects of those injustices on women's opportunities outside the family. In my earlier work on gender disadvantage, I was sensitive to the tension here but left it as a puzzling aspect of the analysis.[32] And some have criticized my analysis because of it, finding it "the politics of mainstreaming."[33] But, in retrospect, it is now clear that there is a sound principled basis for applying equal opportunity ideals to women in the labour market and divorce, but not the family *per se*. Like the labour market, the dissolution of marriage – divorce – can be readily viewed as a competitive process and therefore should be subject to the regulative ideal of equal opportunities.[34] The

---

[32] See, e.g., Lesley Jacobs, 'Equal Opportunity and Gender Disadvantage,' *The Canadian Journal of Law and Jurisprudence, Vol. 7* (1994), p. 66.

[33] Caroline Andrews, 'The Fine Line – Strategies for Change' in François-Pierre Gingras, editor, *Gender and Politics in Contemporary Canada* (Toronto: Oxford University Press, 1995), p. 253.

[34] This doesn't mean that divorce should necessarily be adversarial. It is entirely consistent to favour alternative dispute resolution routes such as mediation over litigation in most divorce cases while still viewing them as competitions.

family is not a competition and should not therefore be regulated by the ideal of competitive equality of opportunity. This viewpoint contrasts sharply with that of some liberal feminists such as Susan Moller Okin who call readily for the application of equality of opportunity to the family.[35] That call reflects a failure to appreciate the limited scope of equality of opportunity as a regulative ideal for competitive procedures and institutions. If equality of opportunity is to be part of a normative response to gender disadvantage, it must function as a regulative ideal on men and women competing as individuals, not on the family.[36]

The shift to equal opportunities along the lines I am pressing here makes for an important contrast with other models of equality of opportunity, including Richard Arneson's theory of equal opportunity for welfare. According to Arneson, "For equal opportunity for welfare to obtain among a number of persons, each must face an array of options that is equivalent to every other person's in terms of the prospects for preference satisfaction it offers."[37] The main idea here is that if you imagine a map for each individual showing the various life choices he or she faces, and in turn the different options that those choices lead to, and so on, where each option is ranked by its prospects for welfare understood in terms of preference satisfaction, the theory requires equivalent maps so that "all persons face effectively equivalent arrays of options."[38] Much of the criticism of Arneson's theory and others that are similar to it concentrate on the fact that Arneson employs welfare as the currency of egalitarian justice.[39] These critics question the appropriateness of welfare understood in terms of subjective preference satisfaction as a way to determine what share of society's benefits and burdens each individual should

---

[35] Susan Moller Okin, *Justice, Gender, and the Family* (New York: Basic Books, 1989), pp. 16–17, 180–86.

[36] Here I concur with the emphasis on individuals, not families, in the response to Okin's position developed by Drucilla Cornell, *At the Heart of Freedom* (Princeton: Princeton Univeristy Press, 1998), ch. 3.

[37] Arneson, 'Equality and Equal Opportunity for Welfare,' p. 85.

[38] Arneson, Equality and Equal Opportunity for Welfare,' p. 86.

[39] Ronald Dworkin, 'What Is Equality? Part 1: Equality of Welfare,' *Philosophy & Public Affairs*, Vol. 10 (1981), pp. 185–246; John Rawls, 'Social Unity and Primary Goods' in Amartya Sen & Bernard Williams, editors, *Utilitarianism and Beyond* (Cambridge, UK: Cambridge University Press, 1982); Cohen, 'On the Currency of Egalitarian Justice'; Thomas Christiano, 'Difficulties with the Principle of Equal Opportunity for Welfare,' *Philosophical Studies, Vol. 62*; Norman Daniels, 'Equality of What: Welfare, Resources, or Capabilities?' in *Justice and Justification* (New York: Cambridge University Press, 1996).

enjoy. And Arneson's principal effort has been responding to this line of criticism.[40]

But an alternative line of criticism could focus instead on Arneson's employment of the idea of opportunity, not welfare. For Arneson, "talk of 'opportunity' is a stand-in for whatever factors affecting preference formation we decide should be treated as matters of individual responsibility"[41] and hence for him, "An opportunity is a chance of getting a good if one seeks it."[42] His point is that by comparison with a theory that requires equality of welfare, equal opportunity for welfare allows individual responsibility to influence the outcome of distributional equality. What I find so problematic in Arneson's theory is the prospect of equalizing opportunity, once the diversity of opportunities is appreciated. The problem here is that in order to equalize the complete sets of opportunities for two or more individuals, it is necessary for all opportunities to be commensurable and for there to be some standard for comparison. Now, Arneson seems to think that welfare or preference satisfaction can serve this purpose in the sense that if each opportunity involves the potential for welfare, this can provide a basis for comparing opportunities. This move does not, however, take seriously enough the diversity in opportunities because what is at stake here is not just diversity in the welfare potential of different opportunities but also diversity along other lines such as what one values including when that is in tension with one's welfare.[43]

Although Arneson sometimes writes about equal opportunities rather than equal opportunity,[44] I suspect that he resists the general shift to the latter that I endorse in order to avoid the so-called indexing problem. This problem arises when an egalitarian theory of distributive justice recognizes a number of different and irreducible goods as

---

[40] See, e.g., Arneson, 'Liberalism, Distributive Subjectivism, and Equal Opportunity for Welfare' and 'A Defense of Equal Opportunity for Welfare.'

[41] Arneson, 'Liberalism, Distributive Subjectivism, and Equal Opportunity for Welfare,' p. 175.

[42] Arneson, 'Equality and Equal Opportunity for Welfare,' p. 85.

[43] See, for a similar point about the importance of diversity, Amartya Sen, *Inequality Reexamined* (Cambridge, MA: Harvard University Press, 1992), ch. 4. Sen does not place the emphasis on the diversity of opportunities but that it is a logical implication of his position, especially if one agrees with Arneson that "[Sen's] Equality of capability is then a notion within the family of equality of opportunity views, a family that also includes the idea of equal opportunity that I have been attempting to defend.' See 'Equality and Equal Opportunity for Welfare,' p. 91.

[44] See, e.g., Arneson, 'Liberalism, Distributive Subjectivism, and Equal Opportunity for Welfare,' p. 159.

possible components in an individual's fair share of the benefits and burdens of social life. The indexing problem asks how we can aggregate such diverse goods so that we have a complete measure of the share size for each individual. Arneson thinks that the indexing problem is insoluble.[45] By allowing for the diversity of opportunities within his theory of egalitarian justice, his theory would have to face an insoluble problem.

The three-dimensional model of equal opportunities as a regulative ideal avoids the indexing problem in a different way. That model appeals to the normative standard of equal opportunities as a justice-based criterion for the governing of individualized competitions for scarce goods and resources. There is nothing in that model that requires aggregating an individual's opportunities across competitions in civil society or indeed across his or her life span. Therefore, the problem of aggregating diverse opportunities does not arise. Indeed, the only way to make sense of equal shares across one's entire life within a competitive model of equality of opportunity would be to assume that one's whole life can be seen as one giant or mega-competition; I trust that such an image is absurd.

What this model of equal opportunities as a regulative ideal takes as a given, however, is that there are certain competitions for allocating some of the benefits and burdens of social life. The competitive opportunities of civil society are the subject of this egalitarian approach. Equality of opportunity therefore functions principally as a regulative ideal for those competitions. It may seem that by accepting these competitions as a given, the three-dimensional model of equal opportunities as a regulative ideal is insufficiently distant and critical of the status quo in civil society to constitute a genuine account of justice. As Ronald Dworkin elegantly puts, "It is part of our common political life, if anything is, that justice is our critic not our mirror."[46] But the model of equal opportunities as a regulative ideal is not a mirror of the competitions it is designed to govern, but functions rather as an independent moral critic of the practices in those competitions. It is important also to recognize the evolving character of institutions and practices of civil society; civil society changes in response to normative regulation and political governance.[47] Part of the challenge of theorizing about social justice is

[45] Arneson, 'Primary Goods Reconsidered,' *Nous*, Vol. 24 (1990), p. 445.
[46] Ronald Dworkin, 'What Justice Isn't' in *A Matter of Principle* (Cambridge, MA: Harvard University Press, 1985), p. 219.
[47] Charles Taylor, 'Invoking Civil Society,' p. 77.

accommodating for this dynamic relationship between the demands of justice and the structure of social institutions and practices.[48]

2.4 BACKGROUND FAIRNESS AND STATUS EQUALITY

Integral to the equal opportunities model I have been developing in this chapter is the three-fold distinction between procedural, background, and stakes fairness. The concern for background and stakes fairness saves that model from the charge that it is merely a formal or empty theory of egalitarian justice. Background fairness reflects the importance placed on a level playing field where individuals compete from starting positions that are governed by fairness. What precisely is required for persons to compete from starting positions governed by fairness? When is the playing field level in the institutions and practices of civil society? What principle should guide our judgments about background fairness in the three-dimensional model of equal opportunities as a regulative ideal?

The single principle of background fairness running throughout the arguments of this book is that the initial starting positions of individuals in any competition are fair when all enjoy status equality.[49] This principle of status equality does not necessarily require that all individuals start a competition with the same amount of wealth or other economic resources. Nor does it necessarily require that all individuals be at the same level of human functioning or some other objective standard of well-being. Neither still does it mean that each individual has the same power to affect an outcome. In ordinary language, the term status derives from the Latin meaning literally 'standing' in society.[50] Status equality as a principle of background fairness requires, therefore, that all persons enjoy the same standing in the competition.

Before elaborating in more detail on this requirement, it may help to give a concrete example of status equality to elucidate the basic idea. The

---

[48] This is part of the basic motivation for the revisions to justice as fairness that John Rawls introduces in *Political Liberalism*.

[49] My development of the idea of status equality has been influenced especially by Thomas Nagel, 'Personal Rights and Public Space,' *Philosophy & Public Affairs*, Vol. 24 (1995); Frances Kamm, *Morality, Mortality, Volume II: Rights, Duties, and Status* (Oxford: Oxford University Press, 1996); and Deborah Satz, 'Markets in Women's Sexual Labor,' *Ethics*, Vol. 106 (1995), pp. 63–85, and 'Status Inequalities and Models of Market Socialism' in Erik Olin Wright, editor, *Equal Shares* (New York: Verso, 1996).

[50] Bryan S. Turner, *Status* (Minneapolis: University of Minnesota Press, 1988), p. 2.

example I have in mind is the presumption of innocence for the accused in criminal trials. At the very foundation of Anglo-American criminal justice is this presumption: Every accused person facing a criminal trial enjoys the same standing of innocence until proven guilty beyond a reasonable doubt in a court of law. This standing is enjoyed by an individual, regardless of wealth, class, race, disability, religion, creed, sex, or nationality. Moreover, even if the accused has been previously convicted of a crime, in each new trial that individual once again enjoys the status enjoyed by all others facing a criminal trial. The presumption of innocence is, in this respect, inviolable; this status cannot be alienated or infringed without being violated.[51] The status equality reflected in the presumption of innocence shapes our judgements about fair trials and their procedures regarding onus of proof, disclosure, evidence rules, and so on. In other words, status equality functions as a regulative ideal of background fairness for criminal trials when those trials are viewed as competitions between the accused and the state. The principle of status equality utilized in this book can be understood as an attempt to abstract from this example of the presumption of innocence.

The very idea of status can be clarified by contrasting it with identity. As Charles Taylor explains it, identity, "designates something like a person's understanding of who they are, of their fundamental defining characteristic as a human being."[52] Identity is therefore a subjective matter in the sense that it is a function of one's *own* understanding, even though that understanding may be shaped partially by others. Status is, in contrast, exclusively a function of factors other than one's own self-understanding. Status is a matter of recognition by others. The presumption of innocence is, for instance, a status because it is exclusively a function of how the court recognizes the accused.

Let me now draw a distinction between *moral status* and *social status*. Historically, social status has been linked by sociologists to social stratification. The main idea is that societies distinguish between different positions individuals can occupy along any of a number of different trajectories including, to cite the most familiar ones, income, ownership of the means of production, race and ethnicity, religion, sex and gender, sexual orientation, education, and disability. Social status is a

---

[51] The inviolability of status is an important theme in Nagel, 'Personal Rights and Public Space.'

[52] Charles Taylor, 'The Politics of Recognition' in Amy Gutmann, editor, *Multiculturalism and The Politics of Recognition* (Princeton: Princeton University Press, 1992), p. 25.

reflection of what position an individual holds in society with respect to one of these means of differentiation. The social status of an individual is therefore his or her standing in this system of social stratification.[53] For many sociologists, because of the conceptual link between social stratification and social status, it is nonsensical to talk about equality of social status.

This makes for a neat point of contrast with moral status. For our purposes, the moral status of an individual is his or her standing in the moral universe. In the history of ethics, the moral universe was often thought by philosophers in the past to be stratified in much the same way sociologists interpret social stratification in contemporary societies. However, for the past two hundred years, under the influence of Kant's moral philosophy, the moral universe has been predominantly viewed (at least by secular moral and political philosophy) as one where all individuals share a common humanity that recognizes the same standing for each, and nothing else in the moral universe has higher standing.[54] In this moral universe equality of status for all individuals, far from being nonsensical, is a moral platitude.[55]

The principle of status equality is at base a claim about moral status. It must be underlined, however, that it is also a principle of background fairness. Status equality identifies a starting position – the same moral

---

[53] At the risk of touching on complex issues in social stratification theory and research, there seems to me no reason why this account of social status cannot be extended to groups as well.

[54] J.B. Schneewind writes of Kant's new vision of the moral universe, "His astonishing claim is that God and we can share membership in a single moral community only if we all equally legislate the law we are to obey . . . For Kant, however, it is not knowledge of independent and eternal moral truth that puts us on an equal footing with God in the moral community. It is our ability to make and live by moral law. The invention of autonomy gave Kant what he thought was the only morally satisfactory theory of the status of human beings in a universe shared with God.' See *The Invention of Autonomy* (New York: Cambridge University Press, 1998), pp. 512–13.

[55] Some commentators on the history of moral philosophy, perhaps most notably Peter Berger, have maintained that this development reflects a departure from the concept of moral status to the concept of human dignity. See Peter Berger, 'On the Obsolescence of the Concept of Honor' in Stanley Hauerwas & Alasdair MacIntyre, editors, *Revisions: Changing Perspectives in Moral Philosophy* (Notre Dame: University of Notre Dame Press, 1983). From the perspective of background fairness, what the concept of moral status retains but the concept of dignity loses is the centrality of 'standing.' My example of the presumption of innocence is about standing and status, and it would seem to me a misdescription to express it in terms of dignity.

status for each and no higher moral standing possible – in a competition that all individuals should enjoy. It is in this respect a benchmark for measuring the background fairness of the competition. But it shouldn't be overlooked that a competition from these initially fair starting positions then ensues, with the requisite upshot that some competitors may emerge as winners, others losers, with the attendant differences in social status. From the perspective of background fairness, this outcome is fair by virtue of the status equality that characterized the competition at the outset.[56] The example of the presumption of innocence can be used to illustrate the intuitive force of the underlying reasoning. Imagine two accused individuals each facing a trial for a similar offence at the same time in different courtrooms. The presumption of innocence for each meets the requirements of status equality. At the outset of their trials, each is presumed innocent, and this affects how they are duly treated during their trials. In due course, however, one accused is found guilty, the other not guilty. At the end of the trials, the status of the individuals is therefore very different. Still, this outcome will not strike most of us as contrary to background fairness; those benchmarks were met by the court's recognition of the presumption of innocence for both individuals.

Although the principle of status equality deals in the currency of moral status, it is essential to recognize that the relationship between social status and moral status is analogous to how most rights theorists view the relationship between legal rights and moral rights. Legal and moral rights are ordinarily thought to share the same structure; this is what makes them both types of rights. But, whilst legal rights exist by virtue of a legal system, moral rights are independent of positive law. An important function of moral rights is, however, to provide a critical perspective on positive law. I don't mean that all moral rights should receive legal recognition; some familiar moral rights clearly shouldn't. There are two especially important aspects of the insight that moral rights bring a critical perspective to bear on positive law. The first aspect is that moral rights often are an inspiration for legal rights. For example, many constitutional theories of freedom of expression are inspired by a moral vision of the right to freedom of expression. The second aspect

---

[56] It is an instance of what Rawls calls "pure procedural justice." This "obtains when there is no independent criterion for the right result: instead there is a correct or fair procedure such that the outcome is likewise correct or fair, whatever it is, provided that the procedure has been properly followed." See *A Theory of Justice*, p. 86.

is that the failings and injustices of existing legal rights, as opposed to, say, the law's silence, are the most discernible focal point for the critical perspective moral rights offer to positive law.

There are two parallel aspects in the relationship between moral status and social status. First, accounts of moral status provide an inspiration for concerns about social stratification and social status. The structure of status in the moral universe can provide a blueprint for the structure of status in society. Second, the requirements of the principle of status equality are best thought of concretely in terms of social stratification and its attending unfairness. The demands of background fairness are approached in this book through attention to the questions of fairness and equality raised by the ascription of social status. As I noted in the introductory chapter, the last six chapters of this book are organized around race, class, and gender as types of social status. These types are, I observed, major sites for inequalities in civil society. The indexes of social status – inequalities in wealth and income, power, and privilege – provide here evidence when the demands of the background principle of status equality are not met.

Why status equality? What makes this the appropriate currency of background fairness in the three-dimensional model of equal opportunities as a regulative ideal? Certainly, among philosophers and economists, when concerns about background fairness have been raised, the predominant focus has been on material inequalities, however they are measured.[57] That is to say, the emphasis has been on income and wealth, access to educational resources, control over means of production, and so on. In more abstract terms, the currency has been goods and resources. This preoccupation with material inequalities has not gone completely unchallenged. Some have emphasized instead the importance of welfare or utility, although it is unclear to me how exactly welfare or utility might inform a principle of background fairness. Others such as Amartya Sen and Martha Nussbaum have argued that the concern should be on the capabilities and functionings of people, and resources and goods only to the extent that they contribute to capabilities and functionings.[58] The principle of status equality constitutes

---

[57] I have deliberately left sociologists out of this generalization.

[58] See, especially, Martha Nussbaum, *Women and Human Development: The Capabilities Approach* (Cambridge, UK: Cambridge University Press, 2000), pp. 4–15, and Amartya Sen, *Development as Freedom* (New York: Anchor Books, 1999), pp. 74–85.

another avenue for challenging the conventional egalitarian emphasis on inequalities in material resources and goods.[59]

The case for the principle of status equality is simple. If the preceding analysis of background fairness in a competition is correct, the basic concern is with the starting positions of competitors. Status is *the* currency of starting positions; the principle of status equality identifies the egalitarian standard of that currency.[60] Resources or goods such as income are mere proxies for the real currency of background fairness. This doesn't mean that they are often a very good proxy, but we shouldn't lose sight of the that they are still proxies, nonetheless.

The principle of status equality differs from, and is much more demanding than, the so-called principle of anti-discrimination. This principle is very familiar, and prevails in litigation around equality rights in Canada, Great Britain, and the United States. At the core of the anti-discrimination principle is the idea that similar things should be treated similarly. This presupposes that whilst discriminatory treatment is inevitable, some discrimination is justified and other discrimination is arbitrary. The anti-discrimination principle prohibits 'arbitrary' discrimination.[61] Much of the initial application of the anti-discrimination principle was on race. So, for instance, Paul Brest, in one of the most influential defences of the principle, says simply, "By the 'antidiscrimination principle' I mean the general principle disfavoring classifications and other decisions and practices that depend on the race (or ethnic origin) of the parties affected."[62] More recently, and especially outside of the United States, the anti-discrimination principle has been readily applied to other classifications including sex and gender, disability, sexual orientation, religion, and age. The anti-discrimination principle can be easily formulated as a principle of background fairness: Starting-positions in a competition are fair when no competitors face arbitrary discrimination.

The growing influence of the anti-discrimination principle in equality rights litigation neatly dovetails with significant developments in

---

[59] Satz makes a similar point in 'Status Inequalities and Models of Market Socialism,' p. 74.

[60] This is something that is lost in David Miller's account of equality of status in 'Equality and Justice' in Andrew Mason, editor, *Ideals of Equality*, pp. 23, 31–36.

[61] Owen Fiss, 'Groups and the Equal Protection Clause,' *Philosophy & Public Affairs* Vol. 5 (1976), p. 109, reprinted in Christopher McCrudden, editor, *Anti-Discrimination Law* (New York: New York University Press, 1991), p. 59.

[62] Paul Brest, 'Forward: In Defense of the Antidiscrimination Principle,' *Harvard Law Review*, Vol. 90 (1976), p. 1, reprinted in McCrudden, *Anti-Discrimination Law*, p. 3.

political philosophy, in particular the contributions of John Rawls. What constitutes arbitrary discrimination? Where is the line between what is arbitrary and non-arbitrary? Rawls in *A Theory of Justice* has provided the best-known answer.[63] For Rawls, this distinction is necessarily a *moral* one. What precisely is arbitrary from a moral point of view? The clearest cases involve factors that are a reflection of one's birth. Race, class, and sex are ordinarily thought of as illustrations of this. Who your parents are is said to be arbitrary from a moral point of view; nobody deserves to have rich or poor parents or parents of a particular race. Likewise, the particular sex-determining chromosomes you receive upon conception seem arbitrary in the same way. What all these factors appear to have in common is that they are the consequence of contingencies – what Rawls calls "the arbitrariness of fortune" over which an individual has no control or choice. The logical implication is that the line demarcating 'arbitrary' discrimination rests on classifications such as race, class, and sex being the result of this "arbitrariness of fortune."[64]

---

[63] Rawls, *A Theory of Justice*, esp. pp. 72–74.

[64] It is not my intention here to press in detail criticisms of Rawls nor the anti-discrimination principle, as my main interest is drawing the contrast between the anti-discrimination principle and the principle of status equality. (Rawls receives much more careful scrutiny in the next chapter.) But it should be noted that others have made some important and relevant criticisms of the anti-discrimination principle. Feminist critics have argued, for example, that in a gendered society, the distinction between arbitrary and justified discrimination routinely assumes a male standard. This has been parlayed into a challenge to the Rawlsian theme that justified discrimination can be traced to choices and personal responsibility. For example, while many pregnancies can be traced to individual choices made by women, discrimination against pregnant women is still unfair. And this is now routinely recognized in statutory law. But the fact that legal measures protecting pregnant women are often represented as special treatment reveals that the male experience is assumed to be the norm, and deviance from that norm the exception, even though most women but no men will experience pregnancy in the course of their lifetimes. Other critics have been very effective in pointing out another fundamental flaw with this approach to background fairness. The flaw is that when the idea of nullifying for natural and social contingencies in initial starting positions is taken to its logical conclusion, any model of equality of opportunity that relies on it becomes indistinguishable from a theory of equality of results. The reason is that at some level, practically any difference between individuals, including differences in talents and skills and effort, is a contingent factor. Hence, concludes Brian Barry, "since anything that makes for different outcomes for indistinguishable entities is ... morally arbitrary, we can reduce this idea of equal opportunity for equals in the relevant respect to that of simple equality of outcomes.' See Brian Barry, 'Equal Opportunity and Moral Arbitrariness' in Norman Bowie, editor, *Equal Opportunity* (Boulder: Westview, 1988), p. 31.

The normative contrast between the principle of status equality and the principle of non-discrimination is stark when we focus on the controversial issue of racial profiling in police. The most familiar example of this type of racial profiling is the police practice of stopping motorists from certain minority groups because their race is grounds for criminal suspicion. Typically, such racial profiling is either *thin* or *thick*. *Thin* racial profiling occurs when police stop motorists solely because of their race. *Thick* racial profiling occurs when police stop motorists for several reasons including their race. For instance, a police officer may stop a black motorist partly because of his or her race but also because in the officer's judgment the motorist was driving erratically. While the concern about police stops tracking racial lines has received the most public scrutiny in the United States, it is also a genuine issue in Canada and the United Kingdom.

At dispute in racial profiling is the extent to which the police use, in Randall Kennedy's perceptive phrase, "a person's race as a proxy for an increased likelihood of criminal misconduct."[65] The term proxy is intended to capture the point that for police who stop black drivers in greater proportions than white drivers, they are not simply stopping the driver because of his or her race but rather because his or her race is correlated to some other trait – namely, a (perceived) increased risk of criminality. The background context is that in the United States, young black men, in relation to the percentage of the total population, are perceived to, and indeed do, commit many more crimes under most statistical analyses. The point is that the use of a proxy of this sort by the police has the appearance of being quite reasonable. Indeed, Kennedy found in his survey of recent American case law that, "courts have broadly *defended* police use of racial proxies by asserting, among other things, that such strategies are realistic."[66] The Canadian courts also don't have a strong record of questioning racial profiling.[67]

While racial profiling is intuitively for egalitarians morally repugnant and the court record dismaying, racial profiling under the anti-discrimination principle raises hard questions that can excuse police

---

[65] Randall Kennedy, *Race, Crime, and the Law* (New York: Pantheon Press, 1997), p. 137.

[66] Kennedy, *Race, Crime, and the Law*, p. 148.

[67] See Sujit Choudhry, 'Protecting Equality in the Face of Terror: Ethnic and Racial Profiling and Section 15 of the Charter' in Ronald J. Daniels, Patrick Macklem, and Kent Roach, editors, *The Security of Freedom: Essays on Canada's Anti-Terrorism Bill* (Toronto: University of Toronto Press, 2001).

use of it. Defenders of racial profiling by police, especially *thick* racial profiling, generally allow that the practice is discriminatory, but hold that this discrimination is justified, given the statistical basis for the use of racial proxies.[68] As Jeffrey Goldberg has put it, "From the front seat of a police cruiser, racial profiling is not racism. It's a tool – and cops have no intention of giving it up."[69] The anti-discrimination principle takes this sort of rationale seriously, and presumably the weak record of American and Canadian courts on racial profiling suggests the influence this principle has on its decision-making.

The principle of status equality requires taking a very different perspective on racial profiling by police. Reliance on racial proxies by the police is, in the terms of this principle, fundamentally an issue of standing. Allowing for racial proxies amounts to ascribing to individuals different standings in criminal investigations based on their race. In other words, individuals do not enjoy a level playing field, with equal starting positions. Some individuals start behind others simply by virtue of their race. Racial profiling is therefore prohibited by the principle of status equality because in essence it amounts to unequal status for some individuals. Thus, under the three-dimensional model of equal opportunities as a regulative ideal where status equality is the appropriate principle of background fairness, policing practices would forbid the use of the tool of racial proxies. There would be no need to engage, as some courts have, the effectiveness or efficiency of that tool in order to judge if it constitutes justified discrimination in the manner that the principle of anti-discrimination demands. The relevant upshot is that the principle of status equality draws a clear line in the sand based on standing, and police practices such as racial profiling cross that line.

2.5 THE IDEA OF STAKES FAIRNESS

Stakes fairness concentrates on the regulation of the outcome or effect of a competition. This distinguishes it from both procedural and background fairness. I suggested earlier that a distinctive feature of the three-dimensional model of equal opportunities as a regulative ideal is the reference to stakes fairness. In effect, stakes fairness has been

---

[68] For some excellent new empirical evidence challenging the effectiveness of racial profiling, see David A. Harris, *Profiles in Injustice: Why Racial Profiling Cannot Work* (New York, The Free Press, 2002), pp. 75–87.

[69] Jeffrey Goldberg, 'The Color of Suspicion,' *The New York Times Magazine* (June 20, 1999), p. 51.

under-appreciated in models of equality of opportunity, and can often be shown to be at the heart of some regulative issues that arise regarding inequalities in civil society. But the concept of stakes fairness shares certain features with other theories of social justice that should be acknowledged.

There are two aspects of stakes fairness that inform the three-dimensional model of equal opportunities as a regulative ideal – concern with what and how much is actually at stake in an individual competition and concern with limiting the effect of the result of one competition on another. At the core of the very idea of stakes fairness is this concern about what and how much is actually at stake in an individual competition. Recall from Section 2.2 that when I introduced it as one dimension of fairness in equality of opportunity, I used an analogy from prize fighting, where it is the norm for professional boxers to share the prize, the difference between the winner and loser being their proportion of the prize. This example expresses the insight that winner-take-all stakes for competitive opportunities are rarely fair.[70] That basic insight defines the role of stakes fairness in the three-dimensional model of equal opportunities as a regulative ideal. Appeals to stakes fairness in subsequent chapters reveal that it is principally a regulatory device to prescribe a wider distribution of the prizes at stake in a competition than a simple winner-take-all scheme.

Constraining an outcome or benefit with an eye to broadening the scope of the distribution has been an important theme in modern economics and political philosophy, even though it has not previously been well developed within a theory of equality of opportunity. Some of the

---

[70] Another analogy based on a controversial public issue may help to sharpen this idea of stakes fairness. Consider the case against capital punishment. Some opponents of capital punishment hold that it is simply wrong for the state to have the authority to kill someone. Others say something to the effect that two wrongs don't make a right. Yet, among the general public, the most frequently cited reason for reservations about capital punishment concerns wrongful convictions. Neither of the two views mentioned here is able to capture fully reservations based on the concern about wrongful conviction; they both hold that capital punishment in any circumstances is wrong. Think about capital punishment from the perspective of stakes fairness. Capital punishment in a modern legal system is a sentence that flows from a competitive trial system between the accused and the state. The relevant question is whether capital punishment makes the stakes too high in this competition. And it is easy to imagine why many people might concur; what wrongful conviction does is highlight how high (and unfair) the stakes are when capital punishment exists. Capital punishment is, to put it bluntly, the ultimate winner-take-all stake.

most familiar principles of welfare economics such as Paretian optimality and the Kaldor-Hicks rule are certainly a reflection of this theme. The single most important philosophical expression of this theme has been by John Rawls. Rawls's theory of justice as fairness is a special case of a more general conception of justice that he formulates in the following way:

All social values – liberty and opportunity, income and wealth, and the social bases of self-respect – are to be distributed equally unless an unequal distribution of any, or all, of these values is to everyone's advantage.[71]

There is a clear sense in which this general conception of justice expresses a possible principle of stakes fairness. The main idea, as Rawls points out, is that, "injustice is simply inequalities that are not to the benefit of all."[72] But this idea is deeply problematic as a standard for stakes fairness within the framework of competitive equality of opportunity. As I noted at the beginning of this chapter, competitions yield winners and losers; this is a constitutive feature of competitive models of equal opportunity. Imagine a competitive Olympic sport such as figure skating. The stakes are familiar: the gold, silver, and bronze medals. Three levels of medals entail a wider distribution than simply winner-take-all. The results of this competition conform to widely held views of stakes fairness, even though the resultant inequalities do not benefit everyone.[73]

There is an even more penetrating problem with this general concept of justice functioning as principle of stakes fairness in a model of competitive equal opportunity. In Section 2.2, I noted that competitions do not have a preconceived winner or outcome. In a competitive model of equal opportunity, the winner is a function of a set of fair rules. And if the winners do not conform to an ideal type, it is perverse to propose changing a set of *fair* rules in order to affect a change in this outcome. If the rules are fair, so too must be the outcome. Any principle of stakes fairness must respect this general framework. This poses, however, a serious difficulty for Rawls's general conception of justice because there is a clear sense in which it has a preconceived fair outcome: The baseline is

---

[71] Rawls, *A Theory of Justice, revised edition* (Cambridge, MA: Harvard University Press, 1999), p. 54. I have made reference to the newly revised edition of *A Theory of Justice* only when the text differs from the original published in 1971.

[72] *Ibid.*, p. 54.

[73] It may be possible to fabricate some sort of scenario where everyone does benefit, but such a fabrication strains our common sense. Rawls stresses this sort of role for common sense throughout his works. See, e.g., *Justice as Fairness: A Restatement* (Cambridge MA: Harvard University Press, 2001), p. 5n5.

equality, and deviations from that baseline are permissible when it is to everyone's advantage.[74] Rules should be designed to affect this outcome, and if they don't yield this outcome, they should be changed. The problem is then one of fit. Stakes fairness requires a certain type of principle, and the general conception of justice seems not to fit that type.

Now, Rawls's own theory of justice as fairness advances the following two principles:

(a) Each person has the same indefeasible claim to a fully adequate scheme of equal basic liberties, which scheme is compatible with the same scheme of liberties for all; and

(b) Social and economic inequalities are to satisfy two conditions: first, they are to be attached to offices and positions open to all under conditions of fair equality of opportunity; and second, they are to be to the greatest benefit of the least-advantaged members of society (the difference principle).[75]

Although Rawls characterizes "justice as fairness" as a special case of the general conception of justice, he emphasizes that certain aspects of the general conception are questionable, especially that it allows for more inequalities than justice permits (in his view), and the two principles correct for this mistake. As Rawls explains it,

The general conception of justice imposes no restrictions on what sort of inequalities are permissible; it only requires that everyone's position be improved. We need not suppose anything so drastic as consenting to a condition of slavery. Imagine instead that people seem willing to forego certain political rights when the economic returns are significant. It is this kind of exchange which the two

---

[74] This parallels an observation Rawls makes about utilitarianism: "Utilitarianism does not interpret the basic structure as a scheme of pure procedural justice. For the utilitarian has, in principle anyway, an independent standard for judging all distributions, namely, whether they produce the greatest net balance of satisfaction.' See *A Theory of Justice*, p. 89. He also writes on p. 79: "The difference principle is, strictly speaking, a maximizing principle." The similarity in structure I am noting here was long ago noted by Robert Nozick in his discussion of end-state principles of justice in *Anarchy, State, and Utopia* (New York: Basic Books, 1974), pp. 153–55.

[75] Rawls, *Justice as Fairness*, pp. 42–43. Rawls has revised these two principles in various ways. I use the most recent formulation here. Compare it with Rawls, *Political Liberalism*, pp. 5–6 (where he also includes reference to the fair value of "equal political liberties") and the original formulation in *A Theory of Justice*, pp. 302–03, as well as *A Theory of Justice, revised edition*, pp. 266–67 (which is a more detailed elaboration of the two principles quoted in the text).

principles rules out; being arranged in serial order they do not permit exchanges between basic liberties and economic and social gains except under extenuating circumstances.[76]

What does this mean for stakes fairness? The fact that Rawls differentiates between the difference principle and the general conception of justice raises the possibility that the difference principle is a plausible principle of stakes fairness, even though the general conception of justice is not.

Indeed, someone might try to represent Rawls's second principle of justice, to use the term I introduce in this chapter, as a three-dimensional model of equality of opportunity, although I don't know of anyone who has done so. After all, the first part of the second principle – fair equality of opportunity – involves reference to procedural fairness and background fairness, and the second part – the difference principle – could be construed as involving stakes fairness. Is this a reasonable reading of Rawls?

Let me suggest two reasons why it is not. The first is that although Rawls labels the combination of fair equality of opportunity and the difference principle "democratic equality," he consistently presents the difference principle as a standard of fairness independent of equality of opportunity, whereas on any variation of the three-dimensional model, stakes fairness is integral to equality of opportunity.[77] For Rawls, the two principles of justice as fairness and their constitutive parts are designed to work in tandem but reflect the distinct values of freedom and equality. Within the second principle, he imagines the requirements of fair equality of opportunity and the difference principle pulling in different directions.[78] Infringements of fair equality of opportunity for Rawls arise when there is an inequality of opportunity. The question for him is when are infringements of fair equality of opportunity justified. The difference principle allows for only one sort of justified infringement: "An inequality of opportunity must enhance the opportunities of those

---

[76] Rawls, *A Theory of Justice, revised edition*, p. 55.

[77] Throughout the discussion here, the difference principle refers only to the second part of the second principle of justice as fairness. This is consistent with how Rawls now insists the term be used, e.g. *Justice as Fairness*, p. 43n3, and *A Theory of Justice, revised edition*, p. 72.

[78] The reason for this may well be a reflection of the sort of tension Derek Parfit highlights between principles of equality and principles that reflect giving priority to the less well off. See 'Equality and Priority' in Mason, editor, *Ideals of Equality*.

with the lesser opportunity."[79] Notice, therefore, that the basic role of the difference principle is to justify unequal opportunities. This contrasts with the primary role of stakes fairness in the three-dimensional model, which is to identify a regulative dimension of what equal opportunities requires.

The second reason is that the difference principle does not fit the principle type required of stakes fairness. I stressed earlier that any principle of stakes fairness must respect the general framework that holds that if the rules are fair, so too must be the outcome. The general conception of justice, I argued, does not fit with this requirement. As Rawls himself has noted, however, the difference principle has the same form as the general conception of justice. "In fact," writes Rawls, "the general conception is simply the difference principle applied to all primary goods including liberty and opportunity and no longer constrained by other parts of the special conception."[80] Does the same objection then apply? I shall say yes, while admitting that this is a complicated issue. Rawls in general frequently characterizes justice as fairness as a case of pure procedural justice where "the essential feature of pure procedural justice is that what is just is specified by the outcome of the procedure, whatever it may be. There is no prior and already given criterion against which the outcome is to be checked."[81] The relevant point is that if all of the constitutive parts of the two principles of justice as fairness reflect pure procedural justice, then it would seem that the difference principle is a good fit for stakes fairness. However, Rawls draws on pure procedural justice principally to characterize fair equality of opportunity[82] and the original position.[83] (Unfortunately, Rawls is not unambiguous about this.[84]) But I believe that it is a pretty safe interpretation of his view. Hence, it is doubtful that Rawls views the difference principle

---

[79] Rawls, *A Theory of Justice*, p. 303. Rawls also writes, "Infringements of fair equality of opportunity are not justified by a greater sum of advantages enjoyed others or by society as a whole," 302. This passage has been deleted from *A Theory of Justice, Revised Edition*, p. 265.

[80] Rawls, *A Theory of Justice*, p. 83.

[81] Rawls, *Political Liberalism, paperback edition* (New York: Columbia University Press, 1996), p. 73.

[82] Rawls writes in *A Theory of Justice, revised edition*, "The role of the principle of fair opportunity is to insure that the system of cooperation is one of pure procedural justice." p. 76. This sentence is slightly revised from the original on p. 87 of *A Theory of Justice*.

[83] This is especially evident in *Political Liberalism, paperback edition*, pp. 72–74.

[84] This is clearly shown by Brian Barry, *Theories of Justice* (Berkeley: University of California Press, 1989), pp. 265–68, 307–19.

as a case of pure procedural justice. And in practical terms, the difference principle seems to embody merely a more constrained version of the general conception of justice. The upshot is that although stakes fairness and Rawls's difference principle are a reflection of similar concerns, the latter cannot be construed as a principle of stakes fairness.

At the start of Section 2.5, I mentioned that there are two aspects to the idea of stakes fairness in the three-dimensional model, one reflecting a concern with how much is at stake in a given competition, the other a concern with limiting the effects of one competition on another. With regard to this other aspect of stakes fairness, the fundamental idea is that winning or losing one competitive opportunity in civil society shouldn't affect one's prospects in a competition for another opportunity. For example, financial success shouldn't translate into better educational prospects; ability to pay or any other similar measurement should not affect the educational opportunities an individual enjoys. In many respects, this aspect of stakes fairness blurs the distinction between this dimension of fairness and background fairness; in effect, the concern can also be represented as one about the initial standing of individuals in a competition. But I use the language of stakes fairness because it seems to me that the most effective way to address the underlying concern here is by regulating the stakes in any given competition. This is the basic insight Rousseau offers when, out of concern about the corrupting influence of wealth, he prescribes that "no citizen shall be rich enough to be able to buy another, and none poor enough to be forced to sell himself."[85]

This second aspect of stakes fairness bears some resemblance to Michael Walzer's vision of a regime of complex equality. For Walzer,

complex equality means that no citizen's standing in one sphere or with regard to one social good can be undercut by his standing in some other sphere, with regard to some other good. Thus, citizen X may be chosen over citizen Y for political office, and then the two of them will be unequal in the sphere of politics. But they will be equal generally so long as X's office gives him no advantage over Y in any other sphere – superior medical care, access to better schools for his children, entrepreneurial opportunities, and so on.[86]

Although Walzer's vision of complex equality is compelling, sceptics have pressed him to explain more precisely where the boundaries for

---

[85] Jean-Jacques Rousseau, 'The Social Contract,' Book II, ch. 11, in *The Essential Rousseau*, translated by Lowell Bair (New York: Mentor Books, 1974), p. 45.
[86] Walzer, *Spheres of Justice*, p. 19.

the different spheres of justice lie. And few have been swayed by his suggestions that the social meanings of goods can guide us in identifying the nature of the spheres and their borders. Ultimately, as he readily admits,[87] Walzer's approach focusses on the injustice of border crossings between spheres and marginalizes concerns about the fairness of the effect or outcome within the sphere of competition. It is the latter – the other aspect of stakes fairness noted earlier – that is at the very core of stakes fairness.

The added dimension of stakes fairness in the three-dimensional model makes it a more comprehensive account of equality of opportunity than two-dimensional models. Consider, by comparison, the theory of equality of opportunity developed by John Roemer. As I noted at the beginning of this chapter, Reomer has been among those egalitarians leading the renewed interest in equality of opportunity. There are certain important points of convergence between Roemer's theory and the three-dimensional model of equal opportunities as a regulative ideal I have advanced here. We share the view that equality of opportunity should be approached from the perspective of a level playing field. There is also agreement that equality of opportunity is not a comprehensive view about fair shares but rather an ideal that can be applied to different spheres of social life.[88] Moreover, Roemer is sensitive to the importance of distinguishing equality of opportunity and meritocracy.[89] Roemer, however, places the idea of responsibility at the very centre of his theory, whereas I regard it as peripheral to the concept of equality of opportunity. But the most fundamental difference is that Roemer's theory of equality of opportunity is a two-dimensional view, whereas mine is three-dimensional. And it can be shown that weaknesses with Roemer's theory stem from his neglect of the third dimension of fairness.

Earlier I used the analogy of a boxing match to explain the importance of the three-fold distinction between procedural fairness, stakes fairness, and background fairness. Although Roemer does not refer to boxing in his exposition of his theory, boxing can also be used to explain the main elements of his theory. Recall that boxers are classified according to their body weight, and matches involve pairing similarly

---

[87] See, especially, the contrast Walzer draws between his vision of complex equality and the preoccupation of most political philosophers with monopoly in *Spheres of Justice*, pp. 16–17.

[88] Roemer, *Equality of Opportunity*, p. 3.

[89] Roemer, *Equality of Opportunity*, pp. 16, 84–85.

classified boxers. In my view, this practice is useful to illustrate the implicit role of background fairness but provides little insight into the precise principle of background fairness that should govern equal opportunities. Roemer seems to find something substantially insightful about this practice in boxing. He imagines partitioning the entire relevant population into *types*, where types are analogous to the weight classifications in boxing between, say, a flyweight and a heavyweight. What determines an individual's membership in a particular type is his or her 'ability,' which for Roemer is a term of art meaning the propensity to transform *circumstances* into achievement.[90] An individual's *circumstances* can be understood as those factors, such as his or her genes, family background, culture, and general social milieu, that are beyond his or her control. (Ability performs the same function in identifying a person's type as body weight determines a boxer's fighting class.) Ability contrasts with 'effort,' which for Roemer is a proxy for that over which a person has control. The implication of partitioning individuals into types based on their ability is that under conditions of perfect competition, any differences in achievement are the result of differences in the expenditure of effort. As Roemer explains it,

We will observe, in all likelihood, a *distribution* of effort levels in each type... *Where* on that distribution an individual sits is, however, by construction, due to his choice of effort... equal-opportunity policy must equalize, in some average sense yet to be defined, the... achievements of all types, but not equalize the achievements within types, which differ according to effort.[91]

To return to the boxing analogy, the reasoning is that if (counterfactually) ability in boxing is simply a function of body weight, then successes or failures in matches between similarly classified boxers would be determined by effort, and equality of opportunity requires equalizing the prizes for the expenditure of effort across weight classifications.

How precisely does Roemer propose to equalize the advantages of achievement across types?

I propose that a distribution of the resource across types be chosen so that for each centile π, the achievement levels of all those at the πth centile of their respective effort distributions are equal. If such a distribution of the resource exists, I deem it to be the equal-opportunity policy.[92]

---

[90] Roemer, *Equality of Opportunity*, p. 2.
[91] Roemer, *Equality of Opportunity*, p. 7.
[92] Roemer, *Equality of Opportunity*, p. 10.

The proposal amounts to the requirement that if you are at, say, the 80th percentile in terms of effort in your particular type, then the advantages of achievement for you should be the same as those of others at the 80th percentile in other types. The principle is that the benefits you receive should be determined by your effort, not your ability. "[L]evelling the playing field," declares Roemer, "means guaranteeing that those who apply equal degrees of effort end up with equal achievement, regardless of their circumstances."[93]

Now, although Roemer's theory of equality of opportunity is admirable for its technical precision, it is possible to put pressure on the broad vision of equal opportunities as a regulative ideal it projects. His theory focusses on the inputs into a competition. By definition, for Roemer, those inputs can be classified as either *effort* or *circumstances*. Achievement in the competition is designed to be a function of the effort input. But it is the nature of competitions that often the outcomes are influenced by factors aside from the input factors, however exhaustively those factors are defined. Indeed, part of the thrill and excitement of, say, a game such as hockey is the unpredictability of the outcome, even when all of the input factors are known entities. And part of the powerful image in our culture of the under-dog winning is a reflection of this. Roemer's theory is sterile in how it envisions competitive opportunities and the dynamics involved in determining who wins and loses.

This sterility stems from the two-dimensional focus on background and procedural fairness. As we have seen, background fairness is indeed essentially a matter of regulating the starting positions or input factors in a competition. But when stakes fairness is added to the tool kit of a theory of equal opportunity, it becomes possible to imagine the normative regulation of competitions in ways that better reflect the dynamic and unpredictability of the outcomes, in effect by regulating what is at stake in the competition, ensuring a broader distribution of the prizes, and limiting how much competitors can gain or lose.

The added dimension of stakes fairness allows us to handle competitions that Roemer's theory is incapable of handling.[94] Specifically, Roemer doesn't allow for competitions across types; his objective is the same distribution of achievement within each type. But sometimes it is compelling to have competitions with competitors from vastly different circumstances, not because those from the most advantaged

---

[93] Roemer, *Equality of Opportunity*, p. 12.
[94] This very important point I owe to one of the anonymous referees.

backgrounds are sure to win but because the outcome of a genuine competition that is not predetermined provides for the possibility that the under-dog can win. Witness Toni Morrison winning the Nobel Prize for Literature, the first African American women to do so. Or the United States Ice Hockey team beating the USSR for the gold medal at the 1980 Winter Olympics in Lake Placid. These outcomes are inspirational, but they also involve, in Roemer's terms, competitions across types. Stakes fairness allows for these sorts of competitions while regulating what is at stake.

2.6 CONCLUSION

This chapter outlines in some depth the three-dimensional model of equal opportunities as a regulative ideal. I have argued that by comparison with one- and two-dimensional views of equality of opportunity, this three-dimensional model is better able to handle egalitarian concerns about the normative regulation of competitions in civil society for scarce resources and goods. I have also sought here to dispel the influential charge that an equal opportunities model is incapable of invoking concerns about substantive justice. My argument has been that the added dimensions of background and stakes fairness move a theory of equality of opportunity from being merely formal to being capable of addressing genuine inequalities of race, class, and gender in civil society. In the next chapter, this account of the three-dimensional model is extended to show why the charge that equality of opportunities magnifies natural inequalities likewise rests on a mistake.

Chapter 3

Equal Opportunity without Natural Inequalities

3.1 INTRODUCTION

At the beginning of the last chapter, I noted two influential objections raised by egalitarians to the general concept of equality of opportunity. The first, which was the principal focus of my initial formulation of the three-dimensional model of equal opportunities as a regulative ideal, holds that equality of opportunity is an inadequate account of egalitarian justice because it is merely formal and empty of a commitment to substantive equality. The second objection makes the accusation that equality of opportunity builds upon and magnifies natural inequalities between persons, and for this reason is not a genuine account of egalitarian justice. It is this second objection that has convinced so many modern liberal egalitarians to give up on the ideal of equality of opportunity.[1] In John Schaar's very influential 1967 critique, equality of opportunity "is really a demand for an equal right and opportunity to become unequal ... [I]t so arranges social conditions that each individual can go as high as his natural abilities will permit."[2] Likewise, Ronald Dworkin charges that equality of opportunity is fraudulent as an ideal, "fraudulent because in a market economy people do not have equal opportunity who are less able to produce what others want."[3] The single most influential execution of this objection came, however, in

---

[1] Although my emphasis here is on later version of this objection, it has in fact an older lineage, receiving expression in, for instance, R.H. Tawney, *Equality* [1931] (London: Unwin, 1964; 4th edition), pp. 105–06.

[2] John H. Schaar, 'Equality of Opportunity and Beyond' in J. Roland Pennock and J. W. Chapman, editors, *NOMOS IX: Equality* (New York: Atherton Press, 1967), pp. 238, 233.

[3] Ronald Dworkin, *A Matter of Principle* (Cambridge, MA: Harvard University Press, 1985), p. 207.

48

John Rawls's 1971 book, *A Theory of Justice*. According to Rawls,

> Equality of opportunity means an equal chance to leave the less fortunate behind in the personal quest for influence and social position . . . intuitively it still appears defective. For one thing, even if it works to perfection in eliminating the influence of social contingencies, it still permits the distribution of wealth and income to be determined by the natural distribution of abilities and talents. Within the limits allowed by the background arrangements, distributive shares are decided by the outcome of the natural lottery; and this outcome is arbitrary from a moral perspective. There is no more reason to permit the distribution of income and wealth to be settled by the distribution of natural assets than by historical and social fortune.[4]

For our purposes, it is noteworthy that Rawls's critique (which I shall henceforth call the "Rawlsian objection to equality of opportunity") relies on two distinct claims. The primary claim is the assumption that there exist natural inequalities in the sense that differences between persons in terms of endowments, talents, and abilities constitute inequalities in nature independently of the effects of social institutions and practices. The secondary claim is that the particular distribution of these differences is such that advantages with respect to some natural endowments are not cancelled out by comparison with other persons because of disadvantages with respect to other natural endowments. It is only the combination of these two assumptions that warrants Rawls's objection that the inequalities resulting from any scheme of equality of opportunity are unfair.

Much of the mainstream discussion and response to the objection that equal opportunity magnifies and increases natural inequalities has taken the Rawlsian objection at face value. Sociologists and economists, for instance, have explored in great depth the extent to which so-called natural inequalities in talents and abilities play a role in generating economic inequalities by comparison with other factors such as inherited wealth and chance, often concluding that the latter play a much greater role in the creation of economic inequality.[5] Among those other egalitarians such as Roemer and Arneson involved in the recent philosophical revival of equal opportunity theories noted in Chapter 2, the scope

---

[4] John Rawls, *A Theory of Justice* (Cambridge, MA: Harvard University Press, 1971), pp. 73–74, 106–107. Rawls leaves this and related passages unchanged in the 1999 revised edition.

[5] See, e.g., the superb study by Lars Osberg, *Economic Inequality in the United States* (Armonk, NY: M.E. Sharpe, 1984).

they give to equality of opportunity is very much in the shadow of the Rawlsian objection. The versions of equality of opportunity they embrace are structured so that the shares of particular individuals are a function of factors independent of their particular natural endowments or skills. The slogan is that their theories aspire to an ambition-sensitive, endowment-insensitive distribution.[6]

It is my view that these other recent defenders of equal opportunity concede too much to the Rawlsian objection. The goal of this chapter is to show why this powerful objection to equality of opportunity is misguided. I attack both assumptions Rawls makes. If either of these attacks succeeds, then the Rawlsian objection to equality of opportunity fails. The principal problem with the Rawlsian objection to equality of opportunity is, I shall show, its reliance on the primary assumption that there exist natural inequalities in talents, skills, and other sorts of natural endowments.[7] The main thesis of this chapter, which I build upon in subsequent chapters, is that the belief in natural inequalities, or what Rawls sometimes calls "inequalities in natural endowments,"[8] is a myth. And when that belief is shown to be a myth, the Rawlsian objection to equality of opportunity collapses because, in effect, equality of opportunity cannot be accused of magnifying or building upon natural inequalities since there is no such thing. All inequalities properly understood are social, and it is incumbent on a theory of egalitarian justice to recognize this fact. There is nothing new about the rejection of the idea of natural inequalities. More than 200 years ago, Jean Jacques Rousseau observed in elegant prose, "Inequalities among men [sic] which are regarded as natural are actually the work of habit and the various ways of life that men adopt in society."[9] What is surprising, from my perspective, is that in response to the Rawlsian objection, egalitarian defenders of the concept of equality of opportunity haven't pointed this out.

Ultimately, my objective in this chapter is to advance an egalitarian theory of equal opportunity that does not operate in the shadow of the concern about natural inequalities. While Rawls responded to this

---

[6] The slogan comes from Ronald Dworkin's 'What Is Equality? Part II: Equality of Resources,' *Philosophy & Public Affairs*, Vol. 10 (1981), p. 311.

[7] I use the terms talents, skills, and natural endowments more or less interchangeably throughout this chapter.

[8] Rawls, *A Theory of Justice*, p. 100.

[9] Jean-Jacques Rousseau, *Discourse on the Origin of Inequality* [1754], reprinted in *The Essential Rousseau*, translated by Lowell Bair (New York: Mentor Books, 1974), p. 170.

concern by supplementing fair equality of opportunity with the difference principle in his second principle of justice, I urge egalitarians to question the very idea of natural inequalities. Instead, I show that all inequalities result from social design, and for this reason can be subject to the regulative ideal of the three-dimensional model of equal opportunities.

3.2 THE ASSUMPTION ABOUT NATURAL INEQUALITIES

The assumption that there exist significant natural inequalities between persons has been an important theme in the history of political thought since Plato. The main idea has been that certain individuals have far greater attributes or endowments in things such as physical strength or intelligence, and that these differences constitute an inequality that is independent of the extent to which they are mediated by the institutions and practices of society. This assumption has received surprisingly little scrutiny by major figures in the history of political thought, aside from Rousseau.[10] The assumption about natural inequalities has been used in different ways by various political philosophers to ground specific institutional arrangements ranging from an autocratic rule by an intellectual elite to limited government designed partly to avoid the equation of 'might' and 'right'. The narrow focus of this chapter is, however, only on the way in which the assumption about natural inequalities has been utilized in an egalitarian critique of the concept of equality of opportunity.

As I noted at the beginning of the chapter, John Rawls in *A Theory of Justice* famously advanced the view that the distribution of abilities and talents among individuals is like a natural lottery, and when distributive shares of income and wealth are an outcome of this lottery, "this outcome is arbitrary from a moral perspective."[11] For him, "No one deserves his greater natural capacity nor merits a more favorable starting place in society . . . Those who have been favored by nature, whoever they are, may gain from their good fortune only on terms that improve the situation of those who have lost out."[12]

The view that there is a natural lottery does not by itself amount to the assumption of natural inequalities. Indeed, the natural lottery idea is

---

[10] Thomas Hobbes also expressed some scepticism about natural inequalities.
[11] Rawls, *A Theory of Justice*, p. 74.
[12] Rawls, *A Theory of Justice*, pp. 101–02.

really mere confirmation that there is incredible natural diversity among persons. The fact of 'natural inequality' for Rawls, or what he sometimes calls "inequalities of natural endowment" also relies on a theory about the production of social wealth.[13] Natural inequality in Rawls involves the claim that those individuals with certain talents and skills such as high intelligence distributed in the natural lottery are by their very nature more valuable in the production of social wealth than those with other less useful endowments. The belief in natural inequality does not rely on the entailment that having a particular natural endowment such as high intelligence is a sufficient condition for the production of social wealth.[14] Other contextual conditions, such as the preferences of others, are also necessary. Nor is the belief that there exist natural inequalities inconsistent with the belief that social wealth should not be distributed in proportion to those who are most instrumental in its production. Indeed, as Rawls characterizes it, part of the task of just institutions is to redress partially, albeit not fully, for natural inequalities.[15]

Underlying Rawls's controversial view of how the economic benefits of the natural lottery in talents and skills should be distributed is a distinction first drawn by John Stuart Mill in 1848 between "the laws of the Production of Wealth, which are real laws of nature, dependent on the properties of objects, and the modes of its Distribution which, subject to certain conditions, depend on human will."[16] Mill's point is that while the causal link between capital and wealth production is natural and unchangeable, the distribution of that wealth among the population is a matter of social and political choice. For Rawls, likewise, "those who have been favored by nature" have a much greater capacity to contribute

---

[13] Rawls, *A Theory of Justice*, p. 100. The phrase "natural inequalities" is now commonplace among sympathetic analyses of Rawls, e.g., Thomas Pogge, *Realizing Rawls* (Ithaca: Cornell University Press, 1989), p. 64; and Will Kymlicka, *Contemporary Political Philosophy* (Oxford: Oxford University Press, 1990), p. 57.

[14] In *Justice as Fairness: A Restatement* (Cambridge, MA, Harvard University Press, 2001), Rawls introduces a distinction between "native endowments" and "realized talents and abilities," saying "native endowments of various kinds (say, native intelligence and nature ability) are not fixed natural assets with a constant capacity. They are merely potential and cannot come to fruitation apart from social conditions," pp. 56–57. Although Rawls does not acknowledge this, the distinction he is drawing has an important legacy in the liberal tradition, most notably in the work of T.H. Hobhouse.

[15] Rawls explicitly rejects any sort of comprehensive redress for natural inequalities on p. 101 of *A Theory of Justice*.

[16] John Stuart Mill [1873], *Autobiography* (Indianapolis: Bobbs-Merrill, 1957), pp. 159–60.

to the social production of wealth than those "less fortunate." But it is a function of a theory of justice, says Rawls, to determine what is a fair distribution of that social wealth. It follows, on his view, that some individuals, and indeed groups, within society are fortunate to be more intelligent, and therefore have a greater capacity to contribute to the production of social wealth than others.

The other key, albeit secondary, claim in the Rawlsian objection to equality of opportunity is that the particular distribution of natural differences between persons is such that advantages with respect to some natural endowments are not cancelled out by comparison with other persons because of disadvantages with respect to other natural endowments. Without this assumption about the distribution of natural inequalities, the attention Rawls draws to natural inequalities would not constitute a knock-down objection to equality of opportunity because it is a logical possibility that for each individual, he or she may gain advantage with respect to some natural inequality but be at a disadvantage with respect to some other, in which case equality of opportunity could not be accused of magnifying and building upon natural inequalities.

This analysis makes transparent the reasoning underlying the Rawlsian objection to equality of opportunity. Equal opportunity models seek to eliminate arbitrary distribution based on social contingencies, but ignore the effects of the natural lottery. For Rawls, however, the natural lottery means that persons have different natural endowments, and given the laws of production of wealth, some will have a greater capacity to contribute to that production than others and generate greater wealth and income for themselves. Hence, by ignoring the moral arbitrariness of the natural lottery, equal opportunity models allow for the natural inequalities that flow from the natural lottery to be magnified and built upon, substantiating the assessment that it amounts to an equal opportunity to become unequal.

3.3 THE MYTH OF NATURAL INEQUALITIES

Despite the distinguished intellectual legacy of Rawls's belief that there exist natural inequalities between persons, natural inequalities are, I suggest, a myth. The root difference between natural inequalities and social inequalities is their primary origin. Whilst social inequalities are said to have have their origins in the functioning of social institutions and practices, natural inequalites are said to have their origins in nature. My insistence that natural inequalities are a myth amounts to the claim that no inequalities have their origins in nature. The relevant upshot of this claim is that the Rawlsian objection to equality of opportunity is therefore without force.

Why do no inequalities originate from nature? The argument I have in mind parallels in structure the famous *"argument from queerness"* pressed by John Mackie against those who hold the belief that there are objective values.[17] (I don't mean here to endorse Mackie's subjective view of ethics but merely to mimic his style of argument.) In effect, whatever the differences between persons that originate from nature, it is odd to characterize them as inequalities. All inequalities must be mediated by social institutions and practices; all inequalities are thus, in the terms I introduce in Section 3.4, by social design, and do not originate in nature. If there is an inequality with its origin in nature, it would be a very strange and unusual type; certainly it would not do to assume simply that it is a token inequality, and that some sort of argument is required. I am not denying that there is a set of certain phenomena that has its origin in nature, but merely that the set does not include inequalities.

Genetic differences are, I suspect, the most frequently invoked evidence of natural inequalities. And if natural inequalities are not a myth, the strongest case for their existence will appeal to the diverse genetic make-up of human beings. Let us then consider the challenge of how to think ethically about genetic interventions in human life implied by the rapidly expanding research on the genetic make-up of a human being. In their seminal book, *From Chance to Choice: Genetics and Justice*, four leading American philosophers, Allen Buchanan, Dan Brock, Norman Daniels, and Daniel Wikler, ask: *"What are the most basic moral principles that would guide public policy and individual choice concerning the use of genetic interventions in a just and humane society?"*[18] For these authors, genetic differences among persons in terms of say cognitive functioning constitute natural inequalities.[19] Like Rawls, these inequalities are a concern for them because they are the result of the 'natural lottery' and affect the opportunities available to an individual. One interesting option these authors explore is the use of genetic interventions to change the outcome of the natural lottery. In other words, they imagine

---

[17] John Mackie, *Ethics: Inventing Right and Wrong* (Harmondsworth: Penguin Books, 1977), pp. 38–42.

[18] Allen Buchanan, Dan Brock, Norman Daniels, and Daniel Wikler, *From Chance to Choice: Genetics and Justice* (New York: Cambridge University Press, 2000), p. 4 (italics in original).

[19] Buchanan et al., *From Chance to Choice*, pp. 17, 63.

that natural inequalities between persons might be reduced through genetic interventions. Ultimately, they reject the idea that genetic interventions should be used for "the elimination of all inequalities in natural assets."[20] Instead, they conclude, "a reasonable public policy must proceed in a conservative manner, focusing on efforts to avoid what are clearly deprivations rather than on striving to achieve the greatest equal distribution of natural assets . . . In practice, this would mean a strong societal commitment to use advances in genetic intervention to prevent or ameliorate the most serious disabilities that limit individuals' opportunities."[21]

What is absent in *From Chance to Choice* is a careful account of why genetic differences give rise to natural inequality as opposed to social inequality. The real genetic differences may be natural but the inequalities that are the concern of the authors are social in origin, not natural. By analogy, sex differences may indeed be natural but nobody seriously characterizes the concern about sex discrimination as an issue of natural inequality as opposed to social inequality; sex discrimination has its origins in society, not nature. *From Chance to Choice* reflects incredible sensitivity to the problem of identifying when precisely a genetic difference counts as a natural asset; there is explicit acknowledgement that these are cultural and historical judgements.[22] Yet, why then assume that the genetic interventions in question are addressing natural inequalities rather than social ones?

An illustration might help. An example of the sort of genetic intervention the authors are entertaining is gene therapy to correct deafness in an unborn baby. Buchanan, Brock, Daniels, and Wikler advance the following:

Our claim is only that the appropriate perspective for estimating whether to prevent or restore loss of hearing in an individual who is not competent to decide for himself or herself (a fetus or a child) is that of a reasonable person confronted with the choice of whether to be deaf or not . . . It may be possible to imagine a world in which a reasonable person, confronted with such a choice, would choose deafness, but this is not our world. To make such a choice reasonable for most people would require an enormous reallocation of social resources, indeed a radical restructuring of our modes of production and social institutions, in order to make it true that for most people who are deaf, the benefits of

---

[20] Buchanan et al., *From Chance to Choice*, p. 82.
[21] Buchanan et al., *From Chance to Choice*, pp. 101–02, 82.
[22] Buchanan et al., *From Chance to Choice*, pp. 80–95.

membership in the deaf community outweigh the limitations on opportunity that deafness brings.[23]

What I think is noteworthy about this argument is that it turns on showing that deafness engenders social inequalities; the disadvantages of being deaf stem from social institutions and practices, not nature. And it is those social inequalities rather than some mythical natural inequality related to being deaf that warrant the conclusion that genetic intervention to prevent deafness in a child or fetus is justified.

The point I am advancing about the social origins of inequality has been rigorously established in sociology, even though it has not been well developed by egalitarian political philosophers. In the next section of this chapter, I draw on the rich sociological debate around IQ to further elaborate and substantiate the claim that natural inequalities are a myth. But even without that added detail, the problem with Rawls's claim about natural inequalities should be apparent. As I noted earlier, Rawls follows J.S. Mill in asserting that there is a natural causal connection between certain natural assets or endowments and the production of wealth. But that in turn relies on the deeply implausible (although at certain points in history, widely held) claim that an economy is governed by 'laws of nature' rather than being a social institution.

I suspect that many egalitarians who have been influenced by the Rawlsian objection to equality of opportunity would readily concede that many of the inequalities that are identified as natural are indeed social, but yet nevertheless insist that there are still some core or basic natural inequalities in endowments, skills, and talents. And the fact that there are such basic natural inequalities is enough to defeat equal opportunity conceptions of egalitarian justice. Even though this defence of the belief in natural inequalities – the shift from pervasive natural inequalities to a set of basic or core inequalities – is easy to anticipate, it has not received any careful philosophical articulation.[24] This is largely because the Rawlsian insistence that there are natural inequalities has not been carefully scrutinized.

What is the best way to understand this insistence that common sense says that there are at least some basic or core natural inequalities between persons? Perhaps the most systematic attempt to capture this view can

---

[23] Buchanan et al., *From Chance to Choice*, pp. 282–83.

[24] I have not found it in print but it has been pressed in response to my inequality-by-design critique of natural inequalities by G.A. Cohen in a series of conversations over the years.

be found in the World Health Organization's approach to disablement adopted in 1980 as an aspect of the international classification of diseases.[25] In its analysis of physical disablement, WHO distinguishes between impairment, disability, and handicap. An impairment is defined as "any loss or abnormality of psychological, physiological or anatomical structure or function."[26] An ocular impairment or disorder of visual function is one such example. A disability is "any restriction or lack (resulting from an impairment) of ability to perform an activity in the manner or within the range considered normal for a human being."[27] Not being able to see is a disability when it is the result of an ocular impairment. The ocular impairment itself is not a disability since the latter necessarily involves an activity. (Seeing is an activity.) A handicap is "a disadvantage for a given individual, resulting from an impairment or a disability, that limits or prevents the fulfillment of a role that is normal (depending on age, sex, and social and cultural factors) for that individual."[28] A handicap is in this sense the social costs an individual bears for having the disability of, for instance, not seeing. Now, clearly, this classification scheme was structured around the recognition that some dimension of disablement involves social inequality. Handicaps are defined exclusively in these terms. Disabilities are trickier, but it seems that they are steeped in benchmark comparisons that are culturally and socially relative. The concept of an impairment, however, seems to capture the response to my inequality-by-design thesis that there are still some core or basic natural inequalities in endowments, skills, and talents. An ocular impairment, for example, seems to denote quite a pure instance of natural inequality, without relying on any (socially constructed) consequences implied by either a disability or a handicap. If this view of impairments is correct, then my criticism of the belief in natural inequalities is misdirected.

Fortunately (for my argument in this chapter) this view of impairments can be shown to be unpersuasive. The difficulty is that any sense

---

[25] My description here of WHO's approach to disablement is drawn principally from Jerome E. Bickenbach, *Physical Disability and Social Policy* (Toronto: University of Toronto Press, 1993), ch. 2. My discussion glosses over many of the complexities of this classification scheme as well as the subsequent and very important refinements to it since 1980. For the purposes of my discussion, those complexities and refinements are largely irrelevant.

[26] Bickenbach, *Physical Disability and Social Policy*, p. 30.

[27] Bickenbach, *Physical Disability and Social Policy*, p. 36.

[28] Bickenbach, *Physical Disability and Social Policy*, p 48.

of impairment involves some sort of comparison to others. The judgement of loss or abnormality requires some sort of benchmark for comparison. (Those with an ocular impairment are said, for example, not to be able to see as well as other persons.) But what is the basis for this benchmark? It could be based on either some sort of social consensus about normality or some sort of notion of basic human functioning. Yet neither of these approaches is consistent with the claim that impairments suggest natural inequalities. The social consensus approach obviously presupposes specific social institutions and practices. But so too does the human functioning approach. Buchanan et al. adopt this approach, for instance, saying, "By a physical or mental impairment we mean an impairment of some aspect of normal functioning for our species."[29] Yet their earlier explanation of human functioning is in terms of "having the characteristics necessary to be a *normal competitor* for desirable social positions."[30] In other words, what constitutes human functioning is going to vary from society to society depending on the design of the competitions for desirable positions and goods.

A real-life example might be helpful.[31] Imagine a deaf lesbian couple planning to have children. The couple are well educated and carefully integrated into the deaf community in Washington D.C., which includes Gallaudet University, the only liberal arts college for the deaf in North America. Is it unreasonable for this couple to utilize the now extensive genetic knowledge about deafness in order to have children that are themselves born deaf? Instead of using this knowledge to prevent deafness, their interest is in using this knowledge to have a deaf child. Perhaps for most of us, this course of action is unwise. But for this couple, having deaf children is integral to their fitting into the community to which they belong; deafness in a child is an asset for these parents. Although it is perfectly plausible to insist that being deaf is an impairment, this example shows that it is absurd to present this judgement as one proving natural inequalities as opposed to social inequalities.[32]

Despite these rather obvious problems with the representation of impairments as denoting natural inequalities, there may still be some

---

[29] Buchanan et al., *From Chance to Choice*, p. 285.
[30] Buchanan et al., *From Chance to Choice*, p. 74. See also p. 127. Emphasis added.
[31] This example is drawn from *The Washington Post*, March 31, 2002, describing a deaf couple who deliberately utilized genetic knowledge to have two deaf children.
[32] My argument here is similar to one made by Anita Silvers, 'Defective Agents: Equality, Difference, and the Tyranny of the Normal,' *Journal of Social Philosophy*, vol. 25 (1994), pp. 162–63.

lingering doubts about my attack on that representation. How can those doubts be explained? Ultimately, I think that in order to appreciate fully that all inequalities are social, it is necessary to appreciate that at their roots, impairments are generally misrepresented as residing in individuals and constituting a problem principally for those individuals. Consider our two examples of ocular impairments and deafness. Both of these are commonly thought of as being features of particular individuals: Person x has a visual impairment or is deaf. As Martha Minow has shown, this is the prevalent manner in which he or she is viewed in legal cases.[33] The legal question then becomes one of accommodation: Was the person with the impairment accommodated to a reasonable standard? Suppose, however, that we adopt a different perspective on phenomena such as ocular impairment or deafness. Instead of viewing it as a problem residing in particular individuals, imagine that it is a problem that resides in relations between persons. On this alternative perspective, in most instances, the tension is between the vast majority and a small minority. In a typical classroom, for instance, deafness and a teaching strategy such as exclusive reliance on sign language are a problem because the vast majority seem not to benefit from such a strategy. But in that case, to say that the problem resides in a particular individual is misleading; the problem of differences between individuals is a relational one.[34]

This perspective is reinforced by one of the major insights into the character of egalitarian justice made by Amartya Sen. Sen has criticized much of the mainstream philosophical literature on equality for failing to appreciate an important aspect of the fundamental diversity among human beings. His main target is Rawls's proposition that when thinking about the distribution of the benefits and burdens of social life, shares for individuals can be measured by what Rawls calls "primary social goods" understood as resources like income, basic liberties, and so on. In Rawls's famous formulation, even though persons may vary in their

---

[33] Martha Minow, *Making All the Difference* (Ithaca: Cornell University Press, 1990), ch. 3.

[34] Any serious concern about inequality would seem to reinforce this alternative perspective on impairments. Equality and inequality are in their essence relational concepts; they involve as a matter of necessity relations between individuals as a basis for making comparisons. But in that case, the very idea of natural inequalities seems misconceived. The type of justice that concerns egalitarians is necessarily comparative and reliant on the existence of social institutions and practices to mediate comparisons between persons.

rational life plans, primary goods are those things that all such plans require for their execution.[35] The relevant diversity that raises problems for primary goods and other similar notions is, according to Sen,

> variations in our ability to convert resources into actual freedoms. Variations related to sex, age, genetic endowments, and many other features, give us very divergent powers to build freedom in our lives even when we have the same bundle of primary goods ... We have to examine interpersonal variations in the transformation of primary goods (and resources, more generally) into respective capabilities to pursue ends and objectives.[36]

Given this diversity, Sen charges many egalitarians with a "fetishist handicap" for being preoccupied with the shares individuals have of particular goods and resources, and urges them to "move away from a focus on goods as such to what goods do to human beings."[37] What matters, he says, is the *relationship* between goods and persons.[38]

I concur with sympathetic critics such as G.A. Cohen who have argued that although Sen is right to emphasize diversity and variation among human beings, he is mistaken to infer from this that the only relevant place where this variation matters for egalitarian justice is in terms of capability to pursue ends and objectives. As Cohen puts it, "What goods do to or for people is not identical with what people are able to do with them."[39] However, I think there is a more radical implication of Sen's argument appreciated by neither Sen nor Cohen. Sen assumes that the morally significant dimension of the variations between persons in terms of what goods do for them resides in those people. But for an egalitarian such as Sen, this can't be right. The importance of the diversity he quite rightly emphasizes is that people vary *by comparison with other people*. But in that case, the variation between persons in terms of the conversion of goods and resources is significant in relational terms. Logically, given the diversity among persons, the other people to whom comparisons are made will affect the extent of the inequality. Hence, rather than appearing to denote some sort of natural inequality, the inequality in question has its origins in social institutions and practices.

[35] Rawls, *A Theory of Justice*, p. 93.

[36] Amartya Sen, *Inequality Reexamined* (Cambridge, MA: Harvard University Press, 1992), pp. 85–87.

[37] Amartya Sen, *Choice, Welfare, and Measurement* (Oxford: Basil Blackwell, 1982), p. 30, 368.

[38] Sen, *Choice, Welfare, and Measurement*, p. 366.

[39] G.A. Cohen, 'On the Currency of Egalitarian Justice,' *Ethics*, Vol. 99 1989), p. 944.

Why, then, do some egalitarians still insist on the moral significance of individual *ownership* of impairments and other kinds of differences? The most compelling answer seems to be that if this sort of proprietorship is given up, it becomes difficult to justify differential but beneficial treatment for particular individuals.[40] Programs such as affirmative action that benefit individuals from certain targeted groups would seem insupportable because the problems are relational, not the problems of particular individuals. While I agree that shifting, as I recommend, to a relational perspective on natural differences between persons requires us to rethink programs such as affirmative action, it is precisely that task I undertake in later chapters, where I show that the three-dimensional model of equal opportunities as a regulative ideal does indeed support affirmative action as well as a host of other social policy and civil rights strategies for pursuing equality.[41]

3.4 INEQUALITY BY DESIGN: LEARNING FROM THE IQ DEBATE

An important upshot of insisting that there are no natural inequalities is that it allows for the possibility that with different social institutions and practices, the relevant social inequalities might not exist. The inequality-by-design thesis holds that inequalities have their origins in the design

---

[40] See, e.g., Bickenbach, *Physical Disability and Social Policy*, p. 234.

[41] The shift I recommend also has implications for one strand of Michael Sandel's well-known communitarian critique of egalitarian liberalism in *Liberalism and the Limits of Justice* (Cambridge, UK: Cambridge University Press, 1982). Following Robert Nozick's argument in *Anarchy, State, and Utopia* (New York: Basic Books, 1974), Sandel seizes upon the insight that Rawls' embrace of the difference principle, which allows for inequalities only when they are to the benefit of the least well off, relies upon the idea of treating natural endowments as collective assets. While Nozick attacks that idea as a betrayal of the Kantian value of individual dignity and respect, Sandel maintains that given the choice between individual ownership of natural endowments and community or collective ownership, Rawls is committed to the latter, and in this respect implicitly relies on an intersubjective conception of the self that presupposes, antecedently, some sort of community (pp. 77–82). While many commentators have come to Rawls' defence, arguing in effect that he does not have to deny individual ownership over natural assets, none seems to have challenged Nozick nor Sandel on the assumption that the choice is a binary one between individual ownership or collective ownership. An alternative is to view the natural assets in relational terms, necessarily social, but not at its root a matter of ownership or proprietorship. Ironically, I suspect that this alternate view would reinforce Sandel's communitarian reading of the difference principle.

of social circumstances. From the perspective of the three-dimensional model of equal opportunities as a regulative ideal, this is significant because it allows for the regulation of that design.

The inequality-by-design thesis has received, as I noted earlier, careful attention by sociologists, especially in the debate over IQ. And proponents of the inequality-by-design thesis in the IQ debate have been an inspiration for the challenge I pose in this chapter to the Rawlsian objection to equal opportunity. Moreover, as I will also show, the IQ debate has spurred an important challenge to the assumption Rawls makes about the distribution of differences between individuals in the natural lottery.

Much of the recent revived debate around IQ was ignited by the publication in 1994 of *The Bell Curve: Intelligence and Class Structure in American Life* by Richard J. Herrnstein and Charles Murray. According to Herrnstein and Murray, *The Bell Curve* "is about differences in intellectual capacity among people and groups and what those differences mean for America's future."[42] The future they anticipate, the roots of which they think are already firmly embedded in existing American society, is one where the existence of two small segments of society has a dramatic impact on the shape of the whole society and therefore on the vast majority of citizens who belong to neither. These two segments are, on the one hand, a small elite at the pinnacle of American society who, regardless of their parents' wealth, attend elite universities, enter prestigious professions, and earn high incomes, and on the other hand, a small group at the bottom of society for whom "[p]overty is severe, drugs and crime are rampant, and the traditional family all but disappears."[43] The tendency in both segments is for increased isolation from the mainstream of society but with the paradoxical consequence that those in the mainstream see their lives shaped increasingly by measures designed to protect themselves from the 'underclass' beneath them and by decisions imposed by the powerful elite above them. Herrnstein and Murray anticipate a time when eventually "the fragile web of civility, mutual regard, and mutual obligations at the heart of any happy society begins to tear."[44] The pressing challenge for American social policy, in their view, is to forestall this. But in order to design social policy with

---

[42] Richard Herrnstein and Charles Murray, *The Bell Curve: Intelligence and Class Structure in American Life, paperback edition* (New York: The Free Press, 1996), p. xxi.
[43] Herrnstein and Murray, *The Bell Curve*, p. xxii.
[44] *Ibid.*

this objective, it is necessary to have an explanation for the existence of these isolated two segments of American society.

The basic explanation Herrnstein and Murray advance in *The Bell Curve* is that membership in these two segments is a function of what they call the "general factor of cognitive ability" or "intelligence."[45] Although they seem to think that reference to "intelligence" has only limited power for explaining most people's social and economic positions, it is their view that membership in the elite segment of society tracks those above the 95th percentile in *measured* intelligence (which, following convention, they call IQ) and those in the underclass below the 5th percentile.[46] In other words, those in the isolated segment at the top are necessarily of high measured intelligence and those at the bottom of low measured intelligence.[47] For Herrnstein and Murray, the important point is that individual membership in these two segments can be explained principally by the IQ of that person rather than by his or her race, gender, sexual orientation, or parents' socio-economic status.

For anyone familiar with the dominant strands of thinking about social justice among contemporary political philosophers, the concessions Herrnstein and Murray make to egalitarian liberals such as Rawls should be striking. As I have emphasized in this chapter, for Rawls the distribution of abilities and talents among individuals is like a natural lottery, and when distributive shares of income and wealth are an outcome of this lottery, "this outcome is arbitrary from a moral perspective."[48] "No one," writes Rawls, "deserves his greater natural capacity nor merits a more favorable starting place in society . . . Those

---

[45] Herrnstein and Murray, *The Bell Curve*, p. 22.

[46] Herrnstein and Murray, *The Bell Curve*, pp. 120–21.

[47] It is noteworthy that the view that those in the underclass are characterized as having a low IQ is in tension with Murray's representation of the underclass in his book, *Losing Ground* (New York: Basic Books, 1984), the so-called bible of the Reagan Administration. The arguments in that book, which made Murray famous, revolve around a hypothetical couple, Harold and Phyllis, responding to existing welfare regulations. The assumption that Murray makes is that this couple is completely rational and highly intelligent, despite being part of the underclass. And based on this assumption, Murray provides an explanation for why, in particular, Aid to Families with Dependent Children (AFDC) caused the breakdown of traditional family units among the poor, and in that way made the poor worse off than if AFDC had not existed. It is generally accepted that this argument was a major impetus for the eventual abolition of AFDC in 1996 welfare reform legislation.

[48] Rawls, *A Theory of Justice*, p. 74.

who have been favored by nature, whoever they are, may gain from their good fortune only on terms that improve the situation of those who have lost out."[49] Subsequently, other influential liberal egalitarians, perhaps most notably Ronald Dworkin, have embraced a similar view, saying that a liberal "theory of economic justice . . . requires that people not have different amounts of wealth just because they have different inherent capacities to produce what others want, or are differently favored by chance."[50] In a surprisingly similar vein, Herrnstein and Murray state "To be intellectually gifted is indeed a gift. Nobody *deserves* it. The monetary and social rewards that accrue to being intellectually gifted are growing all the time, for reasons that are easily condemned as being unfair."[51] In their view, natural assets such as intelligence are a matter of brute luck, and any distributive scheme that tracks such assets does not rely on an appeal to desert. The relevant contrast is to other conservative-minded social policy analysts such as Nathan Glazer who continue to insist on the importance of desert for justifying inequality.[52]

The principal difference, then, between Rawls, on the one hand, and Herrnstein and Murray, on the other, does not turn on whether the distribution of intelligence or other natural endowments is morally arbitrary but how in particular the economic benefits of that distribution should be distributed. Murray, in his 1996 Afterword to *The Bell Curve*, explicitly states his intellectual debt to Rawls, and that *The Bell Curve* should be read as a reaction to Rawls:

When we began work on the book, both of us assumed that it would provide evidence that would be more welcome to the political left than to the political right, via this logic: If intelligence plays an important role in determining how well one does in life, and intelligence is conferred on a person through a combination of genetic and environmental factors over which that person has no control (as we argue in the book), the most obvious political implication is that we need a Rawlsian egalitarian state, compensating the less advantaged for the unfair allocation of intellectual gifts. Neither of us thought that the most obvious implication was the right one . . . But we recognize the burden on us to make the case.[53]

---

[49] Rawls, *A Theory of Justice*, pp. 101–02.
[50] Dworkin, *A Matter of Principle*, p. 207.
[51] Herrnstein and Murray, *The Bell Curve*, p. 442.
[52] Nathan Glazer, *The Limits of Social Policy* (Cambridge, MA: Harvard University Press, 1989), pp. 156–67.
[53] Herrnstein and Murray, *The Bell Curve*, p. 554.

Unlike Rawls, who argues that economic distribution should "work for the good of the least fortunate,"[54] they hold the view that the focus should be on neither the cognitive elite nor the underclass but rather on "the vast majority of Americans."[55]

Like the Rawlsian objection to equality of opportunity, the argument in *The Bell Curve* relies on the belief that there exist natural inequalities. Herrnstein and Murray state, for instance, "Inequality of endowments, including intelligence, is a reality. Trying to pretend that inequality does not really exist has led to disaster."[56] Unlike in the case of Rawls, the foundational role Herrnstein and Murray assign to the belief in natural inequalities has been widely recognized, and has prompted responses by many of the strongest critics of *The Bell Curve*. These attacks on *The Bell Curve* are very persuasive and help sharpen the criticism of natural inequalities I have pressed here.

The most systematic and careful attack on the belief in natural inequalities is provided in the book, *Inequality by Design: Cracking the Bell Curve Myth*, by Claude S. Fischer et al. The following is a succinct statement of this criticism.

We were impelled to write this book by the publication in late 1994 of *The Bell Curve*. That immensely well publicized book was then the latest statement of a philosophy that gained extensive credence in the 1990s: The widening inequalities among Americans that developed in the last quarter-century are inevitable. Because of human nature, because of the nature of the market, because of the nature of modern society, Americans will necessarily divide more and more by social class and race. We reject that philosophy. Besides being morally complacent, it is a doctrine without scientific foundation. Research has shown that 'nature' determines neither the level of inequality in America nor which Americans in particular will be privileged or disprivileged; social conditions and national policies do. Inequality is in that sense designed.[57]

This idea of inequality-by-design challenges not only *The Bell Curve* but also more generally the assumption that there exist natural inequalities and therefore the Rawlsian objection to equality of opportunity.

---

[54] Rawls, *A Theory of Justice*, p. 102.
[55] Herrnstein and Murray, *The Bell Curve*, p. 550.
[56] Herrnstein and Murray, *The Bell Curve*, p. 551.
[57] Claude S. Fischer, Michael Hout, Martin Jankowski, Samuel Lucas, Ann Swidler, and Kim Voss, *Inequality by Design: Cracking the Bell Curve Myth* (Princeton: Princeton University Press, 1996), p. xi.

The core idea of inequality-by-design is a complex one. Fischer et al. distinguish crucially between two dimensions in the design of inequality by way of a metaphor. Imagine that the ranking of affluence or influence in a society is like a ladder. One concern is with why someone ends up on a higher rung whilst someone else ends up on a lower rung. Believers in natural inequalities hold that natural endowments play at least some role in which rung an individual ends up on. Another distinct concern is "why some societies have tall and narrowing ladders – ladders that have huge distances between top and bottom rungs and that taper off at the top so that there is room for only a few people – while other societies have short and broad ladders – ladders with little distance between top and bottom and with lots of room for many people all the way to the top."[58]

The argument of *Inequality by Design* is that both (1) the allocation on the higher and lower rungs, *and* (2) the distance between the rungs is a function of the policies and structures of social and political institutions. As I indicated earlier, the second part of this conjunction is really not in dispute. Herrnstein and Murray, for instance, readily concede that societies can structure ladders in different ways; their book is an argument for structuring those ladders in one way rather than another. The real controversy revolves around the first part of the conjunction.

The basic structure of their objection to the belief in natural inequalities is set out in the following passage from *Inequality by Design*:

Appeals to nature . . . cannot satisfactorily answer even the first question: Why do some *individuals* get ahead and some fall behind? Certainly, genetic endowment helps. Being tall, slender, good-looking, healthy, male, and white helps in the race for success, and these traits are totally or partly determined genetically. But these traits matter to the degree that society makes them matter – determining how much, for example, good looks or white skin are rewarded. More important yet than these traits are the social milieux in which people grow up and live.[59]

This objection says, in other words, that the good fortune that derives from possessing some natural endowments rather than others is not natural but is rather dependent on how much a given society values those endowments. And therefore what Rawls and others characterize as natural inequalities in talents and skills are in fact social inequalities.

---

[58] Fischer et al., *Inequality by Design*, pp. 7–8.
[59] Fischer et al., *Inequality by Design*, p. 9.

The logic is that assessments of what is or is not an advantage require a mechanism for valuing, and all such mechanisms are social,
hence any claims about inequalities in the distribution of advantages or
disadvantages are also necessarily social. Natural inequalities are impossible because they presuppose some sort of 'natural' standard of
value, and no such standard exists.

This general objection to the very idea of natural inequalities is most
clearly illustrated in the view about the relationship between race and
IQ defended in *Inequality by Design*. The provocative thesis advanced
by Fischer et al. is that "a racial or ethnic group's position in society determines it measured intelligence rather than vice versa."[60] If
this thesis is sound, it undermines what I described earlier as the core
of *The Bell Curve*. The explanation underlying their thesis, say Fischer
et al., is that "ethnic groups in lower caste or status positions tend to
score poorly because their position leads to socioeconomic deprivation,
group segregation, and a stigmatized identity, each of which undermines performance on psychometric measures of intelligence."[61]

This explanation fits with both the well-known examples of intelligence testing of immigrants to the United States in the 1920s and the differences in measured intelligence among the same racial or ethnic group
in different countries. During World War I and in the 1920s, at the outset of the widespread establishment of standardized intelligence tests,
prominent researchers, most notably H.H. Goddard, allegedly found
that Jewish immigrants had very low IQs. Looking backwards, these
results are surprising because IQ tests now find that Jewish test takers
outperform all other groups. This inconsistency appears damming for
defenders of IQ tests such as Herrnstein and Murray, although they deny
its relevance to their argument.[62] Alan Ryan in his essay "Apocalypse
Now?," comments, "What it does suggest is that either relative cognitive abilities change more rapidly than Herrnstein believed or that
our estimates of them are less reliable than he thought."[63] Stephen Jay
Gould in *The Mismeasure of Man* provides a systematic analysis of the
results of Goddard and Brigham that seeks to show that rather than
applying IQ tests with the objective of discovering the IQ of Jewish

---

[60] Fischer et al., *Inequality by Design*, p. 173.
[61] Fischer et al., *Inequality by Design*, p. 190.
[62] Herrnstein and Murray, *The Bell Curve*, p. 5.
[63] Alan Ryan, 'Apocalypse Now?,' *The New York Review of Books*, reprinted in Russell
Jacoby and Naomi Glauberman, editors, *The Bell Curve Debate* (New York: Times
Books, 1995), p. 27.

immigrants, these researchers assumed that these immigrants had low IQs and designed and administered tests with the intent of validating this assumption.[64] Fischer et al., in *Inequality by Design*, give this well-known example a different twist. Suppose that we assume that the IQ test results in the 1920s were genuine rather than fabricated as, in effect, Gould maintains. What could explain the discrepancy between results for Jewish test takers now and then? Fischer et al. seize upon the difference in social status of Jews now and then. In the 1910s and 1920s, Jewish immigrants were poor, segregated into certain urban neighbourhoods, denied access to public facilities, institutions, and professions, and hence heavily stigmatized. While anti-Semitism in the United States has not disappeared, there is nothing comparable today. The inference drawn by the authors of *Inequality by Design* is that the low social status of Jewish immigrants explains their poor results on IQ tests. And as their social status improved, so too did their test results.

This conclusion is also supported by cross-national comparisons. Consider, suggest Fischer et al., the example of Koreans.[65] Koreans in the United States as a group do extremely well on IQ tests, well above the average. Their scores are generally comparable with those of Japanese Americans. This contrasts sharply with the IQ scores of people of Korean descent living in Japan. There, Koreans do poorly on standardized tests. What is the relevant difference? In Japan, Koreans have a very low social status. Children often attend segregated schools, isolated from the majority of Japanese descent. They are economically disadvantaged as a group. The point is that as in the case of Jewish immigrants from Eastern Europe at the beginning of the century, the test results finding low IQ among Koreans living in Japan are a function of their low social status in Japanese society.

I now want to draw on another vein of the rich criticism of *The Bell Curve* to put pressure on the other key claim in the Rawlsian objection to equality of opportunity – namely, the assumption that the particular distribution of natural differences between persons is such that advantages with respect to some natural endowments are not cancelled out by comparison with other persons because of disadvantages with respect to other natural endowments. Recall that without this assumption about the distribution of differences between individuals, it is a logical possibility that for each individual, he or she may gain an advantage

---

[64] Gould, *The Mismeasure of Man*, pp. 194–98.
[65] Fischer et al., *Inequality by Design*, p. 172.

with respect to some natural endowment but be at a disadvantage with respect to another, in which case equality of opportunity could not be accused of magnifying and building upon natural inequalities.

The relevant vein of criticism questions the intelligibility of measured intelligence as it is represented by Herrnstein and Murray. These critics make two related claims that are totally relevant to my rejection of the Rawlsian objection to equality of opportunity: (1) A person's IQ cannot be captured by a single number, and (2) the distribution of IQ across a population cannot be represented by a bell curve.

The view that IQ has significant explanatory force derives considerable mileage from the common sense observation that people can be said to be intelligent, and that some appear more intelligent than others. Herrnstein and Murray begin *The Bell Curve* with precisely this sort of observation: "That the word *intelligence* describes something real and that it varies from person to person is as universal and ancient as any understanding about the state of being human."[66] The difficulty for social scientists is moving from this common sense observation to the idea that intelligence can be measured. By analogy, most people believe that 'love' exists and that one can be more or less in love, as illustrated by colloquialisms like 'head over heels in love.' But presumably most of us would be sceptical of any pseudo-scientific project that purports to measure love. Something similar underlies criticism of the concept of measured intelligence.

Although Herrnstein and Murray acknowledge that the concept of intelligence has now engendered a range of competing conceptions, they nonetheless hold to a conception from the 'classical tradition' of psychometrics that treats intelligence as a single general mental ability that is structural rather than as substantial types of acquired knowledge or as a matter of information processing.[67] Following the founder of psychometrics Charles Spearman, they call this unitary mental factor g, and seem to view g as "a general capacity for inferring and applying relationships drawn from experience."[68]

Some influential modern psychologists have developed alternative conceptions of intelligence. Howard Gardner, for example, has advanced a multi-dimensional model of intelligence: linguistic, musical, logical-mathematical, spatial, naturalist, interpersonal, intrapersonal,

---

[66] Herrnstein and Murray, *The Bell Curve*, p. 1.
[67] Herrnstein and Murray, *The Bell Curve*, pp. 19–23.
[68] Herrnstein and Murray, *The Bell Curve*, p. 4.

and bodily kinesthetic. Gardner charges that intelligence in *The Bell Curve* is treated like a black-box phenomenon that need not be explained and can ignore modern scientific findings.[69] For Herrnstein and Murray, g is the factor measured by all standardized tests. The logic is that unlike the distinct dimensions of intelligence such as creativity identified in Gardner's model, g seems to be a common focus of all standardized tests. It follows for them that the scores from any standardized test have some value in the measurement of intelligence. Gardner thinks that this belief in g involves an act of 'faith' rather than an inference towards a conclusion from premises that are supported by modern scientific literature.

Why insist on viewing intelligence as a singular human ability? The obvious answer is that this view makes it more feasible to measure it in individuals and quantify their intelligence in a single number. The more dimensions intelligence is said to have, the more difficult it is to quantify intelligence and rank ordinally the IQs of different individuals. In Gardner's view, we should shift from IQ to "profiles of intelligence" once we appreciate that "no two of us exhibit the same intelligences in precisely the same proportions."[70]

The claim that intelligence is multi-dimensional and cannot be captured by a single unitary number puts pressure on the proposition that the distribution of measured intelligence within a given population can be represented as a bell curve. In its structure, however, Rawls's assumption about the distribution of natural endowments – in his words, "assuming that there is a distribution of natural assets"[71] – is similar to Herrnstein and Murray's views about the distribution of IQ.[72] But that assumption would, likewise, seem to be vulnerable to similar types of objections. If we accept the notion that natural differences are multi-dimensional, the sort of distribution in the natural lottery Rawls is assuming seems impossible. The only plausible way to save Rawls's assumption is by identifying some common natural value that underlies

---

[69] Howard Gardner, 'Scholarly Brinkmanship,' reprinted in Jacoby & Glauberman, *The Bell Curve Debate*, p. 64–65.

[70] Howard Gardner, 'Who Owns Intelligence?,' *Atlantic Monthly* (February 1999), p. 71.

[71] Rawls, *A Theory of Justice*, p. 73.

[72] Ironically, Norman Daniels, one of the best known sympathetic critics of Rawls, pointed out many years ago, as I have here, that the assumptions about the distribution of intelligence across the population derived from "an elitist and racist social theory." See 'IQ, Intelligence, and Educability,' *Philosophical Forum, Vol. 6* (1974–75), p. 64.

the wide diversity of natural assets, endowments, and differences. While in the history of economic and political thought there have been some bold attempts to do this – most notably around the labour theory of value – there is now a broad consensus that philosophically such attempts are misconceived.[73]

3.5 TWO OTHER ISSUES ABOUT NATURE AND JUSTICE

The argument that there are no natural inequalities should be carefully distinguished from two other important issues about justice. The first issue concerns the scope of justice.[74] Is it an injustice when the workings of nature have harmful effects? Is, for example, a destructive hurricane an injustice? Or alternatively is the scope of justice limited to the involvement of social institutions and practices? These questions have prompted a range of competing answers. Nothing in my rejection of natural inequalities commits me to a particular position on this issue. Since the subject of *egalitarian* justice is restricted to inequality, then it follows logically that the scope of *egalitarian* justice does not extend to nature. It is, however, counter-intuitive to hold that egalitarian justice completely fills the space of what justice is. The subject of justice includes more than just equality; certainly, freedom and community are constitutive values of justice.[75] These other values of justice allow for the logical possibility that the scope of justice extends to nature, even if the value of equality does not.

The other issue that should be carefully distinguished from my critique of natural inequalities is the extent to which the domain of justice

[73] The clearest and most concise demonstration of this is by G.A. Cohen, 'The Labour Theory of Value and the Concept of Exploitation' in *History, Labour, and Freedom* (Oxford: Oxford University Press, 1988). While it should be acknowledged that some Marxist economists retain a commitment to the labour theory of value, this commitment seems to be mainly politically motivated, and in spite of the philosophical and conceptual difficulties. I noted in the text that the source of the Rawlsian view on natural inequalities is John Stuart Mill. Mill himself was unclear about his reliance on the labour theory of value – he followed Ricardo in allowing for value other than labour – but in practice, the principal source of value in his political economy was labour. (I have benefitted immensely from conversations and correspondence with my colleague Margaret Schabas on this aspect of Mill scholarship.)

[74] See, e.g., Thomas Nagel, 'Justice and Nature,' *Oxford Journal of Legal Studies*, Vol. 17 (1997), p. 303.

[75] I have argued this in Lesley A. Jacobs, *The Democratic Vision of Politics* (Upper Saddle River, NJ: Prentice-Hall, 1997).

is limited to correcting for misfortune or brute bad luck. Here, the main idea is that inequalities can be justified if they have their origins in an individual's choices but cannot be justified if they are the result of brute bad luck. As I noted in the last chapter, both Roemer and Arneson subscribe to a view of this sort. There is a clear sense in which this view constitutes a way to rethink the relation between justice and nature.[76] Nature is often conceived of as a given, something beyond human control. The logic is that the effects of nature are a matter of luck or misfortune, not choice. And because the domain of justice applies to bad luck, the harmful effects of nature are included in the scope of justice.

Again, my insistence that there are no natural inequalities does not commit me to any defined position on this issue. My concerns about natural inequalities are quite independent of the scepticism I have expressed in Chapter 2 about the view that individual choice and control is always the salient consideration in a judgement about an injustice. Part of that scepticism derives from the difficulty of determining when an individual controls an action or outcome. But even in circumstances when it is beyond dispute that an individual chooses to embark on an action or seeks an outcome, egalitarian concerns about injustices seem to me to arise regularly. Fair treatment of pregnant women in the workplace does not, for example, turn on the extent to which a woman deliberately chose to become pregnant.

3.6 EGALITARIAN JUSTICE WITHOUT NATURAL INEQUALITY

My main goal in this chapter is to save the concept of equality of opportunity in general from the Rawlsian objection by revealing its two main assumptions as flawed. For many sympathetic to Rawls, the argument in this chapter, and in particular singling out for attack Rawls's belief that there are natural inequalities, may seem odd, for Rawls's theory of justice as fairness is widely viewed as a challenge to both natural and social inequalities. In his words, "What the theory of justice must regulate is the inequalities in life prospects between citizens that arise from social starting positions, natural advantages, and historical contingencies."[77] And other liberal egalitarians such as Ronald Dworkin, Will Kymlicka,

---

[76] Buchanan et al., *From Chance to Choice*, p. 83.
[77] Rawls, *Political Liberalism, paperback edition* (New York: Columbia University Press, 1996), p. 271.

and Eric Rakowski have tried to make a case for their own respective views of egalitarian justice by showing that their theories better address the moral arbitrariness of natural and social inequalities than Rawls's own theory of justice as fairness.[78] What substantial difference is there between Rawls's approach and the one I have defended here?

Rawls's approach is presumably quite familiar and well expressed in the following passage from *A Theory of Justice*:

> The natural distribution [of natural talents] is neither just nor unjust; nor is it unjust that men are born into society at some particular position. These are simply *natural* facts. What is just and unjust is the way that institutions deal with these facts.[79]

This passage neatly captures the logic that underlies the Rawlsian objection to equality of opportunity. For it amounts to the claim that equality of opportunity is unjust in its dealings with natural inequalities. It is charged with taking natural advantages and systematically building upon them. I have rebutted that charge by rejecting the assumptions Rawls makes about natural inequalities and its distribution.

But, recalling the discussion in Section 2.5, the concern for Rawls about natural inequalities justifies the difference principle as an independent requirement of social justice designed to work in tandem with equality of opportunity under the rubric of democratic equality. If there are no natural inequalities, there is no need for an independent principle to complement the shortcomings of equal opportunity with regard to natural inequalities. The three-dimensional model of equal opportunities as a regulative ideal is proposed as an egalitarian theory that deals with the multiple dimensions of fairness that also underlie Rawls's second principle of justice, but all within the familiar framework of equality of opportunity.

The most important result of denying the existence of natural inequalities is that this entails all advantages in civil society being social in origins. From the perspective of a regulative ideal, this means that what is or who enjoys an advantage is always in a weak sense a type of social choice that can be the subject of regulation. In effect, inequalities are necessarily by design. Moreover, because inequalities are by design,

---

[78] See Dworkin, 'Equality of Resources', Will Kymlicka, *Contemporary Political Philosophy* , ch. 3 , and Eric Rakowski, *Equal Justice* (Oxford: Oxford University Press, 1991), ch. 6.

[79] Rawls, *A Theory of Justice*, p. 102. Emphasis added.

different civil societies may make substantially different choices that yield richly diverse possibilities. (This design may not be deliberate, but instead might evolve as conventions over time.) An egalitarian society must take responsibility for its particular design of advantages and disadvantages and the respects in which these track perceived natural differences between persons. The task of a competitive model of equal opportunity is to regulate competitions in civil society that contribute to the distribution of advantages and disadvantages between persons.[80] The three-dimensional model of equal opportunities as a regulative ideal identifies procedural fairness, background fairness, and stakes fairness as the standards for performing this function.

3.7 THE VULNERABLE MINORITY APPROACH

My insistence that all inequalities be viewed by design focuses the role of the regulative ideal on the form and substance of that design. In Section 3.3, I highlighted the idea that all inequalities are relational, a problem that resides in relations between persons, not in particular persons. From this perspective, inequalities by design are often a reflection of tensions between the vast majority and small minorities.[81] How should an egalitarian view inequalities by design in light of these tensions?

Although these tensions exist for a wide range of minorities including the poor, the disabled, and sexual minorities, the most familiar context for these tensions concerns racial minorities. Racial minorities are commonly identified as suffering racial disadvantage by virtue of their minority status. I shall make specific reference to race in my effort to distinguish, from the perspective of a regulative ideal, between two broad approaches for thinking about how an egalitarian society should assume responsibility for its particular design for the distribution of advantages and disadvantages and the social inequalities that result. Although this foreshadows my discussion in the next two chapters, the general point about minorities and the design of social inequalities is a theme throughout the rest of the book.

---

[80] Other principles of justice are at issue when, to use the language of the previous chapter, non-competitive opportunities are at issue.

[81] Of course, when the existence of natural inequalities is assumed to be a possibility, inequalities experienced by the minority are often attributed to the natural differences between the minority and the majority. Witness the IQ debate!

The first approach, which I reject, holds that a given race in a particular society should enjoy a share of the advantages and disadvantages that is proportional to their total numbers in that society. Racial disadvantage arises in this approach when the given race enjoys a smaller share than its proportional entitlement. This approach (which I shall call *the proportional entitlement approach*) meshes well with our intuitive reactions to some statistical findings with regard to disadvantage. Consider, for instance, the persistently high rates of poverty amongst African Americans. In 1996, 29.6 percent lived in poverty even though they constitute only 12.7 percent of the total population of the United States.[82] Likewise, in 1990, 23,000 African American men earned college degrees whilst 2,280,000 were in prison or on probation and parole. The ratio is 1 to 99 compared with a ratio of 1 to 6 for white men.[83] These findings seem to derive some force from the implicit appeal to the view that African Americans are being denied a share of society's advantages proportional to their numbers.

Although I appreciate the appeal of the proportional entitlement approach to racial disadvantage, it suffers from some fatal flaws. Certainly the most serious is that it presupposes some sort of straightforward and discernible way to define and mobilize the concept of race. Earlier, I indicated my scepticism about important racial differences having a genetic basis. How else might rigorous racial differentiation be grounded? The broader context, referred to in the Introduction to this book (Chapter 1), is the role law has had in the construction of race and the controversial respects in which race has been reconstructed in legal institutions to maintain the status quo or delay social change. Another flaw with the proportional entitlement approach is that it has the potential to be blind to what are generally perceived to be glaring forms of racial disadvantage. Consider, for example, the persistence of anti-Semitism in the United States. Under the proportional entitlement approach, this would not be racial disadvantage if Jewish Americans enjoy a share of the advantages in American society that is proportionally greater than their numbers warrant.[84] Finally, it should be noted that this approach is in

---

[82] Orlando Patterson, *The Ordeal of Integration* (Washington, DC: Civitas, 1997), p. 28.
[83] Henry Louis Gates, Jr., 'The Two Nations of Black America,' *The Brookings Review*, Vol. 16 (Spring 1998), p. 7.
[84] A parallel problem arises if the approach is extended to other forms of disadvantage such as those surrounding sexual orientation. There is no doubt that gay men are often the victims of hate crimes and suffer mistreatment because of their sexual orientation. But on the proportional entitlement approach, the issue of whether

tension with the general arguments for the three-dimensional model I defended in the last chapter. There I stressed that there are some goods that should be distributed on a competitive basis, with the necessary consequence being that everyone will not enjoy an equally proportional share of them.

The other approach to racial disadvantage (which I shall call the *vulnerable minority approach*) fits more readily with the egalitarian vision driving the three-dimensional model of equal opportunities as a regulative ideal. The root idea is that because all inequalities in the distribution of advantages and disadvantages are social, and that those inequalities are principally the function of design mechanisms based on popular opinion and the views of the majority, vulnerable minorities should be protected from social valuing that has a disproportionate impact.

Racial disadvantage arises when racial prejudice against a vulnerable minority influences social choices about valuing and the design for what constitutes an advantage and disadvantage. For our purposes, the following definition of racial prejudice is sufficient:

Racial prejudice should be understood to include those feelings, values, and beliefs that involve, one way or another, the discounting of a person's interests on account of her race. Racial animosity and hatred are among such attitudes, but less extreme forms of prejudice should also be recognized. For example, simple indifference to the plight of others on account of their race is a form of racial prejudice. So are unfounded beliefs and presumptions about the inferior intellectual or moral qualities of the members of a given race. Racial prejudice is not a single attitude but rather a set of them, distinguished by their tie to ideas and actions that count the interests of those in some racial group as less important than the interests of those in the racial reference group.[85]

this constitutes a disadvantage will turn on the overall share of society's advantages gay men enjoy proportionate to the total population. Anecdotal evidence suggests that, unlike lesbians, gay men may enjoy a disproportionately large share of society's advantages.

[85] Andrew Altman, 'Race and Democracy: The Controversy Over Racial Vote Dilution,' *Philosophy & Public Affairs*, Vol. 27 (Summer 1998), p. 188. Although I endorse here Altman's explanation of racial prejudice and am sympathetic to his theory of racial vote dilution, it seems to me that we differ on three very fundamental points – his assumption of the concept of race as unproblematic, his rejection of disproportionate impact analysis, and the fact that his approach does not stress the idea of vulnerable minorities. The last is especially surprising given his acknowledged intellectual debt in the article to John Hart Ely's theory of judicial review.

But this account of racial disadvantage is incomplete without an explanation of the unique vulnerability minorities face in social choices about the design of advantage and disadvantage. The insight that individuals and certain minorities are vulnerable to the tyranny of a dominant minority obviously has its roots in the political theory of Alexis de Tocqueville and John Stuart Mill. The problem is not simply the majority exercising its will. It is about prejudice entering into the exercise of that will. Perhaps the most famous legal expression of this concern came in Justice Harlan Stone's opinion for the United States Supreme Court in *United States v. Carolene Products Co.*, decided in 1938, when he justified greater judicial scrutiny of legislation when there is *"prejudice* against discrete and insular minorities."[86] His reasoning was that although forms of prejudice may enter any social choices about advantages and disadvantages, minorities are especially vulnerable to prejudice against them by the majority when some version of the majoritarian principle is the basis for reaching decisions about the design of inequality.

The vulnerable minority approach to racial disadvantage assumes that race is an intelligible concept. That assumption is not, however, in tension with my expressed scepticism about the natural origins of racial difference. It is now common to hear calls for the wholesale abandonment of the concept of race, especially in the United States.[87] Although these calls undeniably have their origins in the civil rights movement of the 1960s led by Martin Luther King, there are at present grounds for proceeding with care. While racial classification has undeniably been used insidiously, and race itself is a social construction, it is also paradoxically an important aspect of the identity of African Americans; race is in this respect the part of their cultural heritage that functions to give meaning to the choices they make about their lives. "[T]his country's history of slavery" is not, for example, as Derrick Bell stresses, "an insuperable racial barrier to blacks, but . . . a legacy of enlightenment from our enslaved forebears reminding us that . . . they survived the ultimate form of racism."[88] Racial identity serves to unite the group suffering

---

[86] *United States v. Carolene Products Co.*, 304 U.S. 144, 152–53n.4. Emphasis added. For the significance of this opinion, I am indebted to John Hart Ely, *Democracy and Distrust* (Cambridge, MA: Harvard University Press, 1980).

[87] See, e.g., Patterson, *The Ordeal of Integration*, pp. x–xi.

[88] Derrick Bell, *Faces at the Bottom of the Well: The Permanence of Racism* (New York: Basic Books, 1992), p. 12.

from the racism in its struggle against it.[89] The importance of racial identity to African Americans contrasts sharply to that of 'whites' in the United States. As Patricia Williams puts it, "Whiteness is unnamed, suppressed, beyond the realm of race. Exnomination permits whites to entertain the notion that race lives – over there on the other side of the tracks."[90] Her insight is that abolishing race will mean little to the identity of whites since their identity is not bound up with it, or at least, not to a comparable degree. The general point I am making is that the assumption that race is intelligible on the vulnerable minority approach to racial disadvantage does not reify or essentialize racial differences, but merely reinforces the vulnerable minority status of groupings such as African Americans.

It is possible to distinguish between two distinct realms where the vulnerable minority approach to racial disadvantage has significant implications. One realm is clearly the political realm, understood in orthodox terms as concerned with voting, representation, enacting and passing bills into law, and so on. The issues raised by racial prejudice are complex, and there is a very vibrant debate at present around the implications for political equality. Questions are being raised about a host of issues from racial vote dilution to the relation between the social identity of representatives and the quality of their representation.[91] Broadly conceived, these are issues about political or voting rights. As I stated at the beginning, although I think these are important, it is not my intention to address them in this book. Distinct from voting rights issues are the implications of the vulnerable minority

---

[89] For recent reworkings of this aspect of racial identity, see, e.g., K. Anthony Appiah, 'Race, Culture, Idenity: Misunderstood Connections' in *Color Conscious*; Jeff Spinner, *The Boundaries of Citizenship: Race, Ethnicity, and Nation in the Liberal State* (Baltimore: John Hopkins University Press, 1994); and Ronald J. Fiscus, *The Constitutional Logic of Affirmative Action* (Durham, NC: Duke University Press, 1992).

[90] Patricia J. Williams, *Seeing a Color-Blind Future: The Paradox of Race* (New York: Farrar, Straus, & Giroux, 1997), p. 7.

[91] See, e.g., Abigail Thernstrom, *Whose Votes Count?* (Cambridge, MA: Harvard University Press, 1987); Iris Marion Young, *Justice and the Politics of Difference* (Princeton: Princeton University Press, 1990); Bernard Grofman et al., *Minority Representation and the Quest for Voting Equality* (New York: Cambridge University Press, 1992); Lani Guinier, *The Tyranny of the Majority: Fundamental Fairness in Representative Democracy* (New York: Free Press, 1994); Altman, 'Race and Democracy,' and Melissa Williams, *Voice, Trust, and Memory: Marginalized Groups and the Failings of Liberal Representation* (Princeton: Princeton University Press, 1998).

approach to racial, class, and gender disadvantage for pursuing equal opportunities in civil society. This is my focus in the next six chapters.

3.8 CONCLUSION

This chapter has shown that the belief that there are natural inequalities is a myth and that therefore the Rawlsian objection to the concept of equality of opportunity is without foundations. Equality of opportunity cannot be charged with magnifying natural inequalities because there are no such inequalities. All inequalities are by necessity social. This conclusion lays the groundwork for the detailed analysis of a range of social policy issues with a view to applying the three-dimensional model of equal opportunities as a regulative ideal.

PART II

Race

Chapter 4

Equal Opportunities and Civil Rights: Merit, Standardized Tests, and Higher Education

4.1 INTRODUCTION

The goal of this chapter is to explain how a familiar account of civil rights flows from the three-dimensional model of equal opportunities as a regulative ideal that I have been defending in the last two chapters. The idea that civil rights are grounded in the ideal of equality of opportunity was once widely held but now seems to be in disrepute. This has engendered an intellectual crisis in the sense that civil rights seem to rest on weak foundations, and their defenders have embarked on a search for an alternative or supplementary account of egalitarian justice to ground civil rights.[1] It is my belief that this new search is misdirected and that at least one attractive model of equality of opportunity – the three-dimensional model of equal opportunities as a regulative ideal – can well explain the normative role of civil rights. The main insight I defend is that civil rights are legal devices for promoting status equality as a principle of background fairness.

Although the emphasis is on the idea of civil rights, that idea is notoriously elusive and imprecise. As Lloyd Weinreb has pointed out, "For all the discussion and debate about civil rights, it is striking how little attention is given initially to the question of what civil rights are. There is no well-understood principle of inclusion or exclusion that defines

---

[1] The most common supplement to equality of opportunity is the so-called antidiscrimination principle discussed in Ch. 2.4. See Paul Brest, 'Forward: In Defense of the Antidiscrmination Principle,' *Harvard Law Review, Vol. 90* (1976), reprinted in Christopher McCrudden, editor, *Anti-Discrimination Law* (New York: New York University Press, 1991), and Christopher Edley, *Not All Black and White: Affirmative Action and American Values* (New York: Hill & Wang, 1996), ch. 4.

the category."[2] What I have in mind is the type of trend that flourished in the United States after World War II in a series of statutes culminating in the 1964 Civil Rights Act and the 1965 Voting Rights Act but continued in to the 1990s as evidenced by the passing in 1991 of the new federal Civil Rights Act.[3] These pieces of legislation enacted rights for certain minority groups, especially blacks, intended to protect them from certain forms of discrimination and unfair treatment, and made these rights justiciable through the federal courts.[4] The important legal consequence of these new civil rights is that they complemented both in principle and practice already existing constitutional rights, which regulate government, by imposing these requirements on institutions in civil society.

It is often not fully appreciated that this trend was not unique to the United States. Parallel developments occurred, for example, in both Canada and Britain. In Canada, the Province of Ontario enacted the *Ontario Human Rights Code* in 1962 designed to consolidate all of its previous anti-discrimination statutes.[5] All but one of the other provinces quickly followed suit with their own codes. And in 1977, the Federal Government passed the *Canadian Human Rights Code*. A similar consolidation occurred in Britain with the *Sex Discrimination Act* passed in 1975 and the *Race Relations Act* a year later. In both countries, quasi-judicial forums were established to investigate and adjudicate complaints based on these new statutes. As in the United States, the legal rights they

---

[2] Lloyd L. Weinreb, 'What Are Civil Rights?' in Ellen Paul, Fred Miller, and Jeffrey Paul, editors, *Reassessing Civil Rights* (Cambridge, MA: Blackwell, 1991), p. 1.

[3] Although this type of legislation has flourished since the Second World War, it has its origins, of course, in the Reconstruction Era after the American Civil War.

[4] It is accurate to say that although there was considerable disagreement about the set of minority groups who should be protected by civil rights legislation, there was a consensus that blacks were part of any anticipated set. Less well known is the lack of consensus about including women. The fact that the 1964 Civil Rights Act includes women is largely a consequence of an amendment by opponents of the bill. By amending the bill to include women, these opponents believed that the bill was more likely to be defeated. And even after it passed with the amendment, many supporters of the bill in the Johnson Administration expressly denied that the bill should be used to protect the civil rights of women. See Susan Gluck Mezey, *In Pursuit of Equality: Women, Public Policy, and the Federal Courts* (New York: St. Martin's Press, 1992), pp. 36–42.

[5] Throughout this chapter, I use the term civil rights rather than human rights mainly because the former captures the broad focus of this book on civil society, whilst the latter is often associated with international law and international declarations of bodies such as the United Nations. My argument in this chapter is not directed at international law.

created were designed to complement existing constitutional rights in the sense that their scope extended to institutions in civil society.[6]

Now, the evolution of civil rights over the past fifty years has been characterized by shifting views about the applicability of civil rights complaints to issues in civil society. What may have once been thought not to raise a question of civil rights has often emerged over time as one.[7] For critics, civil rights complaints have evolved and multiplied so much that they have lost any coherent meaning.[8] Rather than being based on principle, civil rights complaints are said to be merely another strategy for pursuing an expressly political agenda. Ironically, those who appeal to civil rights often seem to concur with these critics insofar as when tensions emerged between some civil rights complaints and equality of opportunity – the traditional normative foundations of civil rights – there was little hesitation to look for alternative foundations or to disparage the very idea of foundations. My view, clearly evident in the previous chapters, is that this is a reflection of the failure to recognize the variety of models of equality of opportunity and the robust core of that ideal of egalitarian justice. But I appreciate the importance of looking for new challenges and avenues for civil rights litigation. And I agree that a theory of civil rights must be dynamic enough to provide a rationale for pressing complaints in at least some of these new areas. For these reasons, I outline a theory of civil rights based on the three-dimensional model of equal opportunities as a regulative ideal against the backdrop of an emerging issue in American civil rights litigation – the use of standardized test results in admission decisions by institutions of higher

---

[6] The contrast between constitutional rights and civil or human rights is not intended to ignore the very complex relation between constitutional and civil rights. In both the United States and Canada, the courts have recognized the former as more significant than the latter. The United States Supreme Court treats as redundant a complaint based on a civil rights violation when a complaint based on a constitutional right has already been recognized. See *United States v. Fordice*, 505 U.S. 717 (1990). The Supreme Court of Canada has held that human rights codes must conform with the requirements of the Charter of Rights and Freedoms, and so ordered the Province of Alberta to amend its code to provide protection based on sexual orientation since, in an earlier decision, the Supreme Court had held that sexual orientation was protected under Section 15 of the Charter. See *Vriend v. Alberta* (1998) 1 S.C.R. 493.

[7] The starkest illustration of this in the United States is provided by affirmative action, which in the 1960s seemed only remotely, if at all, a question of civil rights but is now widely viewed as one of the most fundamental civil rights issues. I discuss affirmative action in much greater detail in the next chapter.

[8] See, e.g., Richard Epstein, 'Two Conceptions of Civil Rights' in *Reassessing Civil Rights*.

education. As in Chapter 5 in this book on race, the focus is mainly on the United States. As I explained in the introductory chapter, this is a reflection of my belief that the American experience provides some of the most challenging contexts for thinking about the relationship between race and law.

4.2 STANDARDIZED TESTS IN AMERICAN UNIVERSITIES

It is well known that in the United States, universities and other institutions of higher education utilize the results of scores on standardized tests to make decisions about admission and related matters such as financial assistance and scholarships. This practice, though widespread throughout the country, is especially prevalent in graduate programs and professional schools and those select universities that have a very intense competition for admission into their undergraduate programs. Five standardized tests – the Scholastic Aptitude Test (SAT), the Graduate Record Examination (GRE), the Law School Admission Test (LSAT), the Medical College Admission Test (MCAT), and the American College Test (ACT) – are especially relied upon. These tests are all said to be aptitude tests in the sense that they allegedly test the general proficiency of the candidate rather than something taught or acquired. None claim to measure IQ. This is despite careful documentation showing that there is a high correlation between their results and traditional IQ tests. [9] The fact that American universities are immense consumers of standardized test results shouldn't be surprising since they were pioneers in the design and application of standardized tests. [10] It is worth noting, however, that universities in other English-speaking industrial countries such as Canada and Britain do not rely on standardized test results to anywhere near the same extent.

The reasons American universities rely on standardized tests in admission competitions are often said to be practical. In a large country, where students come from a wide variety of educational backgrounds, there are immense commensurability problems posed by the task of trying to compare, for example, high school grades or college GPAs. Standardized tests that measure general proficiency provide a way to compare students from these diverse backgrounds in competitive

[9] Howard Gardner, 'Who Owns Intelligence?,' *Atlantic Monthly* (February 1999), p. 70.
[10] For a history, see Nicholas Lemann, 'The Great Sorting,'*Atlantic Monthly* (August 1995), 84–100.

processes for admission. Looming behind this rationale, however, is a more complex normative argument about merit and the design of a meritocratic admissions scheme that I shall discuss in the next section of the chapter. For now, it is important to recognize one of the implications of relying on standardized test results to make important decisions about admission into selective universities and professional schools. The context is the well documented 'black-white gap' in test scores across the range of these standardized tests from general proficiency tests such as SAT and LSAT to conventional IQ tests. Although the literature on this gap is immense and controversial, there seems to be a consensus that this gap is about one standard deviation – that is, fifteen points. This means that, in the blunt terms of Christopher Jencks and Meredith Phillips, "the typical American black still scores below 75 percent of American whites on almost every standardized test."[11] The important result is that increased reliance on standardized test results will decrease the likelihood of African Americans being admitted into selective universities and competitive professional schools and graduate programs.

Despite this implication, coupled with increased reliance on standardized test results by American universities over the past thirty years, only very recently has the issue emerged as a site for major civil rights complaints, even though the use of standardized tests in employment contexts has been the site of civil rights complaints for more than thirty years. The landmark 1971 U.S. Supreme Court case, *Griggs v. Duke Power Co.*, for example, involved the use of standardized tests in hiring and promotion decisions. What has been the motivation, especially in states such as California, to rethink the civil rights implications of the uses of standardized tests by universities and colleges?

The most important factor is undeniably the retrenchment of affirmative action in admissions to colleges and universities with selective entry policies across the country, especially in Texas and California. The underlying reasoning seems to be that although the use of standardized test scores has always had potentially adverse implications for the admission of certain racial minorities and women into institutions of higher education, the existence of affirmative action programs mitigated this effect and defused the reliance on tests as a civil rights issue. Indeed, Christopher Edley, who served as President Clinton's principal advisor

---

[11] Jencks & Phillips, 'The Black-White Test Score Gap,' *The Brookings Review, Vol. 16* (Spring 1998), p. 24.

on rethinking affirmative action, has described an important function of affirmative action to be "to correct the problems we've inflicted on ourselves with our testing standards."[12] With the prospect of retrenchment, however, affirmative action no longer would function to mitigate for this impact. While I intend to postpone discussing colour-conscious affirmative action in depth until the next chapter, the role it has played in bringing the present issue to the forefront of the American civil rights movement is undeniable.

4.3 MERITOCRACY REGULATED BY EQUAL OPPORTUNITIES

The fundamental question that concerns me is what makes the use of standardized test results by American universities a civil rights issue. While any response to this question presupposes a general theory of civil rights, the most compelling answer revolves around the familiar defense of standardized test results that they enable universities to identify the most applicants with the greatest merit in a competitive process for admission. Merit is understood in the competition to be a combination of ability and effort.[13] When universities look only at past indicators of merit such as high school grades, however, it is difficult to compare different candidates because of the diversity of educational backgrounds and schools, as noted earlier. Standardized test scores provide a proxy for merit, and are easily compared between candidates. As Iris Marion Young explains:

Standardized tests appear to comply with the requirements of merit evaluation because they are usually procedurally fair. They are blind to race, sex, and

---

[12] Quoted in Abigail and Stephan Thernstrom, 'Black Progress,' *The Brookings Review,* Vol. 16 (Spring 1998), p. 16. Edley in fact embraces a much more pluralistic and complex view of affirmative action. See his account in *Not All Black and White: Affirmative Action and American Values.*

[13] Norman Daniels, 'Merit and Meritocracy' in *Justice and Justification* (New York: Cambridge University Press, 1996), p. 303. There is, however, no consensus among philosophers about how to define merit. As an alternative to my definition, John Lucas in *Responsibility* (Oxford: Oxford University Press, 1993) defines merit as something stemming from an attribute someone *has* as opposed to something someone *does*. In his view, someone merits being on a sports team because of some attribute he or she has. But clearly having an attribute is not sufficient for this merit; it is also required that one attend practices or training, and so on. My point is that when these additional requirements are acknowledged, merit is something like, as I state in the main text, *ability* plus *effort*.

ethnicity. They are *objective* in the sense that when they are used to evaluate individuals we can be sure that all have been evaluated according to the same criteria, and in the sense that for a given individual any scorer will come up with the same score. By quantifying test answers and relying on complex statistical techniques, tests also appear able to measure individual skill precisely and to compare and rank individuals, providing an objective assessment of the most and least qualified.[14]

The major testing agencies in the United States, such as the College Examination Board (CEB), validate this equating of merit and test results by providing ample research showing that test scores are useful predictors of success in a student's first year of study.

Many legal commentators have focused, rightly I think, on this idea of merit as the appropriate grounds for bringing forth a civil rights complaint against some universities for their uses of standardized test results.[15] While the precise details of their commentaries vary, the core line of criticism – the radical critique of merit – is similar and involves four principal steps: (1) Standards of merit and corresponding notions of individual desert are social constructions, not something natural or necessarily cross-cultural. (2) Standards of merit in the United States are set by the 'white' majority, and instruments such as standardized tests that are designed to gauge merit reflect this. (3) Thus, although those outside the 'white' majority often fail to meet this standard of merit as indicated by standardized test results, this is a result of the way standards of merit are socially constructed and not necessarily a failing of individuals from the minority group. (4) Standards of merit in the United States should be socially constructed to reflect also the perspective of these marginalized minorities. The basis for a civil rights complaint (concludes this line of criticism) arises when universities don't accommodate for this perspective.

While clearly the arguments about IQ in the last chapter show that I have considerable sympathy for the radical critique of merit, it is nevertheless wrong-headed, principally because it rests on a *common*

---

[14] Iris Marion Young, *Justice and the Politics of Difference* (Princeton: Princeton University Press, 1990), p. 208.

[15] See, e.g., Richard Delgado, 'Rodrigo's Tenth Chronicle: Merit and Affirmative Action,' *83, Georgetown Law Journal* (1995), pp. 1709–55; Daria Roithmayr, 'Deconstructing the Distinction between Merit and Bias,' *85, California Law Review* (1997), pp. 363–421; Michael Selmi, 'Testing for Equality: Merit, Efficiency, and the Affirmative Action Debate,' *42 UCLA Law Review, (1995)* pp. 1251–1314; Susan Sturm and Lani Guinier, 'The Future of Affirmative Action: Reclaiming the Innovative Ideal,' *84, California Law Review,* (1996), pp. 953–97.

misperception about why a college admissions scheme or indeed any other such practice looks to merit to guide its decision-making. Any scheme based on a merit principle is commonly called a meritocracy. It is, however, a common misperception of a meritocracy to think that the concern with merit derives from a more fundamental belief about what particular individuals deserve.[16] In other words, the radical critique conflates two distinct concepts – merit and desert. The mistaken underlying reasoning is that if an admission scheme wants to identify the applicants with the most merit, it is because those individuals most *deserve* to be admitted. But some careful consideration of this reasoning shows why it is flawed. When merit is understood as a function of ability combined with effort, those individuals with the most merit may not be the most deserving since those two factors may have sources such as genetic good luck that do not warrant praise. In other words, although, those individuals under a meritocratic admissions scheme with the most merit may be admitted, they are not necessarily the most deserving.[17] Moreover, whereas a meritocracy is forward-looking, desert-based praise is backward looking, rewarding individuals for their past exemplary behaviour. Standardized tests are, as I noted earlier, designed to measure aptitude and provide a basis for making predictions about future performance; they do not purport to measure past educational achievements. This makes the results of such tests a poor gauge of desert but a more promising fit for a merit exercise.

If a meritocratic admissions scheme is not designed to admit the most deserving individuals, what other purpose might it serve? The most plausible answer is that such a scheme best serves society's interests or maximizes the educational resources of society.[18] Defenders of a meritocratic admissions scheme would presumably say that since places in a selective undergraduate program or professional school are scarce,

---

[16] A prominent example of this misperception about meritocracy is Michael Sandel, *Liberalism and the Limits of Justice* (New York: Cambridge University Press, 1982), pp. 72–76.

[17] The distinction I am drawing here turns on the claim that a *necessary* condition for deserving something is that its basis be to some extent voluntary. This claim is the subject of considerable debate. See, e.g., David Miller, 'Desert and Determinism,' and Julian Lamont, 'The Concept of Desert in Distributive Justice,' both reprinted in Louis P. Pojman and Owen McLeod, editors, *What Do We Deserve?* (New York: Oxford University Press, 1999). It seems to me that many of the objections about the voluntary condition for deserving something hinge on its being a sufficient condition, not merely a necessary condition.

[18] I follow here Daniels, 'Merit and Meritocracy,' pp. 302–16.

society has an interest in utilizing those places in the most productive way possible. How might this be done? By selecting those applicants with the most merit, since by definition they are the ones with the optimal combination of ability and effort and will therefore make the most productive use of the educational opportunity. The common contrast defenders of meritocracy make is to a scheme that admits applicants with less than optimal combinations of ability and effort; this will by necessity yield lower rates of productivity with society's educational resources, and therefore is not in the best interests of society. The insight that a meritocracy values merit because it promotes the best interests of society reinforces that the notion it is a mistake to equate merit assessment with judgements about what people deserve. As Joel Feinberg has pointed out, "to say 'S deserves X because giving it to him would be in the public interest' is simply to misuse the word *deserves*."[19]

If I am right that the underlying forward-looking rationale for a meritocratic admissions scheme is to maximize the educational resources of society, then this has devastating implications for the radical critique of merit as a basis for civil rights complaints against the use of standardized test results in institutions of higher education. That line of criticism turned on the assumption – expressed in step 4 – that a meritocracy is amenable to perspectives on merit that have their origins in minority groups in the society. In what is, in my view, the most careful presentation of the radical critique of merit including an application to law school admissions, Daria Roithmayr concludes her argument with the following prescription:

> Thus, we are left with the task of reconstructing new meanings for merit by having difficult political reservations about what constitutes social value in the legal profession, whether exams accurately predict the ability of a practicing lawyer, whether case law instruction or practical clinical instruction is more appropriate for certain kinds of law, and finally, whether we want our law schools to become resegregated under an admissions process that looks only at the number of a person's LSAT score and GPA, rather than at the content of her character.[20]

But the underlying assumption here about merit has to be mistaken. Merit in a meritocracy is a function of whatever maximizes the use of

---

[19] Joel Feinberg, 'Justice and Personal Desert,' reprinted in Louis P. Pojman and Owen McLeod, editors, *What Do We Deserve?* (New York: Oxford University Press, 1999), p. 81.

[20] Roithmayr, 'Deconstructing the Distinction between Bias and Merit,' p. 1507.

society's educational resources. This account leaves no room for majority and minority perspectives. What is valued in a meritocracy – merit – necessarily has a universalist character in the sense that it involves a social calculus that transcends majority/minority groupings in society.[21] A minority perspective would therefore only make sense if merit is a function of whatever maximizes the minority grouping's use of educational resources (which would be a non-starter for proponents of meritocratic admissions scheme designed for society as whole).

This argument is reinforced by the noticeable lack of any substantial formulation of a 'minority' perspective on merit that differs in any real way from the prevalent perspective. I don't mean to deny that the educational resources of society can be used more productively by including more members of minority groups. This claim is often used, quite rightly, to justify admitting more African American or Latino students into medical or law school. Latino physicians may be more willing to practice in poor predominantly Latino neighbourhoods and therefore society may be better off enrolling a Latino student than a white student with higher test scores.[22] But this claim does not turn on applying some different standard of merit when admitting the Latino student, nor is it being claimed that the Latino student is more deserving; it merely shows the complexity of calculating what is in the best interests of society.[23]

What basis other than the radical critique of merit might there be for a civil rights complaint against the uses of standardized test scores in institutions of higher education? Recall now that in Chapter 2 I was careful to distinguish between a meritocracy and equality of opportunity. I argued there that the function of a theory of equality of opportunity such as the three-dimensional model of equal opportunities as a regulative ideal is to act as an independent moral critic of competitive processes including presumably meritocratic schemes for determining admission into selective programs and professional schools at institutions of higher education. The foregoing analysis showing that a meritocracy is designed to maximize society's educational resources or serve in society's best interests clarifies the role for equal opportunities as a regulative ideal.

---

[21] The universality of merit is claimed by, for instance, Nathan Glazer, *The Limits of Social Policy* (Cambridge, MA: Harvard University Press, 1989), pp. 94–95

[22] Komaromy et al., 'The Role of Black and Hispanic Physicians in Providing Health Care for Underserviced Populations,' *The New England Journal of Medicine, Vol. 332, no. 20* (May 16 1996), p. 1305.

[23] This is discussed by Ronald Dworkin, *A Matter of Principle* (Cambridge, MA: Harvard University Press, 1985), p. 299.

A meritocratic admissions scheme is insensitive to the particular distribution or pattern of university places among members of society. To
be sensitive to the particular distribution of university places requires
viewing those admitted under such a scheme as individuals rather than
merely as receptacles of merit. When the sole goal is assumed to be the
maximization of merit, however, there is no room for this. As Amartya
Sen and Bernard Williams have observed, in a parallel point about utilitarianism, "Persons do not count as individuals in this any more than
individual petrol tanks do in the analysis of the national consumption
of petroleum."[24] The role of equal opportunities as a regulative ideal is
precisely to introduce, for the sake of pursuing equality, sensitivity to the
particular distribution of places into a competitive admissions scheme
based on merit. But this does not require displacing the meritocratic admission scheme and replacing it with some sort of alternative admission
scheme; it requires only placing constraints and regulations on the competition for meritocratic admission. In other words, the proposal is not
to abolish using standardized test scores in competitive admission decisions but merely to identify limits and constraints on their uses based
on this three-dimensional model of equal opportunities.

The three-dimensional model of equal opportunities as a regulative ideal combines a concern for three dimensions of fairness in a
competition – procedural, background, and stakes. As Iris Marion Young
stated in the passage quoted at the beginning of Section 4.3, however, the
reliance on standardized test scores seems consistent with the ordinary
standards of procedural fairness that are applicable to admissions into
a competitive university or college program. If there are concerns about
the equal opportunities of African American applicants, then they must
reflect our standards of background and stakes fairness that govern the
competition. I shall first discuss briefly the application of stakes fairness
to competitions using standardized test scores, and then concentrate on
background fairness with more in-depth analysis. My intention is to lay
the theoretical groundwork for a theory of civil rights developed in the
next section of this chapter.

From the perspective of stakes fairness, given the disproportionate
impact of using standardized test results on African American applicants, it is especially important that what is at stake in the competition be limited in scope. This raises challenging questions about how

---

[24] 'Introduction' to A. Sen and B. Williams, editors, *Utilitarianism and Beyond*
(Cambridge, UK: Cambridge University Press, 1982), p. 4.

important an undergraduate degree from a highly selective university or a graduate degree or a professional degree is to accessing certain (elite) opportunities in the United States. Are these the only avenues to access these opportunities, or are there alternatives? Stakes fairness demands that given the reliance on standardized tests for admission into these various degree programs, there should exist a range of other avenues to access these opportunities. A model for this has emerged in recent years in the opportunities to provide legal and medical services. In the case of legal services, there are alternative providers of legal services such as para-legals, immigration consultants, and mediators. These providers do not need a law degree to serve the legal needs of their community. The emergence of alternative medical practitioners such as mid-wives and chiropractors, ordinarily with very different training from physicians, are perhaps an even more prominent illustration of how the requirements of stakes fairness might be met. Of course, within the business community, there has long existed a healthy scepticism about the exclusive focus on having a particular degree or professional qualification.

I turn now to the more important application of background fairness. In Section 2.4, I defended with some care the proposition that the principle of status equality should provide the basis for assessing background fairness in a competition in the three-dimensional model of equal opportunities as a regulative ideal. Recall that status equality identifies a starting position – the same moral status for each and no higher moral standing possible – in a competition that all individuals should enjoy. Although I have distinguished moral and social status and insisted that the currency of background fairness be moral status, I also noted that the standard indexes of social status – inequalities in wealth and income, power, and privilege – provide evidence of when status equality is compromised. Why might the use of standardized test scores in admission decisions by universities and colleges be seen as a threat to the status equality of African Americans?

Since Chief Justice Warren's famous opinion against racially segregated public schools in *Brown v. Board of Education*, it has become widely recognized that access to educational institutions is of special importance in the determination of the social status of African Americans.[25] For this reason alone, it might be held that reliance on

---

[25] 'To separate [children] from others of similar age and qualifications solely because of their race generates a feeling of inferiority as to their *status* in the community

standardized tests by institutions of higher education amounts to inferior social status since, given the 'black-white' score gap, the effect is to make institutions of higher education less accessible to African Americans. But I doubt that this reasoning on its own will persuade very many who are sympathetic to using standardized tests in higher education decisions that these uses raise questions about equal opportunity. It seems necessary to provide a more subtle two-pronged argument about the relationship between inferior social status and status equality. Debra Satz has perceptively stressed, "Relationships of unequal status are characterized by lack of reciprocity, hierarchy and lack of accountability."[26] All three are evident in the present context. The important point, as I noted in general terms at the end of the last chapter, is that status equality is especially fragile for vulnerable minorities in competitions where the social construction of advantages and disadvantages reflects the values and interests of the majority.

The first prong of the argument draws attention to the institutional choice to use standardized test scores as a proxy for merit in a competition for university and college places. This sort of social choice reflects a decision about what should count as an advantage – high score results – and a disadvantage – low score results – in an important competitive realm of society. But when the reliance on standardized test scores in university and college admissions became widespread about thirty-five years ago, there was already significant awareness of the black-white gap in scores. It seems pertinent to ask what kind of weight the existence of this gap was given in deliberations around relying on standardized test scores. There may be some grounds for thinking that some of the early proponents of using standardized test scores in admissions decisions embraced this choice precisely because of the black-white test score gap.[27] But even if the decision were not invidious, in hindsight it seems to me nearly impossible to draw any inference other than that blacks at the time were not recognized as having the moral standing that would have made this social choice difficult or very controversial if

---

that may affect their hearts and minds in a way unlikely ever to be undone.' *Brown v. Board of Education of Topeka* 347 U.S. 490 (1954) at 494. Emphasis added.

26 Debra Satz, 'Status Inequalities and Models of Market Socialism' in Erik Olin Wright, editor, *Equal Shares* (New York: Verso, 1996), p. 72.

27 This is suggested, in the case I discuss in some depth later, by some of the plaintiffs' arguments regarding the Mississippi college system. See also the discussion in Roithmayr, 'Deconstructing the Distinction between Bias and Merit,' pp. 1474–87.

their moral status would have been perceived to be equal to that of white Americans. And to continue to act on a social choice made in that context is to reaffirm that view of the moral status of African Americans. No doubt, many people believed at the time that the black-white test score gap would eventually narrow, as indeed it has.[28] Yet this does not excuse or hide the fact that if a similar type of social choice by the majority were being made where there were well-known disadvantageous effects on a minority that enjoyed genuine status equality, it seems hard to imagine that choice being made at all, or at least without severe limitations being placed on it. This is further complicated by the undeniable (well-known at the time) historical contributions the state made to the hindrance of educational opportunities for blacks, which have often been thought to be a contributing factor to the black-white test score gap.[29]

What I am suggesting is that the very fact that standardized test scores gained the currency they have despite the black-white score gap is an indicator that African Americans were not regarded as having equal moral standing. (The demand that all enjoy status equality is I think a less demanding requirement for a collective decision than the requirement that they actually participate in the initial development of standards of merit applied in universities and colleges.[30]) This point is reinforced by noting the contrast to the response to score gaps between men and women on standardized tests. The specific example I have in mind is with regard to the scores of the Preliminary Scholastic Assessment Test (PSAT), which had long been characterized by a score gap between males and females. In 1995, among high school juniors, boys scored on average 48.8 verbal and 50.8 math compared with 48.6 verbal and 47.4 math for girls. Rather than defending the validity of the test scores, the CEB, which sponsors the test, responded dramatically by

[28] William G. Bowen and Derek Bok in *The Shape of the River: Long-Term Consequences of Considering Race in College and University Admissions* (Princeton: Princeton University Press, 1998) point out, for instance, that they found that in admission to selective universities and colleges, the gap between successful black and white applicants in combined SAT scores narrowed from 233 points in 1976 to 165 points in 1989 (p. 30).

[29] Commenting on the difficulty of knowing whether the Fourteenth Amendment in 1868 was intended to be applied to public education, Chief Justice Warren in *Brown v. Board of Education* says, "Education of Negroes was almost non-existent, and practically all of the race were illiterate. In fact, any education of Negroes was forbidden by law in some states." *Brown v. Board of Education of Topeka* 347 U.S. 490 at 494.

[30] The latter requirement is defended by Duncan Kennedy, 'A Cultural Pluralist Case for Affirmative Action in Legal Academia,' *Duke Law Journal* (1990), p. 705.

changing the design of the test. In 1997, the CEB announced that it was adding a writing skills component to the PSAT, anticipating that girls would perform better than boys on the new writing skills examination and thus reduce the performance gap between men and women.[31] This type of response is an indicator that within educational institutions, men and women are perceived to have status equality – the same moral status for men and women and no higher moral standing possible – and that choices of mechanisms for distributing competitive advantages and disadvantages are made in the shadow of that perception with an eye to reciprocity. (I suggest in Chapters 8 and 9 that the same cannot be said about the status of women in the labour market or in legal institutions regulating the family.) Conversely, it is precisely because there is no parallel dramatic response to the black-white score gap – only investigations into its accuracy and causes with a view to addressing those causes – that I suggest no similar perception exists.

The second prong of the argument with regard to background fairness concerns how precisely reliance on standardized test scores denies status equality to individual African Americans. Despite the black-white score gap, it might be said that the use of standardized test scores does not function as an exclusionary barrier against individual African Americans because the barriers it resurrects are not against African Americans *per se* but rather those with low test scores, whatever their racial identity. In other words, the reliance on standardized test results by higher education does not compromise the initial standing of an African American applicant because it does not exclude the applicant from the process. There is an interesting parallel here to the use of racial profiling by the police, discussed in Section 2.4. At issue in that case is the idea that a person's race can function as a proxy for an increased statistical likelihood of criminal behaviour. Recall that the principal justification for the use of racial proxies is more effective crime fighting by the police. Defenders of racial profiling commonly highlight the proposition that innocent persons do not suffer greatly because of it; individuals from minority groups might be delayed more by police practicing racial

---

[31] Somini Sengupta, 'Same Subjects, More Verbs in New P.S.A.T.,' *The New York Times* Sunday, October 19, 1997, p. 16. The article states, "The College Board, which designed the test, added a writing skills examination this year in an effort to raise the test scores of girls." The fact that this goal is represented as completely unproblematic is indicative of the contrast I am drawing. I cannot imagine changing the test to "raise the test scores of African Americans" being regarded as similarly unproblematic.

profiling than whites, but assuming the individuals are indeed innocent, racial profiling does not amount to excluding them from important or valuable opportunities. Proponents of the anti-discrimination principle query whether these discriminatory costs on minorities can be justified. In contrast, the principle of status equality holds simply that racial profiling by police should be prohibited because it amounts to ascribing to individuals different standings in criminal investigations based on their race.

Something similar can be said about the use of standardized tests. Much of the focus is on the *exclusionary* effects of relying heavily on test scores. Yet this often leads us to overlook the *costly* burdens on African Americans of relying heavily on standardized test scores to make admissions decisions in institutions of higher education. The basic difference analytically between exclusionary effects and costly burdens is that the latter make it more difficult for African Americans to be admitted into universities and colleges with selective admissions, not impossible. Why think that there are any costs of relying on standardized tests for qualified African Americans? The most interesting and provocative evidence revolves around indicators of the phenomenon of adaptation among African Americans to the reliance on standardized tests. The phenomenon of adaptation arises when individuals adjust their desires or behaviour to social expectations.[32] In other words, given the expectation that African Americans will score lower on standardized tests, there is some evidence that individual African Americans adapt their behaviour to meet this expectation. Consider two examples of this adaptation. Claude Steele, for example, has found that African Americans do less well on standardized tests when they are aware of expectations based on the black-white score gap and their results are viewed within the context of that expectation.[33] The conservative economist Gary Becker has found that African Americans, along with certain other disadvantaged minorities, make bad decisions about investing in their own

---

[32] This characterization of adaptation draws on the careful review of the recent literature by Martha Nussbaum, *Women and Human Development: The Capabilities Approach* (Cambridge UK: Cambridge University Press, 2000), ch. 2.

[33] In an influential statement of this phenomenon, Claude Steele says of a black student, "The devalued state of his race devalues him and his work in the classroom. Unable to entrust his sense of himself to this place, he resists measuring himself against its values and goals." See 'Race and the Schooling of Black Americans,'*Atlantic Monthly* (April 1992), p. 74. See also 'A Threat in the Air: How Stereotypes Shape Intellectual Identity and Performance,' *American Psychologist*, Vol. 52 (1997), pp. 613–29.

human capital because of the expectations of others about what they are capable of achieving. For Becker, "the *beliefs* of employers, teachers, and other influential groups that minority members are less productive *can* be self-fulfilling," causing the members of the disadvantaged group to "underinvest in education, training, and work skills" – and this underinvestment does subsequently make them less productive.[34] Both of these examples illustrate how adaptation to expectations around standardized test results imposes a costly burden on African Americans and how that cost is borne uniquely by them (and individual members of other similarly situated racial or ethnic minorities). This cost affects the initial starting position of African Americans and would seem to violate the demand of background fairness that in the admissions procedures, all applicants should enjoy status equality.

The characterization of a costly burden just given relies on the test of asking what performance would be like without perceived unequal social and moral status. That test is a counter-factual one that might seem quite speculative. There is, however, some independent evidence to support the conclusions drawn from it. At the University of California, Berkeley, the number of first-year African American students increased by 32 percent from 1981 to 1990.[35] The standard view (expressed in the debate around affirmative action) is that Berkeley increased its freshman African American enrollment by lowering its admissions standard, thereby admitting African American applicants with less merit than had previously been the case. And it follows that one would expect lower graduation rates for African Americans over this period. However, this isn't what happened. Among the entering class of 1981, 31 percent graduated within six years. Among the entering class of 1990, 62 percent graduated by 1996. In other words, rather than seeing a decline in graduation rates, the rates doubled for African Americans at Berkeley over this period. The most plausible explanation is the earlier low rates of graduation reflected 'adaptive' performances, which were adjusted as

---

[34] Gary Becker, 'The Economic Way of Looking at Behavior' (1992 Nobel Address), quoted in Nussbaum, *Women and Human Development*, pp. 126–27. See also Martha Nussbaum, *Sex and Social Justice* (New York: Oxford University Press, 1999), pp. 151–53.

[35] The numbers cited in the rest of this paragraph all come from a letter to the editor of *The New York Times*, April 12, 1998, from Genaro Padilla, vice chancellor of undergraduate affairs at Berkeley. Note that in 1998, with the end of affirmative action in the University of California, African American enrollment declined from 6.8 percent in 1997 to 2.4 percent, which was roughly the level it had been in the early 1960s. See Bowen and Bok, *The Shape of the River*, pp. 35–39.

African American students perceived themselves as having greater status equality as their numbers increased significantly as a portion of the total Berkeley student body.[36]

So far, I have argued that concerns about background unfairness can be raised about the uses of standardized test scores in universities and colleges because of the infringement on the principle of status equality. I have yet to explain how these concerns might warrant the regulation of a meritocratic admissions scheme. For some might say that because it infringes on status equality, we need an alternative admissions scheme that better promotes the value of status equality.

Here, the very idea of status or standing performs some valuable work. Recall that it reflects a concern with the initial starting positions of persons, not the goal or purpose of a competition. Recently, some moral philosophers, in particular Frances Kamm and Thomas Nagel, have argued that status is a unique moral notion because it identifies each person as inviolable in a certain way and therefore grounds constraints on the actions and decisions of others. Nagel explains that,

> moral *status* . . . means that one *may not* be violated in certain ways – such treatment is inadmissible, and if it occurs, the person has been wronged. So someone's having or lacking this status is not equivalent to anything's happening or not happening to him. If he has it, he does not lose it when his rights are violated – rather, such treatment counts as a violation of his rights precisely because he has it.[37]

It follows that moral status is not something that can be aggregated amongst persons. Nor can the status of one person be compromised or enhanced by compromising or enhancing the status of someone else. Status is a value that does not allow for such trade-offs. As Kamm puts it, "Respecting it provides the background against which we may then seek the welfare of persons or pursue other values. It is not our duty to bring about the existence of such valuable persons, but only to respect the constraints that express the presence of value."[38] As I emphasized in Section 2.4, status equality is a regulative ideal about the initial

---

[36] An alternative, cynical, explanation might be that Berkeley relaxed its graduation requirements. In fact, though, this is not supported by the evidence, which shows that while the overall six-year graduation rate increased from 68 percent to 80 percent, it certainly did not parallel the doubling of rates for African Americans.

[37] Thomas Nagel, 'Personal Rights and Public Space,' *Philosophy & Public Affairs*, Vol. 24 (Spring 1995), pp. 89–90.

[38] Frances Kamm, *Morality, Mortality, Volume II: Rights, Duties, and Status* (Oxford: Oxford University Press, 1996), pp. 272–73.

standing of all individuals in a competition; its function is to set constraints on the competition, not provide the point and purpose for the competition.

I trust that the relevance of this philosophical analysis of moral status is clear. Earlier, I stressed that a meritocratic admissions scheme is insensitive to the particular distribution or pattern of university places among members of society and that the role of equal opportunities as a regulative ideal should be seen as a corrective measure for that failing. Status equality sets constraints on any meritocracy not by identifying another value to be maximized but by positing certain inviolabilities of persons in the pursuit of aggregating merit for the sake of making the most productive use of society's resources. An important basis for civil rights complaints in the particular case of universities and colleges relying on standardized test scores to make admissions decisions for selective programs and professional schools is therefore that they have transgressed certain inviolabilities grounded in the status equality of African Americans. Like a court that fails to grant the presumption of innocence to the accused, some uses of standardized test scores in decision-making procedures by institutions of higher education amount to the denial of equal standing for some racial minorities in those procedures.

4.4 THE IMPLICATIONS FOR CIVIL RIGHTS

Let us begin by drawing a useful distinction between a statute and legislation.[39] A statute is the canonical set of sentences enacted by a legislature. Legislation refers to the set of legal rights, duties, responsibilities, powers, permissions, or prohibitions the statute creates or confirms. The examples I used at the beginning of this chapter, including the 1964 Civil Rights Act, the 1965 Voting Rights Act, the 1977 Canadian Human Rights Code, and the 1976 Race Relations, are all statutes. The legislation – the particular set of civil rights that these statutes bring into existence or confirm – is a distinct matter. While the relationship between a statute and legislation is widely contested among legal theorists, it is safe to assume in the case of civil rights statutes that it is necessary at a minimum to have a general theory about what purpose civil rights serve. Following Ronald Dworkin, I shall assume that the distinctive feature of rights is to protect minorities from the excesses of

[39] Ronald Dworkin, 'How to Read the Civil Rights Act' in *A Matter of Principle*, p. 319.

social choices made with a view of what is in the best interests of the majority or the common good. As Dworkin has eloquently expressed it, "[R]ights are political trumps held by individuals. Individuals have rights when, for some reason, a collective goal is...not a sufficient justification for imposing some loss or injury upon them."[40] Rights are an issue in the case of relying on standardized test scores for admissions into colleges and universities because they reflect a social choice based on a collective goal – maximizing the efficient use of scarce educational resources – that imposes an injury upon African Americans. Rights can be of different types. Some types are abstract and moral. Others are specific to particular institutions. Civil rights are legal rights in the sense that they are "an institutional right to the decision of a court in its adjudicative function."[41]

Any general theory of civil rights should not only prescribe civil rights legislation, but it should also be able to explain the phenomenology of existing adjudication that surrounds civil rights legislation. I have just suggested that the transgression of certain inviolabilities grounded in the status equality of African Americans provides a basis for civil rights complaints in the particular case of universities and colleges relying on standardized test scores to make admissions decisions for selective programmes and professional schools. The general theory of civil rights underlying this suggestion is that civil rights demarcate certain inviolabilities grounded in the equal moral status of persons.

This theory has considerable explanatory power with regard to civil rights adjudication involving the uses of standardized test scores by institutions of higher education. I noted that the recent emergence of standardized tests as a major civil rights issue is linked to the retrenchment of affirmative action. Universities with affirmative action programs may be tempted to meet a civil rights complaint by appealing to some sort of 'bottom-line' defense showing that it admits more, say African Americans, despite its reliance on standardized test scores – the point being that their admissions decision-making procedure involves a number of components including reliance on standardized test scores and preferential treatment for certain disadvantaged groups and that the procedure should be assessed as a whole. It is the case, however, that the United States Supreme Court has rejected this 'bottom-line' defense,

---

[40] Ronald Dworkin, *Taking Rights Seriously, New Impression* (Cambridge, MA: Harvard University Press, 1978), p. xi.
[41] Dworkin, *Taking Rights Seriously*, p. xii.

and the courts do not apply a lower standard of liability to universities with affirmative action programmes that mitigated for the impact of reliance on standardized test scores on minorities than the standard they would apply to universities without affirmative action programmes.[42] In other words, civil rights complaints against the use of standardized test scores by an institution of higher education do not hinge on the absence or presence of affirmative action, even if, as Edley says in the passage quoted from note 12, an important function of affirmative action is "to correct the problems we've inflicted on ourselves with our testing standards."

This example clearly illustrates that infringements of civil rights cannot be justified by an appeal to some other more basic value or good.[43] Yet this characteristic of civil rights is inexplicable under the most familiar theory of civil rights in the United States, which holds that civil rights are designed to promote racial equality. This theory has been embraced by Dworkin, among others, who says, for instance, that the 1964 Civil Rights Act "represents a decision by Congress to advance racial equality in education, employment, and other areas, and to end an economic era in which those blacks not wholly unemployed are largely restricted to lower paying and less interesting jobs."[44] The problem the example in the previous paragraph poses is quite simple. If civil rights are intended to promote racial equality, and *ipso facto* an affirmative action program promotes racial equality, it seems entirely consistent to allow for the justified infringement of civil rights when an affirmative action programme offsets the losses in terms of the promotion of racial equality. The bottom line is said to be racial equality, and logically civil rights violations can be justified when that bottom-line is promoted. The problem is, of course, that the American courts reject this bottom-line defence when it comes to civil rights. A virtue of the theory that civil rights demarcate certain inviolabilities grounded in the status equality of persons is the ease with which it can explain what is wrong with a bottom-line defense. Any bottom-line defense, including one that justifies civil rights

---

[42] As the Ninth Circuit Court pointed out in 1996, "The Supreme Court rejected the so-called 'bottom-line' defence [against disparate impact claims]. In doing so, the Court emphasized that Title VII prohibits 'procedures or testing mechanisms that operate as *built-in headwinds* for minority groups." See *The Association of Mexican-American Educators (AMAE) v. The State of California*, 937 F.Supp. 1397 (9th Circuit, 1996) at 1408, quoting *Connecticut v. Teal*, 457 U.S. 440 (19).

[43] I thank Christopher Edley for drawing my attention to the importance of this point.

[44] Dworkin, 'How to Read the Civil Rights Act,' p. 319.

infringements by appealing to the existence of an affirmative action programme, assumes that what matters, or is of value, can be aggregated
and maximized. Status is not a value of that sort. One person's status
cannot, I noted earlier, be traded off or compromised for the sake of
someone else's status. Therefore, if status is the value that civil rights
protect, neither can civil rights.

The strength of the theory of civil rights I am advancing, by comparison with the more familiar theory that civil rights are designed
to promote racial equality, is also evident when we examine the idea
of disproportionate or disparate impact. This idea has proven to be
one of the most influential insights of the litigation over civil rights
in the United States that has been adopted in other nations. The now
classic illustration of such a practice comes from the case of *Griggs v. Duke
Power Co.*, decided by the Supreme Court of the United States in 1971.[45]
In *Griggs*, black plaintiffs challenged the adoption by Duke Power of
the requirement that all successful applicants attain at least a certain
score on a standardized aptitude test and have a high school diploma
for entry into jobs that had previously been held exclusively by whites.
Recognizing the difficulty of establishing that the adoption of these requirements was intended to discriminate against black applicants, the
Supreme Court held that the requirements were discriminatory in their
effect, and ruled in favour of the request of the plaintiffs for the removals
of these requirements for employment. The basic function of the idea of
disproportionate impact in civil rights cases such as this is "to challenge
those specific, facially-neutral practices that result in discriminatory impact and that by their nature make intentional discrimination difficult
or impossible to prove."[46]

The legal standard of 'disproportionate impact' remains controversial in the United States, despite its explicit recognition in the 1991 Civil
Rights Act. It is commonly defended as the logical unfolding of the view
that racial discrimination involves the use of race as a criterion of selection for opportunities or scarce resources. Historical examples of deliberate racial discrimination by governments abound. These examples
typically involve the use of racial criteria in statutes such as the well-
known case of the Virginia statute forbidding inter-racial marriage.[47]

---

[45] *Griggs v. Duke Power Co.*, 401 U.S. 424 (1971).
[46] *Latinos Unidos De Chelsea En Acion v. Secretary of Housing and Urban Development*,
799 F.2d 774 at 786 (1st Circuit, 1986).
[47] *Loving v. Virginia*, 388 U.S. 1 (1967).

But in some cases, criteria appear not to be race-based but are in fact the *functional equivalent* of race-based criteria. The most familiar examples are voting rights provisions in a number of Southern states at the turn of the century that applied literacy tests to all prospective voters except those who had the right to vote prior to the end of the Civil War and their descendants. These cases have also proved not to be especially difficult to classify as racial discrimination. Disproportionate impact cases are distinct from both of these types of cases because they involve a criterion that functions as a race-based criterion but also functions in other legitimate ways too. The standardized test score and high school diploma requirements at issue in *Griggs* have this character; those hiring criteria did not function solely as a race-based criteria. What then makes this an instance of racial discrimination? In *Griggs*, it is surely significant that the hiring practices before the adoption of these new hiring requirements were discriminatory. The new facially neutral practice at Duke Power had a similar effect to the overtly discriminatory past hiring practice, and in this respect compounded the disadvantage experienced by blacks. Thus, Chief Justice Warren Burger reasoned, "practices, procedures, or tests neutral on their face, and even neutral in . . . .intent cannot be maintained if they operate to *freeze* the status quo of prior discriminatory practices."[48] This makes the context very important.[49] In *Griggs*, the context was one where the facially neutral criteria – the IQ test and high school diploma requirements – functioned as a barrier to the racial integration of the workplace. But the Supreme Court was careful not to object to all uses of standardized tests in the workplace but only the arbitrary uses. "If an employment practice which operates to exclude [racial minorities] cannot be shown to be related to job performance," stipulated Chief Justice Burger, "the practice is prohibited."[50] This raises the prospect of the permissible use of standardized test scores if they are job related and required for sound business reasons. The important point is that civil rights have been assumed to regulate the use of standardized tests, not prohibit them completely, even when they have an adverse impact on a minority group in society.

The point I am emphasizing has unfortunately sometimes been obscured by the debate over the precise legal standard to be applied for

---

[48] *Griggs v. Duke Power Co.*, 401 U.S. 424 (1971).
[49] See, e.g., Michael Perry, 'The Disportionate Impact Theory of Racial Discrimination,' *University of Pennsylvania Law Review*, Vol. 125 (1977), pp. 557–66.
[50] *Griggs v. Duke Power Co.*, 401 U.S. 424 (1971) at 431.

assessing whether a particular practice is job-related and reflects sound business reasons. Following *Griggs,* the standard was assumed to be that if the plaintiff demonstrated that certain employment practices had effects or impact that were disproportionate or caused disparity on racial lines, the burden of proof was on the employer to show the business necessity of the practices. In 1989, in *Wards Cove Packing Co. v. Atonio,* however, the Supreme Court rejected that assumption, requiring of plaintiffs that they "demonstrate that the disparity they complain of is the result of one or more of the employment practices that they are attacking . . . [and] that each challenged practice has a significantly disparate impact on employment practices for whites and nonwhites."[51] This shifted the burden of proof from the defendants to the plaintiffs. The Civil Rights Act of 1991 shifted the burden of proof back to the defendants. While I appreciate the technical legal implications of the issue, it must be recognized as a derivative one by comparison with the basic feature of the adjudication, which allows for uses of test scores when they are valid, regardless of their impact.

This feature has particular saliency with regard to the uses of standardized test results by institutions of higher education for it is reasonable to assume that the courts will be much more willing to recognize the validity of those results in educational contexts than in employment contexts. In the latter, unlike the former, there is widespread scepticism about any sort of pencil and paper exercise being used to gauge relevant skills. Suppose that complainants were able to show successfully that a reliance on a particular standardized test score by a particular college or university has a significant disparity in impact on certain racial minorities. Nonetheless, it is likely that a court could be persuaded that the use serves a genuine educational purpose, provided there is some minimal relationship between (1) what the test tests for, and (2) that purpose.

A clear illustration of this is provided in the Ninth Circuit Court's 1996 decision in *AMAE v. The State of California.*[52] At issue in this case was the requirement of the California Commission on Teacher Credentialing that for teacher certification, all individuals have to pass a test in reading, writing, and mathematics known as the California Basic Educational Skills Test (CBEST). The plaintiffs complained that this test requirement had a disparate impact on a class of prospective teachers

---

[51] *Ward's Cove Packing Company v. Atonio,* 490 U.S. 642 (1989).
[52] *The Association of Mexican-American Educators (AMAE) v. The State of California,* 937 F.Supp. 1397 (9th Circuit, 1996).

from minority groups. An important issue raised in the case was the type of validity that the use of the CBEST scores should be subject to. Following the Uniform Guidelines, the court considered three distinct types of validity that might be applied: "[*Content validity*] refers to the extent to which the items on the CBEST are representative of a defined . . . domain of content, in this case, the basic reading, writing, and mathematics skills relevant to the job of teaching . . . [*Criterion-related validity*] refers to the extent to which an individual's score on the CBEST is predictive of some other criterion, usually job performance . . . [*Construct validity*] refers to the extent to which the CBEST is a measure of some hypothetical or psychological construct."[53] The defendants only provided content validity for CBEST. The plaintiffs argued that they should also show criterion-related validity and construct validity. The Court rejected the arguments of the plaintiffs with regard to validity principally on the grounds that neither criterion-related validity nor construct validity conformed to the recommended uses of CBEST scores. The Court explained, "The CBEST . . . does not purport, and was not designed, to predict a teacher candidate's performance on the job . . . [I]t does not purport to measure a candidate's general mental aptitude, intelligence, or any other construct. Rather, it is designed to measure specific, well-defined skills in reading, mathematics, and writing."[54] Since the CBEST was validated for measuring these reading, writing, and mathematics skills, and they have an educational purpose, the Court dismissed the complaint.

From the perspective of someone who holds the theory that civil rights are designed to promote racial equality, trying to make sense of opinions such as this is a real challenge. This is because the goal of promoting racial equality does not seem to be at the centre of the Court's reasoning about content validity. If racial equality were the principle at issue, it seems hard to imagine not also considering criterion-related validity since the job performance of certified teachers seems absolutely relevant to the promotion of racial equality, whereas content-validity seems more peripheral to that concern. The goal of racial equality is such a broad, encompassing one that it seems difficult to explain the careful distinctions between uses of standardized test scores that run through the civil rights adjudication on this issue. A more plausible account of the decision in *AMAE v. California* is that the court did not see the CBEST as a threat to the status equality of minority candidates,

---

[53] *AMAE v. The State of California*, 937 F.Supp. 1397 at 1411.
[54] *AMAE v. The State of California*, 937 F.Supp. 1397 at 1411–12.

provided it was validated for content. It is on this basis that the court was able to distinguish between valid and invalid uses of CBEST.

The general point I am making is that even in disparate impact cases, the role of civil rights is not to introduce some independent value or goal to be promoted by the courts but rather to regulate processes and practices, setting limits and constraints on, for example, the uses of standardized test results. The problem with the popular view that civil rights exist to promote racial equality is precisely that it seems unable to explain this regulatory role since it posits an independent goal – racial equality – that civil rights adjudication would seem intended to promote. By contrast, status equality is indeed a value but not one that is a goal to be promoted. Instead, it provides principles of inviolability that set boundaries on the promotion or pursuit of other goals such as those that characterize a meritocracy. It is thus a regulatory value, and for this reason can so readily explain the regulatory role assumed by civil rights.

Given the black-white test gap, someone may ask quite reasonably why *any* use of standardized test scores is not a violation of status equality. As I have already indicated, this fails to appreciate the extent to which the very idea of disproportionate or disparate impact is inconsistent with the categorical rejection of a practice. The contrast used earlier to illustrate this is between a provision denying voting rights to those whose grandfathers were slaves and the sort of employment practices at stake in *Griggs*. The unfairness of the former is transparent without any appeal to disproportionate impact. The facially neutral character of standardized tests results suggests that in some contexts, they may not be an issue. It is interesting to note that even some of the strongest critics of IQ such as Stephen Jay Gould allow that in some circumstances, IQ test results can have some value.[55] The more important question that can be raised is whether status equality would provide grounds for prohibiting absolutely some uses of standardized test scores. What uses, if any, of standardized test scores might be prohibited by civil rights designed to protect status equality in the admissions policies of institutions of higher education?

The most widespread use of test scores that would be prohibited is the use of a certain standardized test score as a cut-off point for admissions. Although the use of cut-off scores is quite prevalent, it is not well known that this practice also runs contrary to the recommendations

---

[55] Stephen Jay Gould, *The Mismeasure of Man, revised and expanded* (New York: Norton, 1996), p. 185.

of most testing agencies, including the College Board and the Education Testing Service.[56] The objection to using test scores as a cut-off is that standardized test results then constitute an exclusionary barrier for African Americans to higher education. It is not simply that cut-offs make it more difficult for African Americans to be admitted, but rather that they exclude many African Americans from even competing for admission places.[57] Consider, for example, a cut-off score of 160 on the LSAT for admission into a law school. In 1992–93, 25.7 percent of white applicants scored at least 160 on the LSAT compared with 12.7 percent of American Indians, 11.5 percent of Latinos, and 2.9 percent of African Americans. Seen in the context of a social choice about what constitutes advantage and disadvantage, the disadvantages of being a minority for whom the choice to use standardized test scores already has disparate impact are magnified when those scores are used to define an absolute cut-off to entry. Thus, they pose a much greater threat to the status equality of African Americans. A similar point can be made about exclusive reliance on standardized test scores for admission into institutions of higher education.

The importance of protecting status equality by prohibiting the use of cut-off scores is evident if we examination the extensive civil rights litigation surrounding the state universities in Mississippi. These cases had a long history dating back to 1975, when a group of private plaintiffs initiated a class action suit on behalf of all black citizens in the state of Mississippi that complained that Mississippi was maintaining a racially dual university system. The eight public universities managed and controlled by the Board of Trustees of State Institutions of Higher Learning were said to have remained segregated, with five historically

---

[56] See Jim Vaseleck, 'Stop Working and Put Down Your Pencils: The Use and Misuse of Standardized Admission Tests,' 20 *Journal of College and University Law* (1994), p. 406. Organizations that sponsor standardized tests have, however, been criticized for their lack of genuine concern about valid uses of tests and related phenomena such as cheating. These organizations are sometimes said to be more concerned with covering up such problems because of the belief that it would be bad for business. See, e.g, Eric Douglas and Jon Nordheimer, 'Giant of Exam Business Keeps Quiet on Cheating,' *The New York Times* (Sunday, September 28, 1997), p. 1.

[57] Implicit here is a distinction between using test score cut-offs in competitive processes such as admissions and using cut-offs in a certification process where there is not a limited number of people certified. This is extremely relevant for explaining my sympathy with the decision in *AMAE v. State of California*. In that case, the cut-off on the CBEST was 50 percent, but the good at stake – teacher certification – was not subject to a competition and not limited in quantity.

white institutions (HWIs) remaining almost exclusively white and three historically black institutions (HBIs) remaining almost exclusively black. The target of the complaint was the 1961 admission policy of the Board of Trustees requiring all applicants to take the American College Test (ACT) and authorizing each university to set a minimum ACT score for admission into undergraduate programs. HWIs by 1963 all required a score of at least 15 on the ACT. The average ACT score at the time for white students was 18 compared with 7 for black students.

In *United States v. Fordice*, the Supreme Court held that these ad-missions policies were originally adopted for a discriminatory purpose and that their discriminatory effects continued to be felt because the minimum ACT requirements "restrict[ed] the range of choices of en-tering students as to which institution they may attend in a way that perpetuate[d] segregation."[58] The objection was to the use of an ACT cut-off in a system where there was not uniformity with regard to that cut-off in admission standards among all the universities in the public system of higher education in Mississippi. The upshot of using an ACT cut-off without this uniformity was that it functioned to stream black citizens to HBIs. The initial reaction of some civil rights activists to this decision was fear that its effect would be the end of historically black colleges in Mississippi.[59]

In the Fall of 1996, the Board of Trustees implemented a new uni-form policy of admission requirements for all eight public universities in Mississippi. This policy made regular admission conditional on meet-ing one of three possible standards – one based solely on GPA, one based on a combination of GPA and an Enhanced ACT score with an absolute cut-off, and one based solely on a cut-off Enhanced ACT score. The pol-icy also allowed for admission via so-called Spring screening and the Summer remedial programme. The effect of this new policy has been the desegregation, to a considerable extent, of the Mississippi university system.

The new admissions policy introduced two distinctive features into that system. The first feature is obviously the uniformity of admission criteria across HWIs and HBIs. The second feature is that for the *first*

---

[58] *Ayers v. Fordice* 111 f.3d 1183 at 1190 (5th Circuit, 1997) at 1193, quoting *United States v. Fordice*.

[59] Alex M. Johnson, 'Bid Whist, Tonk, and United States v. Fordice: Why Integra-tionism Fails African-Americans Again,' *California Law Review*, Vol. 81 (December 1993), pp. 1401–74.

time since 1961, HWIs allowed for some regular admission that did not require the applicant to meet an ACT cut-off score. The relevant point is that the consequence of the Supreme Court's decision in *United States v. Fordice* is a procedure that recognizes a plurality of standards for regular admission to HWIs rather than sole reliance on ACT cut-offs.

4.5 THE WORRY ABOUT AFFIRMATIVE ACTION

Some readers may worry that the general theory of civil rights I have been defending could be the basis for a powerful objection to affirmative action, understood as a programme or policy that takes group membership or identity into account in order to remedy under-representation of members or certain racial, ethnic, or other minority groups. A familiar objection to affirmative action is that it is unfair because it takes the race or ethnicity of individuals into account, and for some individuals, most notably those in the 'white' majority, this identity counts as a negative factor. Affirmative action is said to violate the civil rights of those individuals because they are in effect being discriminated against on the basis of their race or ethnicity. This objection was at the heart of perhaps the three most controversial cases – *Regents of the University of California v. Bakke*, decided by the U.S. Supreme Court in 1978; *Hopwood v. Texas*, decided by the Fifth Circuit Court in 1996; and *Grutter v. Regents of the University of Michigan*, decided by the Sixth Circuit Court in 2002 and to be heard by the U.S. Supreme Court in 2003 – challenging affirmative action in American universities and colleges.[60] The general theory of civil rights that says that civil rights are designed to promote racial equality gained wide currency principally as a response to this objection. The reasoning is that since affirmative action promotes racial equality, it is nonsense to ascribe to 'white' individuals civil rights against affirmative action.[61] In contrast, the alternative view I have been defending – that civil rights demarcate certain inviolabilities based on status equality – may appear to support those civil rights complaints against affirmative action. After all, affirmative action seems to promote the interests of admittedly disadvantaged minorities but at the sacrifice of some 'white'

---

[60] *Regents of the University of California v. Bakke*, 438 U.S. 265 (1978); *Hopwood v. Texas*, 78 F.3d 932 (5th Circuit, 1996), cert. denied, 116 S.Ct. 2582 (1996); *Grutter v. Lee Bollinger, et. al.* (6th Circuit, May 14, 2002).

[61] The best known statement of this view is by Ronald Dworkin: 'Why Bakke has No Case,' reprinted in *A Matter of Principle*, ch. 14.

individuals. Doesn't affirmative action therefore threaten their status equality and violate their civil rights?

This question should be carefully distinguished from the debate around the validity of the 'innocent persons' objection to affirmative action. That objection criticizes affirmative action,

for being unfair to white males who are displaced by the programs even though they have not themselves caused particular harm to blacks or women. The charge is that such programs are always unfair to the individuals (white or male) against whom the preferential treatment is directed, unless those individuals themselves participated in the discrimination against the now-preferred minorities. If they have not personally participated in the particular discrimination in question, then they are considered innocent, and the imposition of an affirmative action quota that disadvantages them is considered an unfair act of discrimination against them simply because they are white or male.[62]

This "innocent persons" objection has generated some very clever and complex responses among the defenders of affirmative action.[63] But I don't think it is necessary to respond to them at all in order to show that affirmative action does not threaten the status equality of those from the 'white' majority.

The argument throughout this chapter has been that the status equality of African Americans is threatened when a social choice is made to use standardized test scores as a proxy for merit in a meritocratic scheme for admitting students into universities and colleges, given the well documented 'black-white' test score gap. In this context, African Americans are a minority group vulnerable to the effect of a social choice reflecting the majority view about what constitutes an advantage and disadvantage in a competitive process. And civil rights have been represented as a regulative device for protecting status equality under threat in this way.

There is no immediate parallel to be drawn to the situation of someone from the 'white' majority who is displaced by an affirmative action programme. That person is not a member of a vulnerable minority group. Moreover, as is often stressed, affirmative action is not motivated by any sort of invidious discrimination against whites or men.

---

[62] Ronald Fiscus, *The Constitutional Logic of Affirmative Action* (Durham: Duke University Press, 1992), p. 4.

[63] See, especially, Kathleen Sullivan, 'Sins of Discrimination,' *Harvard Law Review*, vol. 100 (1986), pp. 78–98 and Fiscus, *The Constitutional Logic of Affirmative Action*, ch. 1.

Indeed, although this is not always sufficiently appreciated, affirmative action is often characteristically a product of a social choice reflecting the will of the majority. It is not, for instance, a programme imposed by the court as a counter-majoritarian measure. This is true for both Allan Bakke, the white plaintiff in the *Bakke* case, and Cheryl Hopwood, the principal white plaintiff in the *Hopwood* case. In *Bakke*, the subject of the complaint was the affirmative action admissions policy of a state university in California, the University of California at Davis Medical School. In *Hopwood*, the subject of the complaint was the affirmative action programme for admission into a state university in Texas, the University of Texas Law School. In both instances, those affirmative action plans reflected the wishes of the elected legislative assemblies in the state. Indeed, after the Fifth Circuit Court struck down as unconstitutional the University of Texas Law School's affirmative action program in 1996 and the Supreme Court refused to hear an appeal, the Texas Legislative Assembly responded with a new affirmative action policy for state universities – this law guarantees the top 10 percent of the graduating class of every public high school in Texas a place at the public university and campus of their choice – that does not rely on racial classification of applicants to displace from admission some applicants who would otherwise have been admitted. Preliminary evidence suggests that this policy has a similar effect to race-based affirmative action in terms of diversifying the undergraduate student body.[64] This sort of legislative initiative illustrates vividly that affirmative action policy is generally the product of political decision-making guided by familiar principles of majority rule, in which case it is odd to say that those decisions threaten the status equality of members of the majority.[65]

Another consideration in support of this scepticism is that it is doubtful that affirmative action can even be said to have a significant disparate impact on whites, especially in the admissions process to universities and colleges. It is often assumed that not only does affirmative action have an impact on particular displaced individuals like Allan Bakke and Cheryl Hopwood, but that it also has a significant disproportionate impact on white applicants on the whole. For twenty years from 1978,

[64] Jodi Wilgoren, 'Texas' Top 10% Law Appears to Preserve College Racial Mix', *The New York Times*, November 24, 1999, A1, A18.
[65] An outstanding illustration of the point that anti-discrimination initiatives are the product of familiar majoritian politics is provided by Paul Burstein, *Discrimination, Jobs, and Politics: The Struggle for Equal Employment Opportunity in the United States Since the New Deal, New Edition* (Chicago: University of Chicago Press, 1998).

there had been almost no statistical evidence to support or refute this assumption. This gap in the research was filled in 1998 with the findings from the database funded by the Mellon Foundation called "College and Beyond" and reported in a book by William Bowen and Derek Bok titled *The Shape of the River*. Bowen, the former president of Princeton, and Bok, the former president of Harvard, draw on the database to present a very sympathetic picture of affirmative action in universities and colleges. The most relevant finding they presented with regard to the present issue was in their examination of admissions into selective universities and colleges – with existing affirmative action programmes, the probability of admission for white applicants was 25 percent; without affirmative action the probability would rise to 26.5 percent.[66] In other words, contrary to widespread perceptions, the impact of affirmative action on whites as a group in admissions was minimal.

4.6 CONCLUSION

My objective in this chapter has been to show how a general theory of civil rights flows from the model of equal opportunities as a regulative ideal. I have done this by elaborating on the background principle of status equality and showing how it explains some of the major features of civil rights adjudication in the United States better than the more familiar theory that civil rights are designed to promote racial equality. I have also shown why the principle of status equality does not rule out affirmative action programmes. This argument is not in itself an argument for affirmative action. I offer such an argument for race-targeted affirmative action in the next chapter and for sex-targeted affirmative action in Chapter 7 both based on the three-dimensional model of equal opportunities as a regulative ideal.

I have also tried to make sense of the emerging civil rights initiative directed at the use of standardized test scores in American universities and colleges. Rejecting the view that a civil rights perspective rules out any use of standardized test scores, I have made a case for saying that using cut-off test scores in admissions decisions by universities and colleges violates the civil rights of African Americans. For some readers, this may not seem like a very promising or far-reaching conclusion to draw about this emerging civil rights initiative; they may have hoped for much more. But it seems to me very difficult to predict what the

---

[66] Bowen and Bok, *The Shape of the River*, p. 36.

implications would be if universities and colleges ceased to use cut-off scores in their admissions decisions. The practice *of de facto* cut-off test scores is very widespread in American institutions of higher education. Ending that practice may well radically change admissions schemes to universities and colleges.

The fact that civil rights are envisioned in a regulatory role overseeing a meritocratic admissions scheme designed to maximize the use of society's educational resources allows also for some rethinking about merit without appealing to the intellectually fuzzy notion of some sort of minority perspective on merit. An extremely important finding of Bowen and Bok, based on the "College and Beyond" database, is that African American graduates of highly selective universities and colleges, even if they were admitted with lower test scores than their white counterparts, have over the past twenty years made immensely valuable and unique contributions to American society.[67] These findings support the idea questioning the reliance on standardized test scores by universities and colleges without necessarily charging that there is a civil rights issue at stake.

[67] See, e.g., Bowen and Bok, *The Shape of the River*, p. 284.

Chapter 5

Integration, Diversity, and Affirmative Action

5.1 INTRODUCTION

This chapter sets out to defend race-conscious affirmative action as a requirement of the three-dimensional model of equal opportunities as a regulative ideal. As in the previous chapter on race and social policy, my discussion is nested in an American context. I shall follow Paul Brest and Miranda Oshige and understand affirmative action to mean the following: "An affirmative action program seeks to remedy the significant underrepresentation of members of certain racial, ethnic, or other groups through measures that take group membership or identity into account."[1] For our purposes, in competitions for scarce goods such as jobs or university places, affirmative action programmes are significant because they allow the race or ethnicity of certain targeted groups to count as a *plus factor* for individual applicants in the allocation of those goods. This emphasis on race as a plus factor in competitions should be carefully differentiated from the proposal that a certain proportion, or *quota*, of jobs or university places should be set aside for racial minorities. Although quotas are often associated with affirmative action programmes, race-conscious affirmative action programmes in the United States and indeed elsewhere are predominantly of the plus-factor type. And it is this type I intend to explain and defend here.

Although plus-factor affirmative action has been public policy in the United States for more than thirty years, it remains very controversial and has served as a lightning rod for the complex relationship between

---

[1] Paul Brest and Miranda Oshige, 'Affirmative Action for Whom?,' *Stanford Law Review*, Vol. 47 (1995), p. 856. For a discussion about the difficulties of converging on a shared meaning of affirmative action, see Michel Rosenfeld, *Affirmative Action and Justice* (New Haven: Yale University Press, 1991), pp. 42–48.

law, equality of opportunity, and the construction of race. At the centre of the debate is the race-conscious character of affirmative action. Is it fair to take the race of an individual into account in competitions for scarce goods such as jobs or university places? The most influential strand of opposition to affirmative action holds to "the conservative line on race," advocating rigid color-blind social policy and charging affirmative action with transgressing on that ideal.[2] Proponents of affirmative action must be able to show why race-consciousness is permissible or required when some competitive opportunities are at stake.

As I mentioned in Section 4.5, affirmative action has been largely initiated by legislative bodies, presumably motivated by concerns about the public interest and social justice. Separate from ordinary electoral politics, opponents of affirmative action have sought to constrain or prevent legislatures from establishing affirmative action programmes in two distinct ways. One way has been through referendums that are designed to establish legal constraints on legislatures establishing race-conscious affirmative action. Perhaps the best known example of this strategy is the successful 1996 referendum to amend the constitution of the State of California to prohibit affirmative action in all public employment, public education, and public contracting.[3] The other way has been through appeals to the courts to undertake judicial review of legislative action pertaining to affirmative action. For opponents of affirmative action, the strategy of pursuing judicial review has seemed to hold the most promise, and this explains why the courts have been at the centre of the affirmative action debate in the United States.

The revelation that the Black Leadership Forum, a coalition of liberal civil rights groups, played a major role in the settlement in November 1997 of *Piscataway Township Board. of Education v. Taxman*, just weeks before arguments were scheduled to begin before the U.S. Supreme Court, is one of the most visible signs of the effectiveness of this strategy of pursuing judicial review of race-based affirmative action policies. At issue in the *Piscataway* case was the policy of the local board of education to prefer minority teachers over non-minority teachers in layoff decisions in circumstances where the teachers had the same qualifications

---

[2] This phrase comes from Glenn C. Loury, 'The Conservative Line on Race,' *Atlantic Monthly*, November 1997, pp. 144–54.

[3] See Constitution of the State of California, Article I, §31. It is also worth noting that the backlash against affirmative action has not been limited to the United States. The then newly elected conservative government in Ontario, for example, abolished affirmative action in 1995 for the sake of "equal opportunity."

and seniority. The principal justification the board of education provided for this policy was that it served the goal of promoting racial diversity. The Third Circuit Court ruled in 1996 that this policy violated Title VII in the case of a laid-off white teacher, Sharon Taxman. The Supreme Court agreed to hear the appeal in June 1997. The settlement involved a payment of $433,500 in back pay, damages, and legal fees to Taxman. Significantly, the Black Leadership Forum agreed to raise $308,500 of that amount in order to avoid the Supreme Court's making a ruling based on this case, even though the Forum was not a party to the case.[4]

Although the idea of a third-party's paying 70 percent of a settlement is ordinarily hard to imagine, the motives behind the Black Leadership Forum's actions were not difficult to discern. The first stemmed from the perception that the school board's case in *Piscataway* was extremely weak. The fear of civil rights groups was not simply that the decision of the Third Circuit would be upheld but that the Supreme Court would provide a general ruling against affirmative action programs based on the goal of diversity except when employers admitted to prior discriminatory practices. If the Supreme Court were going to consider such a move and, in effect, overturn the legal standards set in *Regents of the University of California v. Bakke*, it would be better for civil rights groups if the case before the Court were a very strong one. The second motive was to buy time. Putting off a major ruling on affirmative action by the Supreme Court was significant in two important respects. First, it allowed for the possibility of a change in the makeup of the Supreme Court. Second, time allowed civil rights groups and others to rethink the theoretical basis for affirmative action. The point, as settlement of the *Piscataway* case makes vividly clear, was that the immediate future was critical in an effort to re-establish in the mind of the public why social justice required the presence of affirmative action programmes for visible minorities, especially African Americans, in the contemporary United States, and how those programmes conformed to prevailing standards of fairness.[5]

Ironically, at the same time that conservative critics of affirmative action in the United States have been achieving significant legal and

---

[4] *New York Times*, 23 November, 1997, p. 1.
[5] I have discussed in more depth the prospects for the U.S. Supreme Court in 'Integration, Diversity, and Affirmative Action,' *Law & Society Review, Vol. 32, no. 3* (1998), pp. 102–03.

political victories over the past decade, some of the leading theoretical architects of the conservative critique of affirmative action in the 1970s and 1980s, most notably Glenn Loury and Nathan Glazer, have come to the defense of affirmative action, and challenged its retrenchment. Glazer now argues that dismantling affirmative action would be "bad for the country."[6] Likewise, Loury claims, "there are circumstances where the ability of a public policy to advance the general interest of all persons is enhanced by taking cognizance of the racial identities of particular persons."[7] This back-pedalling suggests to me that this is indeed a very opportune moment to reinvigorate the philosophical debate around affirmative action and its relation to equal opportunity.

I have already suggested in the conclusion to the last chapter that there is compelling evidence to think that much of the discussion about affirmative action has distorted its impact on groups that have not been targeted for affirmative action. In the case of admission to selective universities, for instance, the abolition of affirmative action would only increase the likelihood of admission for white applicants from 25 percent to 26.5 percent. Opinion polls bear this out insofar as they show that as of 1997, after thirty years of affirmative action, only 7 percent of whites in the United States believed that they had been disadvantaged by affirmative action.[8] This is not especially surprising, given that race-based affirmative action is typically targeted at small racial minorities such as African Americans or Native Americans.[9]

The other side of this observation is the evidence showing that *middle class*, as opposed to *poor*, African Americans are the principal beneficiaries of affirmative action programmes. Affirmative action is credited by Orlando Patterson as "the single most important factor accounting for the rise of a significant Afro-American middle class."[10] Why affirmative action benefits mainly those in the middle class has been succinctly

---

[6] Nathan Glazer, 'In Defense of Preference,' *New Republic*, 6 April 1998, p. 24.

[7] Glenn C. Loury, 'Is Affirmative Action on the Way Out? Should It Be?,' *Commentary*, March 1998, p. 38.

[8] Orlando Patterson, *The Ordeal of Integration* (Washington, DC: Civitas/ Counterpoint, 1997), p. 148.

[9] There is here a striking contrast with affirmative action for women, which targets potentially 50 percent of the population. This suggests to me the importance of have a different rationale for affirmative action for women. See Chapter 8, Section 3.

[10] Patterson, *The Ordeal of Integration*, p. 147.

explained by William Julius Wilson:

[M]inority individuals from the most advantaged families are likely to be disproportionately represented among the minority members most qualified for preferred positions – such as higher-paying jobs, college admissions, promotions and so forth . . . Affirmative action . . . applied merely according to racial or ethnic group membership tends to benefit the relatively advantaged segments of the designated groups. The truly deprived members may not be helped by such programs.[11]

The relevant point is that the beneficiaries of affirmative action are in fact a relatively small group.[12] For these reasons, implementing or retaining affirmative action is unlikely to have any more dramatic effect in the United States on the opportunities for African Americans than would (as I urged in the last chapter) ending the use of cut-offs based on standardized test scores for admission in institutions of higher education and other competitions such as job hirings for positions in, say, police work.

In Chapter 4, Section 4.5, I explained why affirmative action does not put into jeopardy the status equality of applicants who are not members of groups targeted by affirmative action. It does not, therefore, violate the requirements of background fairness. That explanation is not, however, a justification for a policy of affirmative action. The main theme of this chapter is that race-based affirmative action in the United States should be viewed as a requirement of stakes fairness. Recall that the three-dimensional model of equal opportunities identifies three dimensions of the normative regulation of competition. Stakes fairness regulates what is at stake in a competition, ensuring a broader distribution of prizes, and limiting how much competitors can gain or lose. In effect, race-based affirmative action should be viewed as an effective way to promote stakes fairness in competitions for selective university places and valuable jobs in the United States.

---

[11] William Julius Wilson, *The Truly Disadvantaged* (Chicago: University of Chicago Press, 1987), p. 115.

[12] I don't mean to deny here, however, that for this small group affirmative action makes a real difference. At the University of California at Berkeley in 1994, 88 percent of the African American students admitted benefitting from the plus factor of their race in the admissions process. Only 12 percent were admitted solely on the basis of their academic achievement measured by GPA and SAT scores. See Michael W. Lynch, 'Affirmative Action at the University of California,' *Notre Dame Journal of Law, Ethics and Public Policy, Vol. XI* (1997), p. 148.

Rationales for affirmative action are commonly classified as either *forward-looking* or *backward-looking*. Forward-looking rationales identify some purpose or objective that is served by implementing affirmative action. Backward-looking rationales identify affirmative action as a measure for compensating for prior injustices or wrongful treatment. Although backward looking rationales in the case of African Americans seem quite compelling since there is an indisputable history of black slavery and Jim Crow laws, this class of rationales is generally viewed as philosophically problematic both because the principal beneficiaries of affirmative action are not in most cases the victims of slavery or Jim Crow laws and because those who carry the burden of affirmative action were not the agents of these injustices or necessarily the beneficiaries of those injustices.[13] Forward-looking rationales for affirmative action are generally thought to hold much more promise.

While there are many different forward-looking rationales for affirmative action, two have predominated in the public forum and in American legal circles. The first (which I call the integration rationale) views affirmative action programs as a means of including members of racial, ethnic, or other groups who might otherwise have been excluded, intentionally or otherwise, from privileged positions or opportunities in American society. Affirmative action, in this rationale, is one policy instrument among many designed to bring about greater integration of different racial and ethnic segments of society. It has its origins in the civil rights movement of the 1950s and 1960s.[14] The second rationale (which I call the diversity rationale) justifies affirmative action as a means of achieving diversity in the racial, ethnic, and gender makeup of social, economic, and political institutions that historically have been marked by rigid homogeneity. The goal is not that, through integration, members

---

[13] An exception here is Richard Delgado, 'Why Universities Are Morally Obligated to Strive for Diversity: Restoring the Remedial Rationale for Affirmative Action,' *University of Colorado Law Review, Vol. 68* (1997), pp. 1165–72. It is noteworthy that Delgado defends a backward-looking justification for affirmative action only as a complement to a forward-looking one.

[14] Martin Luther King Jr. wrote, for example, in *Why We Can't Wait* (New York: Harper & Row, 1964): "Whenever this issue of compensatory or preferential treatment for the Negro is raised, some of our friends recoil in horror. The Negro should be granted equality, they agree; but he should ask nothing more. On the surface, this appears reasonable, but it is not realistic. For it is obvious that if a man is entered at the starting line in a race three hundred years after another man, the first man would have to perform some impossible feat in order to catch up with his fellow runner," p. 147.

from diverse backgrounds will be absorbed and assimilated into mainstream institutions but rather that the institutions themselves will be transformed to reflect the diversity in American society. The diversity rationale has achieved considerable prominence since the declaration by Justice Powell in his 1978 opinion in *Regents of the University of California v. Bakke* that "the attainment of a diverse student body ... clearly is a constitutionally permissible goal for an institution of higher education."[15]

This chapter advances two closely related claims. The first is that there is a serious drawback to relying solely on either the integration rationale or the diversity rationale for affirmative action, and that these two forward-looking rationales should be conjoined. The second is that ultimately integration and diversity matter because they promote stakes fairness with regard to certain competitive opportunities.

5.2 DIVERSITY OF WHAT? DIVERSITY FOR WHOM?

Although Justice Powell's opinion in *Bakke* is now twenty-five years old, it continues to determine the legal standard for affirmative action programs in the United States.[16] In effect, this standard makes it permissible for institutions to treat the race or ethnicity of a candidate as a plus factor in, for example, the admissions process. The explicit link to the diversity rationale has made this the most compelling legal strategy to rely on for those concerned with successfully defending affirmative actions programmes in the courts.[17] My concern, however, is less with

---

[15] *Regents of the University of California v. Bakke*, 438 U.S. 265 (1978) at 311–12.

[16] The notable counterexample to this claim is the opinion of the Fifth Circuit of the United States Court of Appeal in *Hopwood v. State of Texas*, which upheld a challenge to the University of Texas Law School's affirmative action admissions programme, rejecting the diversity rationale for such a program, saying, "We agree with the plaintiffs that any consideration of race or ethnicity by the law school for the purpose of achieving a diverse student body is not a compelling interest under the Fourteenth Amendment. Justice Powell's argument in Bakke garnered only his own vote and has never represented the view of a majority of the Court in Bakke or any other case ... the classification of persons on the basis of race for the purpose of diversity frustrates, rather than facilitates, the goals of equal protection." *Hopwood v. State of Texas*, 78 F.3d 932 (5th Cir. 1996), at 944. The decision of the Fifth Circuit has most recently been rejected in the decision of the Sixth Circuit of the United States Court of Appeal in a case challenging affirmative action at the University of Michigan Law School. See *Grutter v. Bollinger*, 2002 FED App. 0170 (6th Circuit), at 5–15.

[17] See, e.g., William Bowen and Derek Bok, *The Shape of the River: Long-Term Consequences of Considering Race in College and University Admissions* (Princeton: Princeton University Press, 1998), p. 13

the narrow issue of doctrinal law and more with gaining a perspective on how well the diversity rationale actually justifies affirmative action.

From this perspective, the diversity rationale has important shortcomings, for it is unclear what kind of diversity should be promoted, and for whom. Consider, for example, the situation in the University of California law schools since the end of affirmative action in admissions policies. It is now commonplace to describe the trend as the 'whitening' of these schools.[18] The fact that only one African American enrolled for first year in 1997 at Boalt Hall Law School (Berkeley) is often used to illustrate vividly the trend. But critics of affirmative action have seized on an aspect of the changes in admission in California to highlight an ambiguity in the diversity rationale. Stephan Thernstrom points out that while at Boalt Hall, African American and Latino enrollment dropped considerably in 1997, this was offset partially by a marked increase in Asian American enrollment. At UCLA Law School, African American and Latino enrollment also dropped but Asian American increased significantly. "In fact," says Thernstrom, "minority enrollment at the UCLA Law School has not gone down at all; instead, *it is up 18 percent.*"[19] The trend, in other words, is not towards a 'whitening' of California's universities but rather the displacement of one racial minority by another. How, on the diversity rationale, can a preference be given for one over the other?

A similar problem arises with regard to the beneficiaries of affirmative action. I acknowledged earlier that *middle class*, as opposed to *poor*, African Americans are the principal beneficiaries of affirmative action programmes. The middle-class bias of affirmative action is problematic in the diversity rationale because if the objective of affirmative action is the promotion and protection of diversity, it would seem to follow that programmes should be designed to benefit members from diverse socioeconomic backgrounds proportionately. What the diversity rationale seems incapable of explaining is why affirmative action targets the black and Latino middle class as opposed to either poorer African Americans and Latinos or poorer whites.

---

[18] This description is frequently used in the mainstream media. See, e.g., Brent Staples, 'The Quota Bashers Come in from the Cold,' *New York Times*, 12 April 1998, sec. 4, p. 12.

[19] Stephan Thernstrom, 'Farewell to Preferences?,' *The Public Interest*, Winter 1998, p. 42.

The problems I am raising here about the diversity rationale parallel ones pressed by sympathetic critics of diversity such as George Sher. Sher concludes, however, that when faced with the twin questions of diversity of what and for whom, we must ultimately rely on a backward-looking defence of affirmative action with all of its complicated ethical and historical baggage. He claims that "when we ask why the [diversity] argument focuses only on certain groups, we are invariably thrown back on the injustice or discrimination that their past members have suffered."[20] It is my view that Sher and others fail to entertain the very plausible suggestion that conjoining the diversity rationale with the forward-looking integration rationale for affirmative action can provide us with answers to the questions of diversity of what and for whom.

5.3 TAKING INTEGRATION SERIOUSLY AGAIN

The integration rationale for affirmative action reflects a concern for those members of racial, ethnic, or other groups who are marginal or excluded from privileged positions or opportunities in American society. Affirmative action is justified on this rationale as a means of integrating those members into the institutions and social networks that regulate those privileged positions and opportunities. Until twenty-five years ago in the United States, there was no serious alternative to the integration model of race relations as a bedrock for the civil rights movement. Racial integration was the vision that drove much of the pursuit of racial equality, captured most forcefully by the decision of the U.S. Supreme Court in *Brown v. Board of Education* to reject the 'separate but equal' doctrine. Racial segregation was the antithesis of equality; integration was its realization. Through integration, blacks and other visible minorities would gain access to the economic and social opportunities that in the past they had been denied.

The real strength of the integration rationale is that it provides, unlike the diversity rationale, a basis for identifying which groups in society should be the legitimate beneficiaries of affirmative action. In effect, the targeted groups are those that in a stratified social structure have been left behind in the equitable distribution of the benefits of social life. Unlike a minority subject to occasional mistreatment, the groups targeted by affirmative action are those that have been subject to a "pervasive

---

[20] George Sher, 'Diversity,' *Philosophy & Public Affairs*, Vol. 28 (1999), p. 90.

pattern of oppression."[21] Significantly, the analysis of who should be the beneficiaries of affirmative action is *in essence* a sociological one, not a historical one, with an attendant emphasis on wealth, income, and power, even though an eye to what has happened in the past is necessarily bound up in any such analysis.

The integration rationale therefore provides an important corrective to the shortcomings with the diversity rationale. As Deborah Malamud puts it, "The diversity rationale is unconvincing unless it is coupled with an understanding that race-based economic inequality stands in the way of achieving diversity without affirmative action."[22] The reason why the enrollment trends at University of California law schools are troublesome is that, regardless of who is replacing them, the displaced groups – African Americans and Latinos – are in orthodox sociological analyses amongst the least advantaged in American society. Likewise, targeting the black middle class makes sense if the concern of affirmative action is with both integration and diversity because, based on standard socioeconomic measures such as housing, work, and income security, the black middle class in the United States is "systematically worse off than the white middle class, and is thus systematically at a competitive disadvantage in a white-dominated economy and society."[23] The attraction of the integration rationale for affirmative action is precisely that it places those at the socioeconomic margins of society at the forefront of its concern. When the integration rationale is combined with the diversity rationale for affirmative action, it is thus possible to address the twin questions of diversity of what and for whom.

But the ideal of integration has fallen on hard times. Critics challenge both the integrity of the integration rationale and its effectiveness. The example of school desegregation nicely illustrates the integrity problem. Justice Warren in *Brown v. Board of Education* highlights how segregation has a detrimental effect upon the hearts and minds of 'colored' children, and maintains that integration with white children will be of intangible benefit to 'colored' children. Yet there is nothing in that famous decision about the benefits to white children of being integrated with black children. Integration is seen as a one-way street. And this is highlighted

---

[21] This distinction between minorities is drawn by Robert Cover, 'The Origins of Judicial Activism in the Protection of Minorities,' *Yale Law Journal*, Vol. 91 (1982), p. 1304.

[22] Deborah C. Malamud, 'Affirmative Action, Diversity, and the Black Middle Class,' *University of Colorado Law Review*, Vol. 68 (1997), p. 941.

[23] Malamud, 'Affirmative Action, Diversity, and the Black Middle Class,' p. 967.

by the fact that as school boards in the southern United States desegregated in the 1950s and 1960s, tens of thousands of black teachers and principals lost their jobs.[24] Just imagine black professionals teaching or disciplining white children!

The diversity rationale can be understood as the antidote for this concern about the integrity of the integration rationale. What Justice Powell stressed in *Bakke* is the benefits for everyone of having a diverse student body. It is not only the minority students who benefit from access; the educational experience of white students is also enhanced by having fellow students, teachers, and administrators who come from a diverse racial background. Viewed in this light, Powell's decision should be seen as an important corrective to Warren's unanimous decision in *Brown* a quarter-century earlier.

The context for challenging the effectiveness of the integration ideal is one in which racial tensions seem to be heightening, housing segregation in urban areas is on the rise, and the federal courts have made a series of decisions that indicate little sympathy for civil rights complaints. Perhaps the best known expression of this view has been made by Derrick Bell who writes, for example, in *Faces at the Bottom of the Well*,

> For years I believed law was the answer... Now, though, I'm convinced that racism is a permanent part of the American landscape... [Integration] is just another instance that black folks work for and white folks grant when they realize – long before we do – that it is mostly a symbol that won't cost them much and will keep us blacks pacified. It is an updated version of the glass trinkets and combs they used in Africa a few centuries ago to trick some tribes into selling off their brothers and sisters captured from neighboring tribes.[25]

And this scepticism about integration is not just an American phenomenon. For instance, Cecil Foster, in an account of the Canadian experiment with integration, calls it a "shell game" that in many respects is a charade.[26]

Much of this criticism of the effectiveness of the integration ideal, especially in the United States, has in fact been historically based, to the extent that it involves the claim that the United States has pursued the

---

[24] See Derrick Bell, *And We Are Not Saved: The Elusive Quest for Racial Justice* (New York: Basic Books, 1987), p. 266n3.

[25] Derrick Bell, *Faces at the Bottom of the Well: The Permanence of Racism* (New York: Basic Books, 1992), pp. 18, 92.

[26] Cecil Foster, *A Place Called Heaven: The Meaning of Being Black in Canada* (Toronto: HarperCollins, 1996), p. 140.

integration route for fifty years and there has not been much progress for African Americans. Significantly, this is a point of convergence between conservatives and critical race theorists. Orlando Patterson in his book *The Ordeal of Integration* – a vigorous defence of integration – offers two lines of argument in response to this criticism. The first line emphasizes that much of the problem is in "perception."[27] For Patterson, integration is characterized by numerous paradoxes that suggest that very little about it is straightforward and clear; the prevalent perception, even among social scientists, is to make simple inferences from perceived phenomena. One perception Patterson focusses on is the common one that racial tensions are on a rise. It is often inferred from this observation that integration is therefore a failure. Patterson turns it around; increased tension is, he thinks, an inevitable outcome of increased integration. His reasoning is that "as individuals in both groups meet more and more, the possibility for conflict is bound to increase."[28] Racial tensions in everyday life are, to adapt a famous quip from Marx, the "birth pangs" of the journey towards an integrated society. Likewise, while Patterson concedes that housing segregation on racial lines persists in urban areas in the United States, he highlights the dramatic increase in African Americans' satisfaction with their housing from 45 percent in 1973 to 74 percent in 1997.[29]

The second line of argument Patterson that pursues details evidence showing how much progress, relative to whites, African Americans have made in their standards of living over the past forty years. The background here is the well-documented fact that by comparison with whites, blacks in the United States during the 1990s had significantly lower standards of living, were more likely to live in poverty, faced a racial income gap, and had a much less secure membership in the American middle class.[30] The response pursued by Patterson is to emphasize that despite these inequalities, African Americans have made immense progress in their social and economic circumstances by comparison with whites, and, therefore, rather than concluding that integration has been a failure, it should be credited with this progress.

[27] Patterson, *The Ordeal of Integration*, p. 16.
[28] Patterson, *The Ordeal of Integration*, p. 51.
[29] Patterson, *The Ordeal of Integration*, p. 47.
[30] The most influential statement of these facts is Andrew Hacker, *Two Nations: Black and White, Separate, Hostile, Unequal* (New York: Ballantine, 1992).

For many, it may seem that by emphasizing how much progress African Americans have made, it is logical to infer from this that there is no longer a need for affirmative action.[31] But such an inference misconstrues a vital step in a successful defense of affirmative action at the general level of public policy. What pessimistic analyses of African American progress since the 1960s in effect do is play into the hands of neoconservative critics of affirmative action. It is not a coincidence that many of the most influential neoconservative critics of affirmative action also challenge the cogency of most of the welfare state programs that were integral to the vision of the Great Society of the late 1960s. Charles Murray is probably the leading example of such a critic. His book, *Losing Ground*, famously called for the federal government to scrap its entire welfare and income-support structure for people of working age on the grounds that although such programs were intended to help the poor, they had in fact made them worse off.[32] The general policy implication is that ambitious 'liberal' programs targeted to improve the conditions of disadvantaged groups are ultimately self-defeating, and hence should not be undertaken. The upshot of Murray's argument is, of course, that not only are programs such as welfare misconceived, so too is affirmative action, which, despite its lofty ambitions, will make racial minorities worse off. At the core of Murray's argument is the claim that the poor were worse off in terms of their standard of living after the expansion of Aid to Families with Dependent Children (AFDC) and the spending of billions of dollars by governments than before this expenditure. When analysts of race relations paint a bleak picture, they are ironically supporting Murray's claim. AFDC has now been abolished, even though social policy analysts have systematically and conclusively challenged Murray's findings.[33]

The broader point is this. Affirmative action is an ambitious social policy that presupposes that it is possible to undertake large-scale

[31] An important example is Stephan and Abigail Thernstrom, *America in Black and White: One Nation, Indivisible* (New York: Simon & Schuster, 1997). See also, for instance, James Q. Wilson, 'A Long Way from the Back of the Bus,' *New York Times Books Review*, 16 November 1997, p. 10.

[32] Charles Murray, *Losing Ground: American Social Policy 1950–1980* (New York: Basic Books, 1984), p. 227.

[33] Several of the most important studies are Sheldon Danziger and Daniel Weinberg, editors, *Fighting Poverty* (Cambridge, MA: Harvard University Press, 1986); Wilson, *The Truly Disadvantaged*; David Ellwood, *Poor Support* (New York: Basic Books, 1988); and Christopher Jencks, *Rethinking Social Policy* (New York: HarperCollins, 1992).

interventions in the way social and economic decisions are made to the benefit of a particular targetted group.[34] Whilst most critics directly attack affirmative action on the grounds of unfairness, neoconservatives are also challenging that presupposition. At issue here is the "possibility" of politics, to use Stein Ringen's apt phrase.[35] Commencing in the 1960s, the United States experimented with a large-scale intervention of this sort designed to improve the circumstances of African Americans. If we conclude that this experiment was a disaster, then any effort to renew a commitment to affirmative action would be undermined because the presupposition on which such a social policy is based would, given the historical record, seem misconceived. In other words, any serious effort to rethink the basis for affirmative action must embrace the historical legacy of government intervention to improve the circumstances of disadvantaged groups.

5.4 THE VALUE OF DIVERSITY AND INTEGRATION

Thus far in the discussion, I haven't explained why either diversity or integration is valuable. Nor have I shown how they provide a justification for affirmative action. I show the connection to affirmative action in Section 5.5. Here I intend to explain within a framework of the three-dimensional model of equal opportunities the value of diversity and integration to stakes fairness. The structure of my argument is that whilst the diversity and integration rationales identify the purpose of affirmative action, the three-dimensional model of equal opportunities as a regulative ideal posits the underlying value of stakes fairness.

Why does diversity matter? If one assumes that there exist in the world a plurality of practices and beliefs regarding religion, ethnicity, language, and so on, there are quite compelling instrumental reasons for building diversity into our institutions of civil society – namely, so that they reflect efficient economic strategies for adapting to a globalizing

---

[34] My brief synopsis here is an over-simplification. Although neo-conservatives couch their challenges in terms of all welfare state-type policies, the specific character of their challenges is directed principally at so-called *targeted* as opposed to *universal* benefits. This means that if social policies provide universal access, they side-step the neo-conservative objections. I have argued this at length in Lesley Jacobs, *Rights and Deprivation* (Oxford: Oxford University Press, 1993), ch. 8.

[35] Stein Ringen, *The Possibility of Politics: The Political Economy of the Welfare State* (Oxford: Oxford University Press, 1987).

economy and changing ethnic makeup and demographics in the do-mestic markets.[36] But there are also less instrumental reasons for believ-ing that diversity matters. Diversity is a reflection of the differences in cultural identity between persons. What function does cultural identity perform for us? It provides the context for the choices we make in our lives. As Will Kymlicka puts it, "The range of options is determined by our cultural heritage. Different ways of life are not simply different patterns of physical movements. The physical movements only have meaning to us because they are identified as having significance by our culture, because they fit into some pattern of activities which is cultur-ally recognized as a way of leading one's life."[37] Without that cultural identity, our lives would be impoverished in their meaning. The relevant point is that if we assume the fact of pluralism, and yet fail in our institutions of civil society to acknowledge this diversity, we in effect make fragile the meaning of some people's lives.

This explanation about cultural identity and diversity can be directly linked to the idea of stakes fairness. Stakes fairness rejects winner-take-all schemes, seeking a wider distribution of prizes, and limiting the potential losses to an individual in a given competition. With regard to cultural identity, what is at stake is very significant – the cement that gives a person's life meaning. The logic of stakes fairness holds that individuals should not have to risk their cultural identity in order to have access to the competitive opportunities in the institutions of civil society. For instance, an individual should not have to compromise his or her religious practices with regard to say headgear, prayer, or holy days in order to attend an educational institution or participate in the labor market. The additional consideration here, of course, is that it is the cultural identities of minorities that are most at risk and face the greatest threat of being overwhelmed by a foreign dominant culture. In other words, it is members of minority groups who are most vulnerable to the risk of losing control over the meaning of their lives. And hence

---

[36] See, e.g., Bill Ong Hing, *To Be an American: Cultural Pluralism and the Rhetoric of Assimilation* (New York: New York University Press, 1997), pp. 156–57.

[37] Will Kymlicka, *Liberalism, Community, and Culture* (Oxford: Oxford University Press, 1989), p. 165. This feature of culture is now widely recognized, even by con-servatives. Thomas Sowell states, for instance, "Cultures are particular ways of accomplishing the things that make life possible – the perpetuation of the species, the transmission of knowledge, and the absorption of the shocks of changes and death, among other things." See Thomas Sowell, *Migrations and Cultures* (New York: Basic Books, 1996), p. 379.

they are logically the targetted groups in the promotion of diversity.[38] By promoting diversity in civil institutions, threats to the cultural identity of minorities are diminished in accordance with the requirements of stakes fairness.

While the explanation just given for valuing diversity may be contested by some, it is much less contentious than the explanation I shall now give about the relationship between integration and stakes fairness. Integration should be carefully distinguished from assimilation. Assimilation involves absorbing some groups into a more dominant group. Assimilation is in direct tension with the value of diversity, and is generally regarded by members of minority cultures as a threat to the background context that gives their lives meaning. Integration, in contrast, exists when members of minority cultures have access to and participate in the mainstream institutions of civil society and governance. Integration may lead to assimilation, but its practice is perfectly consistent with members of cultural minorities maintaining the distinct cultural identities that are integral to sustaining what gives meaning to the lives they live. A federal state such as Canada is a clear illustration of how one can imagine integration without assimilation.[39] In Canada, as in the United States, there is a division of powers of jurisdiction between the Federal Government and the provincial governments. It was designed in 1867 expressly to recognize the distinctive cultural identity of francophones in Quebec while at the same time integrating them into the mainstream institutions of civil society, especially the economy, of the rest of what was then British North America.

Racial integration in the United States is often presented as a valuable instrument for defusing racial tensions. If true, for whites this would seem to be a very compelling reason for supporting integration. But, as noted earlier, the road to integration may in fact exacerbate racial tensions precisely because it increases the actual interracial points of contact. The upshot is that if integration is valuable principally because

---

[38] The argument I rely on here is not, however, a reason for the intergenerational preservation of diversity, as Charles Taylor has perceptively pointed out. See 'The Politics of Recognition' in Amy Gutmann, editor, *Multiculturalism and the Politics of Recognition* (Princeton: Princeton University Press, 1992), pp. 40–41. A defence of intergenerational diversity would have to rely on a much more contentious theory of cultural pluralism such as that advanced by Hing, *To Be an American*, pp. 154–55.

[39] I discuss this specific case in some depth in 'Federalism and National Minorities,' *University of Toronto Law Journal*, Vol. 49 (1999), pp. 295–304.

it defuses racial tensions, then this is a very contingent justification. And I suspect that some of the decline in support of integration in the United States is a reflection of relying too heavily on this justification.

The principal value of integration, I suggest, lies elsewhere than the defusing of racial tensions. Integration for African Americans is valuable because it gives them potential access to a much greater share of the competitive opportunities at stake in civil society than when they are segregated from the rest of American society. The reasoning is simple. Historically, blacks have enjoyed far fewer opportunities than whites. Without integration, it is hard to see how the opportunities for African Americans or any other historically disadvantaged group can increase significantly since segregation of historically disadvantaged groups would seem to perpetuate their smaller share of the total opportunities in society. My claim here about the value of integration – that it is a valuable instrument for broadening the distribution of competitive opportunities at stake in institutions of civil society so as to include African Americans and other minority groups such as Latinos – does not entail a related claim that has sometimes been made about racial segregation in the United States – namely, that segregation of institutions such as public transportation and schools is objectionable principally because it denies blacks important opportunities for education and self-advancement.[40] My view on segregation, as I explained in the last chapter, is that it also threatens the status equality of African Americans, and not just their share of opportunities.

Support for this argument about why integration is valuable comes, I think, from William Julius Wilson's analysis of new urban poverty. Wilson has shown that the distinctive feature of inner city ghettos is the lack of jobs caused by societal changes. In effect, unlike the robust black inner city neighbourhoods of two generations ago, the distinctive characteristic of the new ghettos is the much higher levels of joblessness.[41] For Wilson, the new urban poverty means precisely, "poor, segregated neighbourhoods in which a substantial majority of individual adults are

---

[40] The contrast between the two complaints about segregation – *one opportunity-based*, the other *status-based* – is carefully explored in Bernard R. Boxill, 'Washington, Du Bois, and Plessy v. Ferguson,' *Law and Philosophy*, Vol. 16 (1997), pp. 299–330. See also Gerald J. Postema, 'The Sins of Segregation,' *Law and Philosophy*, Vol. 16 (1997), pp. 221–244.

[41] William Julius Wilson, *When Work Disappears: The World of the New Urban Poor* (New York: Vintage Books, 1996), p. 18.

either unemployed or have dropped out of the labor force altogether."[42] The relevant point for our discussion is that Wilson doesn't think that segregation explains the increased poverty rates in these neighbourhoods; they have long been segregated, but the dramatic increase and concentration of poverty has happened in the past twenty-five years.[43] However, he does think that segregation constitutes a major barrier to pursuing equal opportunities for African Americans in those neighbourhoods, given the inequalities that presently exist.

> Segregated ghettos are less conducive to employment and employment preparation than are other areas of the city. Segregation in ghettos exacerbates employment problems because it leads to weak informal employment networks and contributes to the social isolation of individuals and families, thereby reducing their chances of acquiring the human capital skills, including adequate educational training, that facilitate mobility in a society. Since no other group in society experiences the degree of segregation, isolation, and poverty concentration as do African-Americans, they are far more likely to be disadvantaged when they have to compete with other groups in society, including other despised groups, for resources and privileges.[44]

The inference I am making from Wilson's work, based admittedly on a study of a marginalized group within the black community, is that integration for African Americans is valuable because it facilitates a broader distribution of the benefits and prizes at stake in competitions for select university places and employment in civil society.

My argument about the value of integration is an instrumental one in the sense that I have assumed that equal opportunities is a regulative ideal in competitions and that integration is a necessary instrument for promoting stakes fairness. This view of integration differs from the way others have sometimes valued integration.[45] Sometimes, people have imagined that an integrated community is intrinsically valuable, and

---

[42] Wilson, *When Work Disappears*, p. 19.

[43] This contrasts with the views, for instance, of Douglas Massey and Nancy Denton, *American Apartheid: Segregation and the Making of the Underclass* (Cambridge, MA: Harvard University Press, 1993). The general claim I am making about the value of integration is also supported by their more provocative position on the effects of segregation.

[44] Wilson, *When Work Disappears*, p. 24.

[45] The distinction I am drawing here parallels the distinction between integration as a process and integration as an ideal community, drawn by Alex M. Johnson, 'Bid Whist, Tonk, and United States v. Fordice: Why Integrationism Fails African-Americans Again,' *California Law Review*, Vol. 81 (1993), pp. 1401–70, but with a very different purpose in mind.

not just of instrumental value. It seems to me, however, that such a view is in tension with the claim that diversity within the institutions of civil society is a requirement of stakes fairness. And because I endorse that claim about civil society, I have argued only that integration has instrumental value derived from its potential to broaden the distribution of the competitive opportunities so that they become more inclusive of African Americans and other vulnerable racial minorities in the United States.

5.5 THE RATIONALE FOR AFFIRMATIVE ACTION

Since I have just provided a succinct account of why integration and diversity are valuable, it might seem that this constitutes a sufficient rationale for affirmative action. But this conclusion is premature. For thus far I have not adequately justified why affirmative action in particular is required, nor why it should be 'colour-conscious'. Critics of affirmative action might readily agree with me about the value of diversity and integration but yet not see why this warrants the sort of public intervention or social engineering that affirmative action involves. After all, integration and diversity would also seem to be of value for practically any immigrant group, but few proponents of affirmative action advance a blanket type of affirmative action. As I noted at the beginning of this chapter, affirmative action targets only particular ethnic or racial groups, and this demands a justification. The colour-conscious character of affirmative action also needs to be defended. The challenge often made is that it seems conceivable that integration and diversity can be promoted without resorting to policies that rely on classifying individuals on the basis of their race. The question here is why must affirmative action schemes rely on racial categories rather than use a less controversial proxy such as socio-economic class as the basis for preferential treatment in hiring and admission decisions?

The first challenge requires an explanation as to why it is appropriate to target particular groups – in this case African Americans – for affirmative action. Consider the distinction between acculturation and structural integration.[46] Acculturation is the function of the capacity of a minority group to adapt and change in response to the dominant or majority group. Structural integration, on the other hand, is a function of the capacity of the dominant or majority group to be inclusive and

---

[46] See Hing, *To Be An American*, p. 167.

accommodate minorities in its associations and institutions. The upshot is that whereas failure to acculturate is the responsibility of the minority group, the lack of structural integration is the responsibility of the dominant group in society. It is indisputable that until at least the 1960s, African Americans experienced the lack of structural integration. Many proponents of the civil rights initiatives in the 1960s rightly viewed those initiatives as measures designed to facilitate structural integration for blacks. The fact that those initiatives were and continue to be popular with white Americans suggests that there is a commitment to taking seriously their responsibility for structural integration. Why aren't those civil rights initiatives enough? Why involve affirmative action?

The most compelling response is that even if the responsibility for structural integration is now being fulfilled, there remains the legacy of the failure to fulfill that responsibility that continues to have an impact on the opportunities and prospects for African Americans today. My claim is not that affirmative action should be seen as a way to compensate for historical wrongs done to blacks. Nor am I suggesting that affirmative action be viewed as an instrument for extracting punitive damages from whites for the behavior of their ancestors. In contrast to these two viewpoints, the perspective on affirmative action I urge is forward-looking insofar as it involves the claim that the problem affirmative action is designed to remedy is the effect of the lack of structural integration in the past on the future opportunities of African Americans. The most notable effect is on the social networks available to African Americans. Social networks are crucial ingredients for access to valuable goods and opportunities in society. A recent study found, for instance, that 57 percent of Americans found jobs through personal contacts compared with only 37 percent who found jobs through formal processes.[47]

My proposal that race-based affirmative action be viewed as a remedy for the effects of past discrimination on the current social networks of African American follows Orlando Patterson.[48] Paterson singles out

---

[47] John David Skrentny, *The Ironies of Affirmative Action* (Baltimore: John Hopkins University Press, 1996), p. 60.

[48] Although I follow Patterson in his rationale for race-based affirmative action, I disagree with him that affirmative action for women should be justified in the same way – that is because women have been excluded from valuable social networks. As I explain in Chapter 8, a much more compelling justification for affirmative action for women can be made by reference to the unfair burden of domestic labour carried by women and the effects this injustice within families has on women's opportunitities in the labour market. See also my articles, 'Equal Opportunity and Gender Disadvantage,' *The Canadian Journal of Law and Jurisprudence*, Vol. 7 (1994),

in particular the fact that African Americans alone "were systematically shut out of the emerging industrial revolution at the end of the
nineteenth century, preventing them from developing those critical patterns of behavior and cultural tools necessary for keeping in phase with
the nation's changing economy."[49] The long-term consequence of this
exclusion is that in terms of human capital, African Americans have
been disabled in their access to two key ingredients – the valuable capital of personal and family networks and the almost immeasurable cultural capital of being integrated into the mainstream of the industrial
culture. Whilst speculating here as an armchair sociologist, I would
suggest that the lasting legacy of this exclusion is evident in, for example, the perception that African Americans at the end of the twentieth
century were at the margins of the current revolution in information
technology.[50] The emphasis on the significance of social networks also
captures some of the more complex dimensions of racism in the United
States. It readily explains why, for instance, the issue of inter-racial
marriage is so significant. It is well known that in the United States,
black-white marriages remain very few in number and far lower in
proportion than intermarriage in other visible minorities such as Asian
and Jewish Americans. Yet, intermarriage between different racial and
ethnic groups seems a key ingredient for access to and development
of social networks.[51] The exclusion – legal and social in the past, social
now – of blacks from this process indirectly threatens the opportunities
and human capital of African Americans. And perceptively explains
why, from an egalitarian perspective, laws such as the infamous prohi-
bition in the state of Virginia against black-white marriages was such
an important site of legal conflict.[52] A similar point can also be made
about the lack of racially integrated church congregations, another very
important context for social networking in the United States.

It is also important to realize that the American federal government
played a significant role in the curtailment of the social networks of
African Americans. Often the emphasis has been on the role of state

---

pp. 61–72, and 'Equity and Opportunity' in Francois Gingras, editor, *Gender and
Politics in Contemporary Canada* (Toronto: Oxford University Press, 1995).

[49] Patterson, *The Ordeal of Integration*, p. 121.

[50] See Anthony Walton, 'Technology versus African-Americans,' *Atlantic Monthly*
(January 1999), pp. 14–18.

[51] Orlando Patterson, 'Affirmative Action: Opening up Workplace Networks to Afro-
Americans,' *The Brookings Review, Vol. 16* (Spring 1998), p. 18.

[52] See the U.S. Supreme Court decision in *Loving v. Virginia*, 388 U.S. 1 (1967).

governments in the segregation of African Americans. And the federal government has been represented as either a reluctant opponent of segregation or as turning a blind eye to it. But as a matter of historical record, the American federal government did play a large role in perpetuating racial segregation in the labor market and stifling the integration of African Americans into the emerging industrial economy of the first half of the twentieth century. Not only were the military and the civil service segregated, the immense government interventions in the private labor market of that period excluded African Americans. Programs such as the 1933 United States Employment Service, designed to help the unemployed find jobs, segregated black workers and aided them only in finding traditional 'black' dominated occupations in the lowest-paid sectors of the economy.[53] Perhaps the most striking evidence comes from the government-regulated apprenticeship programs. These programs were the main entry into skilled labor and the trades in the United States, and virtually excluded African Americans. A NAACP report written in 1960 found that, based on the existing participation rates in apprenticeships, it would "take Negroes 138 years, or until the Year 2094 to secure equal participation in skilled craft training and employment."[54] The relevant point is that apprenticeships are probably the most obvious example of a social network that enhances the opportunities of an individual in the labor market.

What affirmative action has done, and continues to do, is break down the barriers of access to the forms of human capital that African Americans had been excluded from in the industrialization of the United States. It provides an admittedly artificial substitute for the social networks from which African Americans have historically been excluded. It promotes, in other words, the twin goals of diversity and integration in the workplace and post-secondary education so as to include African Americans. And eventually as those social networks mature and integrate African Americans, affirmative action will no longer be necessary. This justification for affirmative action readily explains why affirmative action, as opposed to some other social policy initiative, is appropriate. The targeted problem is the exclusion of African Americans from certain forms of human capital, in particular cultural capital and social

---

[53] This is systematically argued by Desmond King, *Separate and Unequal: Black Americans and the US Federal Government* (Oxford, Oxford University Press, 1995), ch. 6.

[54] Quoted on p. 101 of King, *Separate and Unequal*.

networks. Affirmative action is especially effective at redressing these forms of human capital. Moreover, it provides a compelling explanation for what I described earlier as the fact that *middle class*, as opposed to *poor*, African Americans are the principal beneficiaries of affirmative action programs. In effect, the focus on these particular forms of human capital presupposes that the target of affirmative action is necessarily those African Americans in the middle class. As Patterson puts it,

[A]ffirmative action was never intended to help the poorest and least able members of the minority classes and women. It is, by its nature, a top-down strategy, meant to level the field for those middle- and working-class persons who are capable of taking advantage of opportunities denied them because of their gender or ethnic status. For the underclass and working but chronically poor, an entirely different set of bottom-up strategies are called for.[55]

The defense of affirmative action in terms of exclusion from particular forms of human capital then neatly explains both the social policy design of affirmative action and the demonstrated effects of implementation.

There is also a broader point that can be made about affirmative action. Critics of affirmative action often characterize it as a policy that is antithetical to the very idea of equality of opportunity. But some reflection should suggest that this charge against race-conscious affirmative action rests on a mistake, at least insofar as affirmative action is assumed to be a policy that counts the race of some applicants as a plus factor. (It is, I think, trickier if affirmative action involves quotas. The argument in this chapter has been centred around the idea of race's counting as a plus factor.) Recall from Section 2.2 that at the core of the three-dimensional model of equal opportunities as a regulative ideal is the reliance on competitive procedures as a means for achieving an egalitarian distribution of certain scarce resources or goods. Critics of affirmative action rarely seem to appreciate that at a very basic level, affirmative action reflects a commitment to the reliance on competitive procedures in this way. What affirmative action entails is counting race as a plus factor in that competition; it is not antithetical to the very idea of competition but merely a regulative refinement designed to ensure a competition with greater fairness.

Someone may say, however, that the tension with equality of opportunity arises because of the color-conscious character of affirmative action. After all, from a historical perspective, the language of equal

---

[55] Patterson, *The Ordeal of Integration*, p. 155.

opportunity was deployed to eliminate laws and social practices that discriminated against blacks because of the colour of their skin. Why not design social policies that are not colour-conscious but use some alternative such as class to give an advantage to African Americans? For many proponents of affirmative action, it has been thought sufficient to show that using anything as a proxy for race, in particular socio-economic class, in affirmative action programmes will result in those programmes not benefitting African Americans in great numbers. The reason is quite simple. Although African Americans proportionately are much more likely to be poor than whites, in sheer numbers there are far more poor white Americans than poor black ones. Hence, any programme directed at helping those from poor households without regard to race will be swamped by white applicants.[56] By contrast, race-conscious affirmative action really makes a difference to African Americans and other under-represented minorities. In the recent court challenge to affirmative action at the University of Michigan Law School, it was accepted that if race were eliminated as a factor in the year 2000 admissions process, under-represented minority students would have made up only 4 percent of the entering class rather than the actual 14.5 percent.[57]

But there is also a more principled basis for rejecting the use of a proxy for race such as socio-economic class. This principle has been succinctly explained by Amy Gutmann:

The 'class, not race' proposal . . . fails by the color blind test of fairness; it does not treat like cases alike. It discriminates against blacks by giving a boost only to students who score low because of disadvantages associated with poverty, but not to students who score low because of disadvantages that are as credibly associated with their color . . . The best available evidence suggests that color

[56] For statistical projections, see Linda Wightman, 'The Threat to Diversity in Legal Education: An Empirical Analysis of the Consequences of Abandoning Race as a Factor in Law School Admissions Decisions,' *New York University Law Review*, Vol. 72 (1997), pp. 1–53, and Bowen and Bok, *The Shape of the River*, ch. 2. Many proponents of race-based affirmative action also affirm class-based affirmative action. Richard Delgado recommends, for instance, that minorities 'forswear affirmative action unless it also includes poor whites. White ethnics and people of color – those who join the new coalition, at any rate – would agree to work together to subvert and replace the array of standards, social practices, and old-boy networks that now hold back the progress of both.' See 'Rodrigo's Tenth Chronicle: Merit and Affirmative Action', *Georgetown Law Journal*, Vol. 83, 1995), p. 1747.

[57] *Grutter v. Bollinger.* 2002 FED App. 0170P (6th Circuit) at 4.

and class are both obstacles, with interactive effects in the lives of a majority of black Americans.[58]

The important point is that the colour consciousness of affirmative action is, as Gutmann shows, a logical implication of a colour-blind principle that reflects a concern about class disadvantage.

But I also think that at least some of our reservations about race-based affirmative action stem from a failure to distinguish between two ways in which people interact with other people – as individuals in face-to-face interactions and as representatives of agencies such as governments, corporations, and civic and community institutions.[59] Face-to-face interactions require that we treat everyone with the same respect and dignity. Representational interactions, on the other hand, allow for some variation in how individuals are treated insofar as that treatment should be a reflection of the deterministic effects of social constructions such as race, class, and gender.

Critics of colour-conscious policies often fail to recognize this distinction between types of interactions, and therefore mistakenly apply the normative standard of one type of interaction to the other type. Face-to-face interactions should indeed be colour-blind. In this type of interaction, it is wrong to let the racial identity of the person you are interacting with influence how you treat him or her. In my own interactions with students, it might be said to be wrong for me to treat individual students differently because of racial considerations, for this would be a failure to acknowledge each individual as an autonomous agent.[60] This doesn't mean that I shouldn't be sensitive to differences in their individual needs and concerns, but that remedial solutions for societal racism do not rely on face-to-face interactions. Addressing societal racism rather is in the domain of representational interactions. Representatives in corporate, communal, civic, and governmental roles should therefore not be colour-blind but instead must be sensitive to those circumstances that warrant affording some people special treatment – in particular, in those circumstances where some people have faced harsh social conditions such as racism that have impeded control

---

[58] Amy Gutmann, 'Responding to Racial Injustice' in K. Anthony Appiah and Amy Gutmann, *Color Conscious: The Political Morality of Race* (Princeton: Princeton University Press, 1996), pp. 145, 143.

[59] This is Patterson's distinction from *The Ordeal of Integration*, p. 115.

[60] Randall Kennedy, 'My Race Problem – and Ours,' *Atlantic Monthly* (May 1997), p. 60.

over important areas of their lives and equal opportunities across their lifetimes.

The important upshot is that what is at stake in affirmative action is representational interactions, not face-to-face interactions. Affirmative action is a policy designed to guide the decisions of institutions and their representatives. It has a colour-conscious character precisely because it is designed to address the legacy of racism in the competitive opportunities of civil society. When critics object to this colour-conscious character and maintain instead that social policy should be colour blind, they are appealing to the norm for guiding face-to-face interactions and hence committing a kind of category mistake.

Although I am saying here that representational interactions can be colour conscious, I admit that there is a real danger in allowing institutions and social policy to be so. How governments and legal institutions define race shapes pervasively the discourse of race in the broader society. And certainly in the United States, this role has not been a laudatory one.[61] It may therefore be tempting to abolish any racial classification in representational interactions even though that would make race-based affirmative action impossible. But, as I argued in Section 3.5, the real burden of doing so will fall on minorities, not on the white majority for whom their racial identity is marginal. The relevant lesson I draw instead from the use and abuse of racial classifications is that they be used with great care and be narrowly tailored to particular purposes such as those of diversity and integration served by race-based affirmative action.

5.6 CONCLUSION

At the beginning of this chapter, I pointed out how the out-of-court settlement of *Piscataway Township Board of Education v. Taxman* just weeks before the case was to be argued before the U.S. Supreme Court indicated the importance of rethinking the normative foundations for affirmative action in the United States. The civil rights groups that were instrumental in achieving this settlement viewed the case as an extremely weak one to test the court's views on affirmative action. I have argued in this chapter that the point of affirmative action is the promotion of both diversity and integration. Neither goal is sufficient on its own to ground the distinctive features of colour-conscious affirmative action. The difficulty of

---

[61] See Michael Omni, 'Racial Identity and the State,' *Law and Inequality*, Vol. 15 (1997), pp. 7–24.

resting a policy exclusively on the diversity rationale is exemplified in *Piscataway Township Board of Education v. Taxman*. The principal reason the board of education gave for counting race as a plus factor among similarly qualified employees when there were layoffs was that this promoted diversity among the teaching staff. If the argument I presented earlier is sound, it follows that more needs to be done to justify racial preferences in the situation of layoff decisions between otherwise identically qualified individuals. This can probably be done by reference to human capital-type considerations such as the importance of promoting social networks for African Americans, networks in which high school teachers can play a very significant role, and the responsibility school boards and other social institutions have in the promotion of a significant African American middle class.

The broader theoretical point of this chapter is to show how the idea of stakes fairness can serve as the value underlying diversity and integration in a defense of race-conscious affirmative action. In this respect, the argument offered here complements the one advanced in the last chapter about status equality underlying civil rights. Taken together, the two chapters illustrate how the three-dimensional model of equal opportunities as a regulative ideal with its innovative account of procedural, background, and stakes fairness can further our understanding of the normative foundations of important and pressing issues regarding race and public policy.

PART III

Class

Chapter 6

Justifying Workfare

6.1 INTRODUCTION

The last two chapters focussed on the idea of race as a form of disadvantage and on legal remedies inspired by the three-dimensional model of equal opportunities as a regulative ideal. The activities of the courts and policymakers in the United States provided the context for the arguments I advanced in those chapters. The main reason is that by comparison with other advanced industrial countries, Americans have a wealth of experience – a litany of successes and failures – with race-explicit law and social policy. This chapter and the next shift the focus from race to class.

Class references generally involve two components – social differentiation and ranking. They are, first of all, a way to highlight similarities between some individuals while differentiating them from others. "Class labels," notes Christopher Jencks, "provide a short-hand device for describing people who differ along many . . . dimensions simultaneously."[1] Class is not, however, just about social differentiation. It also denotes a system of ranking order, or what sociologists sometimes call "social stratification."

Theories of class differ with regard to which forms of social differentiation are primary in explanations of class ranking or social stratification. Marxists, for instance, refer to the ownership and control of the means of production. Sociologists typically highlight social differentiation based on the sources of income – for example, from paid work, inheritance, capital investments, welfare, and so on. Many economists stress

---

[1] Christopher Jencks, *Rethinking Social Policy* (New York: Harper Collins, 1992), p. 201.

wealth and income. Other social scientists emphasize cultural variables such as family structure and attitudes toward and participation in mainstream social institutions such as schools, labour markets, and churches to explain social stratification.

My interest in class in this book arises because of the often-cited finding that the class background of individuals affects the range and quality of the opportunities they are presented with over the course of their lives. The concern for egalitarians is that some individuals are denied equal opportunities because of the class membership of their parents. While liberals have traditionally been concerned with ending the privileges resulting from having parents from advantaged classes, egalitarians have largely focussed on challenging the obstacles resulting from being born into families from the least-advantaged classes. This concern is often expressed in principles and slogans such as "giving priority to the worst off" or "the war on poverty."

Over the course of the twentieth century, the modern welfare state with its distinctive combination of macro-level economic policies and redistributive social policies was often represented as a mechanism for reducing the effects of class on realizing equal opportunities for all, as opposed to simply equalizing incomes. Early defenders of the modern welfare state were often explicit about this function. T.H. Marshall, writing in 1949 about the establishment of the welfare state in Britain after World War II, explained, for instance:

The extension of the social services is not primarily a means of equalizing incomes. In some cases it may, in others it may not. The question is relatively unimportant; it belongs to a different department of social policy. What matters is that there is a general enrichment of the concrete substance of civilized life, a general reduction of risk and insecurity, an equalization between the more and less fortunate at all levels – between the healthy and the sick, the employed and the unemployed, the old and the active, the bachelor and the father of a large family. Equalization is not so much between classes as between individuals within a population which is now treated for this purpose as though it was one class. Equality of status is more important than equality of income.[2]

---

[2] T.H. Marshall, 'Citizenship and Social Class' (1949), reprinted in Robert Goodin and Philip Pettit, editors, *Contemporary Political Philosophy: An Anthology* (Oxford: Basil Blackwell, 1997), p. 309.

The analysis in this chapter assumes a perspective on the programs of the welfare state similar to that of Marshall's, one that highlights class-abatement rather than the end of class.[3]

A basic cornerstone of the welfare state is its income support programs for the poorest households in society. These programs – often placed under the general rubric of "welfare" – range from public housing and food stamps to cash transfers. For the past twenty-five years, these programs have been subject to brutal criticism by conservatives in most advanced industrial countries for being ineffective at fighting poverty and making the poor worse off. In the United States, for instance, this has engendered a huge scholarly reassessment of income-support programs for the poor. The findings have for the most part shown that such programs do indeed make the poor better off.[4] Despite the fact that many of the attacks on welfare are without foundation, there can be little doubt that they have had a tremendous influence on how welfare is viewed by the general public and public officials.

The social policy context for this chapter is set by the efforts in a number of advanced industrial countries to reform welfare by introducing so-called workfare requirements. Welfare operates through redistributive transfers. Redistributive transfers, whether in-kind or cash, are payments by the government to an individual or household that does not arise out of current productive activity. Workfare measures, in contrast, make such payments conditional on the individual's performing some sort of work or participating in a job-training scheme. Britain, Canada, and the United States have each been the site of major legislative reform based on workfare since the mid-1990s. In Britain, as a component of the Labour government's New Deal, the 1999 Welfare Reform and Pensions Bill introduced work requirements for those on the dole. In Ontario, Canada's largest province, general welfare and family benefits under the social assistance system were changed in 1996 into the Ontario Works program, which requires recipients to join an employment plan

---

[3] "Class-abatement" is Marshall's phrase: "Class-abatement is still the aim of social rights, but it has acquired a new meaning. It is no longer merely an attempt to abate the obvious nuisance of destitution in the lowest ranks of society. It has assumed the guise of action modifying the whole pattern of social inequality." From 'Citizenship and Social Class,' p. 306.

[4] See, for instance, the excellent review in Rebecca M. Blank, *Its Takes a Nation: A New Agenda for Fighting Poverty*, paperback edition (Princeton: Princeton University Press/Russell Sage Foundation, 1998), ch. 4.

designed to prepare and get them jobs. Most other provinces now have similar schemes. In the United States in 1996, the federal government enacted the Personal Responsibility and Work Opportunity Reconciliation Act, which abolished the existing welfare program, Aid to Families with Dependent Children (AFDC), and replaced it with block grants to individual states, encouraging them to design their own systems of public assistance with mandatory job-search components.

This chapter sets out to justify workfare based on the three-dimensional model of equal opportunities as a regulative ideal. After a preliminary discussion designed to explain and make sense of workfare programs, I show that the three most familiar (non-egalitarian) normative justifications for workfare – those most often advanced by conservative critics of welfare – each have serious flaws. My intention here is to show that there is a real vacuum with regard to the normative foundations of workfare. I then argue that the three-dimensional model of equal opportunities outlined in Chapter 2 can fill this vacuum and provide compelling grounds for implementing workfare.

Justifying workfare on an egalitarian basis is controversial. Egalitarians have for the most part had a knee jerk reaction against workfare. Certainly that was my initial response, for instance, in my 1993 book, *Rights and Deprivation*.[5] But in this book, I am urging a normative reconsideration of workfare; this represents a genuine opportunity to rethink and replace welfare systems that historically egalitarians have long thought are flawed. Ultimately, the problems with workfare are not at the level of principle but at how individual schemes are being implemented and administered. By clarifying the normative basis for workfare, the agenda for reform will hopefully become clearer.

By utilizing the three-dimensional model of equal opportunities as a regulative ideal to defend workfare, I also intend to demonstrate that the theory of egalitarian justice advanced in this book reaches out to embrace policy initiatives that are often thought to be beyond the scope of egalitarian social policy. In the previous chapters on race, I have defended stances on civil rights and affirmative action that are familiar

---

[5] Lesley A. Jacobs, *Rights and Deprivation* (Oxford: Oxford University Press, 1993), pp. 197–202. My views on workfare shifted in the course of working on a co-authored multi-disciplinary book, *Workfare: Does It Work? Is It Fair?* (Montreal: Renouf/Institute for Research on Public Policy, 1995) by Patricia M. Evans, Lesley A. Jacobs, Alain Noel, and Elisabeth B. Reynolds. See also my newspaper article, 'Replacing Welfare with Workfare,' *The Globe and Mail* (Toronto), April 29, 1994).

territory for egalitarians. Here my views are more those of a maverick, at least among egalitarians. Egalitarians have typically responded to the policy crisis around income support for the poor by calling, perhaps dogmatically, for more welfare and the establishment of basic incomes for all. My focus on workfare is intended to show that when the idea of stakes fairness is taken seriously, this encourages more innovative and imaginative responses to the retrenchment of the modern welfare state. The moral imperative of egalitarian justice should be to fight poverty and inequality, not save welfare. If the United States provided much of the setting for my discussion of race, thinking about social programs for fighting poverty in Canada provided the impetus for my discussion of workfare.

6.2 MAKING SENSE OF WORKFARE

Before examining normative arguments for workfare, it is important first to clarify the social policy I am interested in finding justifications for. For workfare is often used to refer to a broad range of social programs. Recall, as I noted earlier, that workfare evolved largely as a corrective to welfare understood as programs using in-kind and cash transfers targeted at the poorest in society. Workfare involves making work a condition of beneficiaries' receiving cash or in-kind benefits.

This suggests that social policies based on workfare have two features that are especially important to highlight and account for in a normative argument for workfare. The first is that benefits are not given unconditionally, subject only to standards such as those suggested by the language of needs-testing or means-testing. The distinctive condition workfare sets is the work requirement. I shall elaborate on what fits under the rubric of "work" in a moment. The second feature of workfare is that it is concerned with only a certain segment of society – the poor or least advantaged.

This two-fold emphasis succeeds at both identifying what is distinctive about workfare and providing a definition that is flexible enough to include a full range of workfare-type schemes. Workfare is not unique in its concern about the transition from welfare to work. The belief that work is preferable to welfare is widespread and certainly not very controversial. Hence, governments with assistance plans for its unemployed or neediest citizens have long been paying attention to the transition from welfare to work. Typically, however, programs that have been put in place to address the transition from welfare to work have been voluntary. What makes workfare unique is its mandatory feature.[6]

This two-fold emphasis also allows considerable scope for accommodating different designs of workfare. Many of these designs differ along the lines of what constitutes work. In practice, most workfare programs accept the notion that the work requirement is met provided the individual is either working in the familiar sense of that term or in a job training scheme or in school. There is also considerable division over the issue of whether the jobs should be public works jobs supplied by the government or jobs based in the private labour market. In the United States, leading liberal social policy analysts such as William Julius Wilson and Mickey Kaus favour the idea of public sector jobs.[7] In Ontario, by contrast, the Ontario Works program is organized around jobs being provided by private firms and other non-governmental organizations.

There is also a range of views about the quality of work at issue. A common criticism of workfare is that it necessarily involves low-skilled, poorly paid work with few long-term prospects. Certainly, it is the case that many proposals have indeed involved only work of this calibre. For example, Mickey Kaus in his influential book, *The End of Equality*, outlines a scheme under which the government would set up job sites, and practically all of the labour would be manual – cleaning, painting, filling potholes, and so on. Moreover, it must be conceded that any comprehensive workfare program will involve work of this type. However, I would like to stress that workfare does not necessarily have to involve work that lacks intrinsic value and requires few skills. The Works Progress Administration (WPA) is a historical example that illustrates my point that workfare can involve useful, dignified, high-skill, and meaningful jobs.[8] WPA was an important part of President Franklin Roosevelt's 1935 New Deal scheme for addressing the high levels of

---

[6] Likewise, there is nothing unusual about egalitarians' arguing that work is indeed special and warrants special attention in social policy, but what is generally lacking is an egalitarian justification for the mandatory requirement that makes workfare distinctive. See, for instance, Richard Arneson's otherwise excellent article, 'Is Work Special? Justice and the Distribution of Employment,' *American Political Science Review, Vol. 84* (1990), pp. 1127–147.

[7] William Julius Wilson, *When Work Disappears* (New York: Vintage Books, 1996) and Mickey Kaus, *The End of Equality* (New York: Basic Books, 1992).

[8] See Jonathan Kesselman, 'Work Relief Programs in the Great Depression' in J. Palmer, editor, *Creating Jobs* (Washington, DC: The Brookings Institutions, 1978). I am grateful to Frank Swartz for drawing my attention to the specific details of the WPA to illustrate my claim.

unemployment in the United States at the time. It was a program under which the government provided work on a wide range of projects to more than three million people. Roosevelt's vision of WPA emphasized work that was socially useful, as opposed to so-called "make-work" projects. Most people associate WPA with the building of infrastructure projects such as highways, bridges, airports, parks, and so on. However, an important component of the WPA was projects designed specifically for artists and writers. These included, for example, a project for writers to produce travel guides to various regions of the United States, guides that are unique and still have a significant readership among tourists.

Issues of design also arise in relation to the question of what sort of programs it is necessary to have in place to support workfare. Some proponents of workfare advocate simply adding a work requirement as a condition for receiving social assistance. Others defend some version of fair workfare that includes support programs such as child care, dental and health care coverage, housing benefits, and job training.[9] Still others, such as Robert Solow, point out the complicated implications workfare has for the wage market, in particular driving down wages at the bottom end, and defends earned income tax credits and minimum wage increases as a component of workfare.[10]

Ultimately, this chapter treats the design of workfare in the same manner that I approach all general questions about the design of social programs throughout this book, in effect as a function of the normative justification for the particular policy in question. This means that we need to sort out initially the value and purpose of a program and then we can work out the details of the design.

6.2.1 *Three Flawed Arguments for Workfare*

Although the three most familiar normative arguments for workfare lack an egalitarian flavor, a careful examination of them helps to clarify the basic ingredients of a successful egalitarian justification for workfare. It is important to keep in mind that often these three arguments are not carefully distinguished; instead, the claims of some arguments are conflated with those of others. From the point of view of critically

---

[9] See, e.g., Christopher Jencks, *Rethinking Social Policy*, pp. 233–34, and Amy Gutmann, 'Introduction' to Robert M. Solow, *Work and Welfare* (Princeton: Princeton University Press, 1998), p. x.

[10] Solow, *Work and Welfare*, pp. 27–43. Se also Joel Handler, 'Welfare Reform in the United States,' *Osgoode Hall Law Journal*, Vol. 35 (1997), pp. 302–307.

evaluating them, this initial task of clearly distinguishing each argument is fundamental. I assume that the general objective of each is to defend the implementation of something like a workfare program with the two features I have just emphasized.

6.2.2 *The Argument from Desert*

Few ideas about the theory of the welfare state have proven to be more controversial than the notion of a 'deserving' poor. The main idea that has driven such a notion is that sound social policy should allow us to distinguish among the poor and disadvantaged between those who deserve help from the government and those who do not. Among social policymakers and political elites, this notion has been harshly received over the past thirty years. Defenders of the modern welfare state, especially in Canada and Western Europe, have regarded such a notion as reminiscent of an earlier, less progressive stage in redistributive social policy, one that we associate with Victorian Poor Law. Despite this hostile reception, the idea of a deserving poor appears still to have a strong residual appeal among the general public.[11] Some have sought to defend workfare over welfare on the grounds that as a social policy measure, it identifies and helps only the deserving poor. This defence gives workfare a populist flavor.

This argument from desert for workfare involves two especially important elements. The first revolves around the question of who exactly are the deserving poor. The deserving poor, according to this argument, are those who are willing to work but, because of bad luck, do not have the opportunity to do so. The supposed contrast is with those who are poor and disadvantaged because they are lazy and irresponsible. The second element has to do with what sort of social policy might track this standard of desert. Typically, the cash handouts that are characteristic of welfare and other similar sorts of social assistance are said not to be sensitive to this standard of desert. Workfare, by contrast, is defended because it tracks desert, so understood. Workfare schemes are said to

---

[11] This has been the subject of some interesting empirical studies in the United States indicating a strong correlation between social programmes that purport to track 'desert' and public support for those programmes. See Fay Lomax Cook and Edith J. Barrett, *Support for the American Welfare State* (New York: Columbia University Press, 1992), ch. 4; and Jeffrey A. Will, *The Deserving Poor* (New York: Garland Press, 1993).

reward only those willing to work. It denies benefits to those who are indolent.

Recall from Section 4.3 the difference between merit and desert. Whilst merit is a matter of what best serves society's interests, desert involves a judgement about the worth of an individual. The contemporary philosophical debates about desert are multi-faceted and complex. It is worth noting that there is in fact little agreement about even the value of the concept of desert. Some modern moral and political philosophers think that it is at the very core of justice.[12] They question how it is possible to even conceive of justice without a prior understanding of the concept of desert. At the other extreme, some utilitarian philosophers believe the concept has no real role in a theory of morality.[13] For them, desert is an empty notion without the sort of critical potential we associate with the concept of justice. Others accept the idea that while the concept may be important, it is such a vague and imprecise standard that we are ill-advised to give it a foundational role in our notions of social justice. Still others give desert a primary place but insist that it is but one among a series of competing values, including equality.[14] Their view is that justice requires us to strike a balance among these various values. We cannot expound here in any depth on this controversy within philosophical circles. At a minimum, the existence of this debate suggests that we should exercise some caution about social policy reform predicated on a view of desert.

Even more relevant to workfare is the debate about the bases of desert. Typically, desert claims have a triadic character: person x deserves y by virtue of z.[15] What z refers to is the basis of desert. As Joel Feinberg boldly puts it, "Desert without a basis is simply not desert."[16] Philosophers disagree about the precise bases of desert, although most seem to recognize a plurality of bases. The argument about workfare relies in

---

[12] Alasdair MacIntyre, *After Virtue* (Notre Dame: University of Notre Dame Press, 1981), ch. 17.

[13] J.J.C. Smart, 'An Outline of a System of Utilitarian Ethics' in *Utilitarianism: For and Against* (Cambridge, UK: Cambridge University Press, 1973).

[14] See, for example, David Miller, *Social Justice* (Oxford: Oxford University Press, 1976); and Michael Walzer, *Spheres of Justice* (New York: Basic Books, 1983).

[15] See, e.g., Owen McLeod, 'Contemporary Interpretations of Desert' in Louis P. Pojman and Owen McLeod, editors, *What Do We Deserve?* (New York, Oxford University Press, 1999), p. 62.

[16] Joel Feinberg, 'Justice and Personal Desert,' reprinted in *What Do We Deserve?*, p. 73.

the first instance on a single basis for the deserving poor: the willingness to work. Yet, most proponents of this argument also acknowledge other bases of desert. Few defend, for instance, applying a work requirement to the elderly or those who suffer severe physical or mental disabilities. Likewise, no one seriously defends workfare for children. (In Canada in 1993, 37 percent of the recipients of welfare were children. In 1995, just before AFDC was abolished in the United States, 67 percent of the individuals benefitting from it were children.) But even for those who are 'employable,' the issue is a good deal more complex. Some of the strongest proponents of workfare admit, for example, that a distinctive disadvantage suffered by the poor and long-term unemployed is a lack of confidence, not lack of willingness to work *per se*.[17]

The debates about the relationship between the bases of desert and responsibility even further complicate the point. Few people seriously challenge the claim that family background significantly influences life chances. This is disturbing because, as numerous political philosophers have emphasized, the family one is born into is a matter of luck; a child is not responsible for the particular family he or she is born into. Does this curtail all related claims about desert? Even more controversial, as we saw in Chapter 3, is the effort to extend this reasoning from family background to the possession of natural endowments. The main idea here is that what natural endowments you have is a matter of genetic luck; it seems that, like your family background, those endowments cannot be said to be something you 'deserve.'

The especially problematic feature of the argument from desert for workfare, then, is that it relies on an implausibly narrow account of the basis for the poor to be deserving. Workfare may indeed track who is deserving if the only basis is willingness to work. Yet, once it is acknowledged that there is a plurality of desert bases, it becomes harder to insist that workfare is a better way to track desert than welfare, with its traditional reliance on redistributive transfers. It is difficult to imagine a workfare program designed to accommodate all of the differences among those who might be said to be 'deserving.' If we did want to design a single social program that tracks desert bases with all their complexities, it seems much more plausible to implement some sort of

---

[17] Lawrence Mead, 'The New Welfare Debate: Workfare Will Transform Passive Recipients' in Beverly Fanning, editor. *Workfare vs. Welfare* (Hudson, WI: Gem Publications, 1989), p. 61.

guaranteed basic income that allows for desert-based inequalities above the social minimum.[18]

6.2.3 The Argument from Self-Respect

Here, I express some doubts about the argument that workfare is preferable to welfare because it better promotes the self-respect of the individuals who benefit from these sorts of government programs.[19] This argument relies on a particularly powerful critique of the reliance on redistributive cash and in-kind transfers that prevails in existing social policy. This critique can be briefly summarized:

1. Redistributive transfers are designed to meet an individual's needs.
2. Among any individual's needs is having self-respect, where self-respect is understood as "one's belief that one lives up to certain [socially determined] standards that define what it is to be a person of worth, a person entitled to respect."[20]
3. In our society, the most important socially determined standard for measuring one's self-respect is the idea that one works for what one receives.
4. Redistributive transfers such as welfare involve payments that have not arisen out of current productive activity.
5. Therefore, redistributive transfers have a self-defeating aspect in that they frustrate some of the needs of the recipient in the course of meeting other needs he or she has.

It is not my intention to challenge the cogency of this critique of redistributive transfers. I believe it successfully pinpoints a genuine problem with conventional social policy. The inference I am concerned with challenging is the further claim that workfare is therefore a better way to meet the needs of individuals.

---

[18] An argument more or less to this effect has been made by Philippe Van Parijs, *Real Freedom for All* (Oxford: Oxford University Press, 1995). See, for a similar argument, Joseph Carens, 'Compensatory Justice and Social Institutions,' *Economics and Philosophy*, Vol. 1, no. 1 (April 1985), pp. 39–67.

[19] In this section, I draw heavily on my discussion in *Rights and Deprivation*, pp. 197–202.

[20] J. Donald Moon, 'The Moral Basis of the Democratic Welfare State' in Amy Gutmann, editor, *Democracy and the Welfare State* (Princeton, NJ: Princeton University Press, 1988), p. 32.

This normative defense rests on the argument that workfare, unlike redistributive transfers, does not threaten the recipient's self-respect and therefore cannot be said to have a self-defeating aspect to it. This argument appears plausible because under a workfare scheme, the unemployed and disadvantaged are given the opportunity to meet their own needs by working for what they receive. But notice that this defense of workfare depends on the further inference that the use of workfare does not threaten the self-respect of the unemployed and disadvantaged. There is, however, an elementary problem with this inference.

Suppose that an individual is given a job because he or she is part of a workfare scheme and not because he or she 'earned' it. What I question is whether anyone who is given a job in this fashion will not experience some degree of threat to his self-respect, if indeed self-respect does require that one works for what one receives. The puzzle is how exercising the opportunity to work provided by a workfare scheme would not have the effect of undermining an individual's self-respect, thus introducing a self-defeating aspect into the use of workfare as a way to meet needs.[21] After all, if one has to take up a job offer from a government workfare program, it is hard to see how, from the perspective of self-respect, this would be any different from accepting a redistributive transfer.

Someone might respond that although it is true that the use of workfare does have a self-defeating aspect, it is still preferable to the use of redistributive transfers because it undermines the self-respect of the recipient less than does the use of transfers. The validity of this response depends on just how much redistributive transfers do in fact undermine the self-respect of the recipient. I shall make three remarks, which combined are intended to show that, contrary to what some proponents of workfare claim, the negative effects of welfare on self-respect are unlikely to be significantly different from those arising from workfare measures.

First, notice that the argument outlined here does not actually establish the fact that all redistributive transfers designed to meet needs pose a threat to self-respect. Consider two distinct ways in which a transfer to someone might be said to be redistributive. It might be either redistributive *between* different people or redistributive *across* one person's life. A social program providing everyone with the same benefits is

---

[21] Jon Elster, 'Is There (or Should There Be) a Right to Work?' in Gutmann (ed.), *Democracy and the Welfare State*, p. 74–75.

an example of a program redistributive between people if it is funded through a progressive income tax with the effect that high earners are subsidizing the benefits received by low earners. A mandatory contribution scheme for old-age pensions is an example of a program that is primarily intended to be redistributive across one person's lifetime. The idea is that people contribute when they are young and working so that they have an income when they are older and no longer working. (This is still an example of a redistributive transfer because the payment of the pension does not arise out of current productive activity.) Redistribution in this second sense – across one person's life – was the primary objective in the setting up of the British and Canadian welfare states after the Second World War. It is hard to see how the use of transfer payments that are redistributive across one person's life would threaten the recipient's self-respect.

My second, and more important, remark concerns the empirical claim that the degree to which a redistributive transfer threatens a recipient's self-respect is a function of whether society regards that transfer as an act of charity or as the fulfillment of a right required by social justice. The received view is that a rights-based redistributive transfer regarded as a requirement of social justice will not pose a threat to the recipient's self-respect.[22] Provided that the society's safety net is regarded as just, reliance on welfare will not have a harmful effect on the self-respect of the beneficiary. The key, therefore, is to sustain the view that welfare is indeed a just social policy.

My final remark requires pointing out a certain irony in the views of conservative critics of welfare. Many conservatives lament that now there is said to be little stigma attached to accepting welfare. As Gertrude Himmelfarb described it in a 1998 commentary, "In recent decades, we have witnessed a deliberate, conscious effort to create a system of welfare (no longer called relief) that is 'value-free', that eschews all moral distinctions and judgments by providing welfare as a matter of right, with no sanctions and no stigma attached to it."[23] What these proponents of workfare yearn for is a situation where receiving welfare is devastating to one's self-respect. But in that case their argument that workfare is better than welfare at preserving individual's self-respect is circular.

---

[22] See R. Plant, H. Lesser, and P. Taylor-Gooby, *Political Philosophy and Social Welfare* (London: Routledge & Kegan-Paul, 1980), pp. 22–25.

[23] Gertrude Himmelfarb, 'Comment' in Solow, *Work and Welfare*, p. 82.

6.2.4 *The Argument from Social Responsibility*

So far, I have argued that, on normative grounds, workfare is difficult to defend on the basis that it tracks desert or that it better promotes self-respect. I turn here to the argument that the normative foundations of workfare rest on the potential of workfare programs to promote social responsibility. This argument has been tremendously influential in both the United States and Canada.

The background context for this argument is a public arena where the language of rights is perceived to be on the increase, and indeed is so pervasive that practically all political issues are expressed as either the violation of rights or the fulfillment of rights. This dominance of rights discourse has not, however, gone unchallenged. Canadian critics have argued that the legalization of issues of social justice constitutes a threat to our democratic institutions and have urged a retreat from the obsession with rights.[24] In the United States, a central theme of a range of writings on the issue of individual rights has been that the dominance of rights discourse has had a devastating impact on public institutions. The practice of rights supposedly engenders a deeply rooted individualism that threatens the sense of community and shared commitment that is foundational to American public life.[25] Citizenship is said to involve not only rights, but also to entail fundamental duties.

Advocates have seized on this argument to defend workfare.[26] The problem, it is said, with viewing welfare benefits as an issue of rights or entitlements is that this has led to a neglect of the social responsibility of the welfare recipient. In a scheme involving redistributive transfers, individuals stand on their rights and demand benefits. They focus, in other words, on what they are owed. But this neglects what they owe

[24] The most influential Canadian statements are by my colleagues, Michael Mandel, *The Charter of Rights and the Legalization of Politics in Canada, second edition* (Toronto: Thompson, 1994), and Allan Hutchinson, *Waiting for Coraf: A Critique of Law and Rights* (Toronto: University of Toronto Press, 1995).

[25] The now classic sociological statement is Robert Bellah et al., *Habits of the Heart: Individualism and Commitment in American Life* (New York: Harper and Row, 1985). The most influential philosophical statements are by Michael Sandel, *Liberalism and the Limits of Justice* (Cambridge, UK: Cambridge University Press, 1982); 'The Procedural Republic and the Unencumbered Self,' *Political Theory, Vol. 12, no. 1* (February 1984), pp. 81–96; and 'Morality and the Liberal Ideal,' *New Republic, No. 190*, May 7, 1984, pp. 15–17.

[26] The most influential statement is Lawrence Mead, *Beyond Entitlement: The Social Obligations of Citizenship* (New York: The Free Press, 1986). See also his more recent book, *The New Politics of Poverty* (New York: Basic Books, 1992).

their political community in return. The implicit idea is that a scheme of social welfare presupposes a measure of reciprocity; people are required to make contributions to the scheme, not just withdrawals. Making the practice of welfare rights and entitlements central to a scheme of social welfare distorts this idea of reciprocity. This case for workfare rests on the claim that workfare programmes are designed to correct the imbalance between rights and duties. The main idea is that the work requirement for the collection of welfare benefits is a mere reflection of what the recipient owes to his or her community, as a matter of duty. Workfare, unlike the existing social assistance programs, imposes social responsibility on people. And the importance of social responsibility has been overlooked in our social policy because of our ill-conceived obsession with rights.

Much of the power of the argument from social responsibility in favor of workfare derives from the background claim that rights and duties are closely linked. I do not intend to dispute that background claim,[27] nor indeed the proposition that social policy, like other realms of public policy, should be more sensitive to social responsibility. However, it seems to me that there is a relatively simple, but nonetheless *decisive*, problem with this argument from social responsibility.[28] The problem is that while defenders of workfare who rely on the argument from social responsibility may be right to say that social policy should be concerned with promoting social responsibility among welfare recipients, they fail to show that workfare is a better way to do this than other social programs such as, for example, a scheme that enables individuals from a wide range of socio-economic backgrounds to work on community projects organized by volunteer and charitable societies.

Let me explain. Proponents of the argument from social responsibility typically emphasize that long-term recipients of welfare not only do not work, but more specifically behave differently from mainstream Canadians and Americans because they have not internalized the commitments to work and to making a contribution to society. Existing social policy supposedly promotes this form of 'dependency' and a

---

[27] In fact, I have advanced elsewhere a theory of rights, which I call the "person-affecting theory of rights," that is sensitive to precisely this point. See *Rights and Deprivation*, ch. 2.

[28] For some more complicated, empirical criticisms, see, for example, William Julius Wilson, *The Truly Disadvantaged* (Chicago: University of Chicago Press, 1987), pp. 159–63; and David Ellwood, *Poor Support* (New York: Basic Books, 1988), ch. 5. For a partial response, see Mead, *The New Politics of Poverty*, chs. 5–6.

parasitic approach to others in their political community. These defenders of workfare lament for a time when everyone accepted his or her social responsibilities and shouldered a share of the burden. The question I am pressing is why they think we should introduce workfare to promote this sense of social responsibility, rather than some other social programme.

The force of this question can be illustrated by reference to Britain. There it is widely believed that over the past twenty years, there has been a significant decline in people's acceptance of this sense of social responsibility. However, the most cogent policy responses have not involved an appeal to workfare. For example, in 1994, the Commission on Social Justice proposed what it called a Citizens' Service. The principal objective of such a service is "the renewal of this country's civic life."[29] The main idea is that young adults from all different socio-economic backgrounds be given the opportunity to join a program for an average of three months, participating in volunteer service activities in return for a small stipend and some sort of educational or UI credit. The point would be to promote the social responsibilities of citizenship by educating young people about, and involving them in, the public sphere of their political community. From the point of view of promoting social responsibility, this sort of program is superior to workfare because it is directed at everyone, not just the poor and disadvantaged. After all, if one takes seriously the claim that the dominance of rights discourse has led to the decline in social responsibility, then this decline must also be prevalent among people other than the poor and disadvantaged.[30] Hence, programs designed to promote social responsibility should be directed at all citizens.

This reasoning is reinforced by recent studies of what people on welfare actually think about social values such as personal responsibility, fairness, work, and so on. Contrary to those who claim that those on welfare function outside the mainstream values of society, these studies consistently show that there are no significant differences in terms of

---

[29] James McCormick, *Citizens' Service, The Commission on Social Justice Issue Paper, Vol. 10* (London: Institute for Public Policy Research, May 1994), p. 1.

[30] Someone might say that, unlike the unemployed, other citizens are bearing their fair share of social responsibilities by working and paying taxes. For this reason, only the unemployed should be targetted for social programs promoting social responsibility. But, presumably, few people seriously think that only the unemployed shrug social responsibility. My point is that once this is conceded, then the case for workfare based on social responsibility is doubtful.

values between the Canadians or Americans on welfare and those who are not.[31]

My objection, then, to the argument from social responsibility is that while it may be right to say that we should have social programs that promote a sense of social responsibility and the idea that rights and entitlements entail duties, it is doubtful that this warrants the introduction of workfare. At a minimum, a careful analysis of proposals such as the Citizens' Service in Britain is necessary to show why we should introduce workfare instead of these alternative programs not just targetted at the poor and least advantaged in society.

6.3 WORKFARE AND THE RELEVANCE OF STAKES FAIRNESS

We are now in a position to consider whether the three-dimensional model of equal opportunities as a regulative ideal is capable of providing normative foundations for workfare. Why might that egalitarian model for regulating competitions be relevant to the workfare debate? Workfare and welfare are both best thought of as corollaries to the labour market. The presumption is that most people will participate in the regular labour market and satisfy their wants and needs through income earned in that market. The very issue of workfare and welfare arises only for the relatively small number of households for whom the regular labour market fails. It is in this sense that social programs such as this are characterized as a safety net. The metaphorical reference is of course to the trapeze artist who functions far above the net, and rarely falls; being caught by the net is an extraordinary event. The contrast in social policy terms is with, for instance, public education, which is assumed to be utilized by practically everyone. Public education is rarely described as a safety net! It is significant that the labour market is a type of competition – it has rules and regulations, prizes and rewards, winners and losers.

In Chapter 2, I argued that as a normative regulator of competitions, an equal opportunities model raises questions of fairness on three distinct dimensions – procedural, background, and stakes. Labour markets generate familiar issues of both procedural and background fairness.

---

[31] For Canadian findings, see Solow, *Work and Welfare*, pp. 7–10, and Christopher McAll, 'Le Cercle Vicieux De L'Aide Sociale,' *Policy Options*, Vol. 16, no. 4 (May 1995), pp. 29–32. For American findings, see Wilson, *When Work Disappears*, ch. 3.

Standard legislation and policies in advanced industrial countries – labour and workplace safety standards, workers' compensation plans, minimum wages, statutory overtime requirements, and so on – all can be viewed as devices for promoting procedural fairness *within* labor markets. Distinct from these measures are those designed to address issues of fairness that come *before* the markets.[32] This is the domain of background fairness.

Labour market competitions also raise questions, however, about what I have called stakes fairness. Recall from Chapter 2 that stakes fairness is concerned with the distribution of benefits and burdens within a competition. Is it fair, for instance, to have a winner-take-all scheme? The different payouts from labour market competition are well known. Some occupations provide high incomes and generous benefits; others do not. International comparisons suggest, perhaps surprisingly, that there are similarities between countries in the rankings of occupations according to difference of earnings and the size of the differentials.[33] This is familiar material, and some egalitarians are well known for urging labour markets where the earnings differentials are minimal or non-existent. These prescriptions raise, in turn, complicated questions about how labour markets could even function with equal incomes; egalitarians have responded with some superb suggestions.[34]

The traditional egalitarian preoccupation with earning differentials between those working has led to the neglect of what is a far graver instance of stakes unfairness – namely, the differentials in benefits between those working and those unemployed. Labour market competition means not just that some people get jobs with higher incomes than other people but also that some people don't get jobs at all. The actual percentage who don't succeed at all in the labour market varies greatly from country to country. The United States since the mid-1990s has been witnessing some of the lowest levels of unemployment in the past thirty years. Elsewhere in the OECD, levels of unemployment have stayed higher. This makes the issue I am raising more visible there. Philippe Van Parijs, writing with a view of the effect of high levels of

---

[32] I am utilizing here the standard distinction in labour economics between discrimination *within* labour markets and discrimination *before* labour markets. See Henry Phelps Brown, *Egalitarianism and the Generation of Inequality* (Oxford: Oxford University Press, 1988), p. 518.

[33] Brown, *Egalitarianism and the Generation of Inequality*, p. 398.

[34] See especially Joseph Carens, *Equality, Moral Incentives, and the Market* (Chicago: University of Chicago Press, 1981).

unemployment in social democratic welfare states in Western Europe, has attempted to rethink what is the fundamental class division within welfare state capitalist societies.[35] The class division he emphasizes is between those with stable, decently paid jobs and those deprived of access to such jobs, such as the unemployed and the casually employed. Van Parijs' insightful observation is that from the perspective of distributive justice, the basic contrast is no longer between workers and capitalists but rather between the employed – those with job assets – and the job poor. For twenty-five years, Western Europe and Canada have experienced consistently high levels of unemployment. The consequence is that those who have stable jobs have a valuable asset that is distinct from, for example, the skills and talents they might have, presumably because some of the (involuntary) unemployed have similar skills. Moreover, a job is an asset not only in the sense that it generates a wage but also in nonpecuniary ways, such as, for example, the benefits to health, self-esteem, social networks, and pension funds.[36] The relevant point to my analysis is that labour market competitions not only distribute jobs; they also distribute these other job assets. And the pressing issue of stakes fairness arises because the biggest losers in the labour market are in a sense doubly disadvantaged; not only do they not get jobs with earned incomes, but they also are excluded from these other job assets.

Cash payments to those without jobs can certainly function as a *partial* remedy for the effect of labour market competitions. This is in effect the role welfare and unemployment insurance payments perform. And the higher the rates of these payments, the more effective they are at lifting out of poverty households lead by the unemployed. Rebecca Blank makes an interesting comparison between Canada and the United States to illustrate this point.[37] Although poverty among single-parent

---

[35] This paragraph and the next two draw on points I initially made in a review of Van Parijs in *Economics and Philosophy*, Vol. 11, no. 1 (April 1995), pp. 197–203, and 'The Second Wave of Analytical Marxism,' *Philosophy of the Social Sciences*, Vol. 26, no. 2 (June 1996), pp. 279–92.

[36] For a superb study of these other disadvantages of unemployment, see Patrick Burman, *Killing Time, Losing Ground: Experiences of Unemployment* (Toronto: Thompson, 1988).

[37] Blank, *It Takes a Nation*, p. 142. Others have emphasized that by comparison with other countries, Canada fares poorly in its use of social assistance to aid single-parent families since in the Netherlands, for instance, the social safety net compensates so much that poverty rates of single-parent families are similar to those of two-parent families. See Anne-Marie Ambert, *Divorce: Facts, Figures and Consequences* (Ottawa: Vanier Institute of the Family, 2000), p. 12.

families is a major problem in both countries, and work behavior in these families is similar, it is significant, she thinks, that in Canada the level is about one-third lower than in the United States. The reason, argues Blank, is that Canadian public assistance is much more generous, noting that in the mid-1980s, cash transfers were twice as much as in the United States.

If, however, the analysis of the double advantage of having a job – the income and the other job assets – is persuasive, no matter how high the level of welfare payments is set, there is no way to redress for the unemployed not enjoying these other assets. Moreover, more radical reforms to welfare such as adding pension benefits won't address the more subjective benefits of having a job. This is a serious problem for proponents of a basic income such as Van Parijs. While I concur with him about the diagnosis of long-term unemployment, a basic or guaranteed income is not the appropriate remedy.

The analysis suggests to me instead that the most effective means to deliver the assets of having a job to the unemployed is precisely by supplying them with jobs. Workfare measures make income transfers from the government conditional on the individual's performing sort of work or participating in a job training scheme. In addition to income, this sort of work also provides individuals with job assets such as social networking, mental and physical health, self-esteem, and so on. The real virtue of workfare schemes is, then, that, by contrast with simple guaranteed income programmes, they are capable of addressing the stakes unfairness of labour market competition with regard to job assets.

This insight is reinforced by studies of low-status jobs, sometimes pejoratively described as "McBurger" jobs. Sceptics of my claim about the virtue of workfare may say that while some jobs do indeed have the additional assets I allege, this is not the case with the sorts of jobs people will likely perform as a requirement of workfare. Katherine Newman, in a detailed anthropological study of young people working at fast food restaurants in Harlem, found even there precisely the sorts of benefits of working – social networking, enhanced self-esteem, self-discipline – that I suggest workfare may offer.[38] The point is that simple cash transfers

---

[38] Findings presented in a talk at the Harvard Law School, March 1998. They have now been published in Katherine S. Newman, *No Shame in My Game: The Working Poor in the Inner City* (New York: Russell Sage Foundation/Knopf, 1999). See also the review by Michael Massing, 'The End of Welfare?,' *The New York Review of Books*, October 7, 1999, pp. 22–26.

through, say, an unconditional basic income scheme will not provide those benefits.

The argument for workfare I am advancing, based on the stakes unfairness of labour market competition, explains a standard feature of workfare plans that is neglected in the three arguments I criticized in Section 6.3. The standard feature in question is the assumption that workfare requirements are principally for the long-term unemployed. In most instances, it is assumed that for those unemployed for short periods of time, cash transfers through either unemployment insurance or welfare should be used. By focussing on the assets of having a job in addition to earned income, I think this assumption is perfectly understandable. The reason is that the assets of having a job or not are rarely significant in the short term. They are really assets of holding a stable job or, conversely, the burdens of being unemployed for a long time. Consider, for instance, the example of health.[39] Certainly, in the United States, when one loses his job, he also loses his health care insurance coverage. In both Britain and Canada, however, this is not the case because health care is publicly funded and universally accessible. But losing health care insurance should not be confused with being unhealthy; the guaranteed coverage assured people in Canada and Britain even if they lose their jobs does not guarantee health. The significant finding is that the long-term unemployed suffer more from ill health, regardless of whether universal access to health care exists. And it is not the case that their poor health causes the unemployment; the causal relationship appears to be the reverse.

A careful critic of workfare may agree with everything I have said so far but deny that this constitutes a persuasive argument for workfare. What I have shown, this critic might say, is that work is indeed preferable to welfare, and that governments should, therefore, make getting the unemployed jobs a priority. The controversial feature of workfare, continues this critic, is not the emphasis on work but rather the mandatory character of the participation, in effect, the requirement that in order to receive public assistance, recipients must work. And I have failed thus far to ground that basic feature of workfare.

Let me now respond to this critic. The common ground we share is that work is really important to the lives of individuals in our society; this may be a contingent feature of our society, but it is nevertheless

---

[39] Richard Wilkinson, *Unhealthy Socieites: The Afflictions of Inequality* (London: Routledge, 1996), pp. 59–60, 67.

an undeniable one. To be excluded in our society from work is therefore unfair, even if excluded individuals are given cash payments that approach what they would have earned holding a job. An example illustrates the point. Much of the effort in the disability-rights movement in Canada has recently been directed at making educational institutions more accessible to the disabled, and at challenging barriers that prevent those with disabilities from pursuing certain employment prospects. Implicit in this initiative is the astute observation that work provides the best means for disabled Canadians to realize control over their own lives. This reflects a significant shift in social policy from providing the disabled with cash redistributive transfers to emphasizing work and training opportunities. The slogan is that those with disabilities have the right to employment. Workfare, like the disability rights movement, is radical because it proposes to take seriously the right of the unemployed to employment.

From this perspective, workfare is a progressive social policy because it enables the poor and disadvantaged to exercise their right to employment. In labour market competitions, those who don't get jobs suffer from the stakes unfairness of being denied not only earned income but also the other assets of holding a job. The three-dimensional model of equal opportunities as a regulative ideal requires that this stakes unfairness be addressed. Workfare can be justified as an egalitarian supplement to the labour market because it provides benefits to the otherwise unemployed that those who hold jobs get from the labour market. (This is not to deny that exercising opportunities to work provided by a workfare program may undermine an individual's self-respect to some degree.) Unlike the argument from social responsibility, the emphasis is on what workfare does for each individual citizen, as opposed to what it does for the civic life of the political community. The focus is on workfare as a programme for fulfilling the right to employment of all citizens in an egalitarian society, rather than on the duties of welfare recipients to contribute to the well being of their community.

This shift, in the context of a discussion of workfare, to the language of a right to employment may be surprising. One reason is that workfare is frequently regarded as a social policy antagonistic to the rights of welfare recipients. (This is, of course, a central theme in the arguments about social responsibility and desert, discussed earlier.) In particular, the fact that workfare compels those drawing benefits to work, rather than making it voluntary, has struck many as contrary to the very notion of a right to employment. But it seems clear that this objection rests on a conceptual mistake about the nature of rights. There is nothing problematic about saying someone has a right to something and then compelling him or her to exercise that right. Perhaps the clearest example is the right to education. In Canada and the United States, few people question that children have a right to education. Nonetheless, in these jurisdictions, we compel children to attend school. Furthermore, programmes such as government social security and old-age pensions are often described in terms of rights. Yet, these programs are mandatory; contributions are involuntary and deducted at the source of the income.

In fact, by viewing workfare from the perspective of the right to employment, and noting the parallel to other so-called welfare rights such as education and old age income security, this provides some insight into why workfare is mandatory. The standard textbook reasons why social programmes such as education and old age pensions are mandatory are familiar enough: collectivizing risk, assurance that others are participating, combating myopic tendencies.[40] Exactly the same reasons would seem sufficient to make workfare mandatory. Critics of workfare who reject those reasons are, I suggest, questioning not only workfare but also the main pillars of the modern welfare state. The irony, then, is that whilst these critics typically represent themselves as defenders of the status quo welfare state, they are in fact fuelling attacks on most progressive redistributive social policies.

There is, furthermore, a more complex reason why workfare is mandatory that also parallels the mandatory participation in public schemes to provide pensions and public education. My argument here has been that workfare can be justified as an egalitarian supplement to the labour market because it provides, as a requirement of stakes fairness, benefits to the otherwise unemployed that those who hold jobs get from the labour market. This account highlights public responsibility to remedy for an unfair dimension of labour market competition. A well-known pitfall with voluntary public schemes in modern welfare states is that they often become marginal and easily subject to cost-cutting measures. Ironically, by making workfare mandatory, this prevents public decision-makers from shirking their responsibility to those who fail to get jobs in the labour market and not taking their rights seriously. This amounts, in other words, to a claim that the mandatory character

---

[40] See, e.g., Nicholas Barr, *The Economics of the Welfare State, new edition* (London: Weidenfeld & Nicolson, 1993), chs. 4–5.

of workfare does not necessarily entail paternalistic treatment of the beneficiaries of workfare.

6.4 CONCLUSION

In this chapter, I have shown how the three-dimensional model of equal opportunities as a regulative ideal can provide the normative foundations for workfare. Utilizing the idea that everyone has a right to employment, I have argued that workfare with its mandatory work requirements can be viewed as a device for fulfilling the rights of the long-term unemployed. It should be readily apparent that this justification for workfare is unique to a three-dimensional approach to equal opportunity. Recall from Chapter 2 that what distinguishes a three-dimensional approach from the more familiar two-dimensional approaches advanced by Rawls and other egalitarian liberals is the introduction of the dimension of stakes fairness. This dimension of stakes fairness is, I have argued here, fundamental for appreciating the disadvantages facing those who experience longer term unemployment in competitive labour markets. Workfare has been defended as an egalitarian remedy for this dimension of stakes unfairness in that competition.

It must be acknowledged, however, that this argument is principally one for favouring workfare over welfare. Andrew Levine has commented, "To make the case that the state ought to accord such a right [to paid employment] – by promoting full employment policies and/or serving as an employer of last resort – one would have to show that for some individuals, the benefits of employment are such that nothing can adequately substitute for them."[41] Levine sets the standard too high. In my analysis, unregulated labour markets impose costs on those who don't get jobs that raise serious concerns about stakes fairness. Welfare and other similar forms of social assistance are viewed as attempts to remedy for this unfairness. Workfare is preferable to welfare because in effect it is a more comprehensive remedy, addressing not only the lack of earned income but also some of the other benefits of having a job. The case for fulfilling the right to employment here is not, therefore, that there is no substitute for work but that one sort of social program – workfare – better addresses the stakes unfairness of the labour market than another – welfare.

---

[41] Andrew Levine, 'Fairness to Idleness: Is There a Right Not to Work?,' *Economics and Philosophy*, Vol. 11 (1995), p. 263.

Chapter 7

Universal Access to Health Care

7.1 INTRODUCTION

So far in this book, I have been concerned to show the dynamic possibilities of the three-dimensional model of equal opportunities as a regulative ideal with regard to a range of issues in law and social policy. I now intend to illustrate the limits of that theory of equality of opportunity. Specifically, I have insisted that equality of opportunity is an egalitarian ideal applicable only when there should be a competition for resources. It follows that that concept is silent in cases where competition for resources is inappropriate. It is my view that many proponents of equality of opportunity have failed to appreciate its boundaries. And they have weakened the case for equality of opportunity by trying to utilize it everywhere in law and social policy. This chapter sets out a principled basis for limiting the application of equality of opportunity. The example I shall use to illustrate the limitations of equal opportunities as a regulative ideal is health care. After making a case for why competition for health care is counter-intuitive as evidenced by the widespread commitment to universal access, I point out the pitfalls of egalitarian efforts to ground universal access to health care when they assume either an equality of opportunity approach or some other approach that emphasizes competition.

7.2 THE SIGNIFICANCE OF UNIVERSAL ACCESS

Part of the challenge of showing the application limits of the theory of equality of opportunity is selecting an example of a non-competitive opportunity. Any such selection is bound to be controversial, for someone is bound to insist that the selected example is in fact wrongly classified. I have, for the purposes of this chapter, selected health care as an example of a non-competitive opportunity to illustrate my general point about equality of opportunity. And for those readers who find this controversial, I ask them to suspend their scepticism and try to keep the overall objective of the chapter in mind. But first let me explain why I think health care involves a non-competitive opportunity.

It is my view that whatever might be the fair way to allocate scarce health care resources, competition is an inappropriate device for that allocation. In other words, individuals should not be treated as competitors for health care. Health care should not be regarded as a prize. Although tragic choices about health care resources are inevitable, those who are the beneficiaries of modes of health care allocation and those who are not cannot be described as winners and losers, respectively. And because competition is not suitable for health care allocation, equal opportunity theories have little purchase here. A different principle for allocating health care is called for. I do not here offer such a principle; my objective is principally to show that a competitive model of equal opportunity is a misapplication in the case of health care. I intend here in this Section 7.2 to make a case for adopting this view of health care – that it is unsuitable for competition – by showing that it underpins the widely held commitment to universal access. The significance of universal access to health care is that it makes sense only if health care is unsuitable for competition, that it involves what I called in Section 2.3 a non-competitive opportunity.

Part of the appeal of the concept of equality of opportunity, I am suggesting in general, stems from appreciating the complexity of social justice. While some philosophers have searched for a single principle or value as the basis for allocating and distributing the benefits and burdens of social life, most on reflection have appreciated that such a quest reflects a failure to appreciate the diversity of the benefits and burdens at issue. It seems to be a gross over-simplification of the idea of social justice to try to find one single principle. The greater challenge is not so much to recognize the diversity of goods and the implication that different principles may come into play, but to identify the basis for saying which principle is applicable.

Most efforts to meet this challenge have sought to offer a principled basis for identifying which, if any, of society's goods and resources should be immune from allocation through the market. In an influential paper written many years ago, Bernard Williams argued that the basis for distributing a particular good is part of the very idea of what that particular good is. Williams claimed, for instance, that "the proper ground of distribution of medical care is ill health; this is a necessary truth."[1] Critics such as Robert Nozick responded that Williams' claim is unhelpful because something like the "necessary truth" Williams identifies with health care can be said about practically any good or service; for example, "The only proper criterion for the distribution of barbering services is barbering need."[2] The force of Nozick's charge is that since haircuts should obviously be subject to market allocation, so too should health care. In an important revision to Williams' view, Michael Walzer argued that whilst there is nothing in the essence of particular goods about how they should be distributed, each has a "social meaning," and how they should be distributed is a function of that meaning. In effect, says Walzer, "distributions are patterned in accordance with shared conceptions of what the goods are and what they are for."[3] Since social meanings are historically contingent, there is no basis for saying that some good should always be distributed in this or that way. But for now those meanings provide a basis for distribution. On this view, the analogy Nozick draws between health care and barbering breaks down because of differences in the "social meaning" of those goods. Sympathetic critics of Walzer, in turn, have questioned how social meanings are constructed and whether they can perform the sort of critical role required of principles of social justice.[4]

An alternate account to both Williams and Walzer has been provided by Margaret Jane Radin, who highlights the distinction between fungible and non-fungible goods. In effect, non-fungible goods are those we associate with our personal identity, with who we are. Examples might be a wedding ring or a home. Fungible goods can, in contrast, be completely replaced or exchanged.[5] The value of the latter is well captured by markets in a way that the value of the former is not. Since health care would seem to be bound up with our personal identity, and hence can be said to be a non-fungible good, it can be inferred from Radin's account that

---

[1] Bernard Williams, 'The Idea of Equality' (1962), reprinted in Robert E. Goodin and Philip Pettit, editors, *Contemporary Political Philosophy: An Anthology* (Oxford: Basil Blackwell, 1997), p. 471.

[2] Robert Nozick, *Anarchy, State, and Utopia* (Oxford: Basil Blackwell, 1974), p. 234.

[3] Michael Walzer, *Spheres of Justice* (New York: Basic Books, 1983), p. 7.

[4] See, e.g., Ronald Dworkin, 'What Justice Isn't' in *A Matter of Principle* (Cambridge, MA: Harvard University Press, 1985) and Susan Moller Okin, *Justice, Gender, and the Family* (New York: Basic Books, 1989), ch. 6.

[5] Margaret Jane Radin, 'Property and Personhood,' *Stanford Law Review*, Vol. 34 (1982), pp. 960, 986–88.

markets in health care are inappropriate or should be circumscribed. A serious problem with Radin's account is the deeply subjective character of the relationship between a type of good and people's personal identities. Health may be extremely important to some people but not to others.

I find all of these approaches wrong-headed. It seems to me that the focus on what should and should not be subject to market allocation does not get at the core of the challenge of identifying the basis for saying which principle is applicable when a complex array of principles of social justice are acknowledged. The running example of health care illustrates this vividly. The concerns about health care and social justice are not principally about the use of markets. They revolve instead around access to health care. Markets constitute part of the debate but they are not at its center.

Much of the discussion about health care is framed by contrasts between the American health care system and those found in Canada and Western Europe. The two main concerns about the United States are familiar: (1) Huge numbers of Americans without any health care insurance and significant numbers who are underinsured – in 2000, about 45 million and 20 million respectively. (2) The large expenditure on health care as a percentage of the Gross Domestic Product in comparison with other OCED countries – the commonly noted irony is that although the United States far outspends all other nations on health care, it does so without providing coverage to all of its citizens. The best known comparisons are with the Canadian health care system. Canada provides health care insurance for all of its citizens whilst its gross per capita spending on health care was 55 percent of that of the United States in 1995.[6] Moreover, in terms of measures such as infant mortality, Canada does much better. But in other respects, the American system is clearly superior, especially with regard to the availability of expensive technology. This translates into, for instance, much higher success rates in cancer treatment. The five-year survival rate for American women with breast cancer is 84 percent, 12 percent higher than in the country (Germany) with the second highest survival rate.[7]

---

[6] Pat and Hugh Armstrong with Claudia Fegan, *Universal Health Care: What the United States Can Learn from the Canadian Experience* (New York: The New Press, 1998), p. 104.
[7] *New York Times*, Thursday, February 10, 2000, A14.

Neither the successes nor the failures of the American health care system seem easily attributable to the reliance on markets. Certainly in the United States, markets in the provision of health care are widespread. But the belief that there are not similar markets in, for instance, Canada is misleading. In Canada, as in the United States, most hospitals are private, not-for-profit institutions. Physicians are paid predominantly on a fee-per-service basis and compete among themselves for patients. Prescription drugs are produced and sold by privately owned pharmaceutical companies (although compulsory licensing is more widespread in Canada than in the United States, leading to more less expensive generic drugs on the market.) The principal difference is that in Canada there is a single payer – provincial governments – for medically necessary services, whereas in the United States there are multiple payers including state governments, the federal government, insurance companies, and individuals. This difference may affect the particular character of the markets in health care in each country but does not negate the existence of markets in both countries.

If there is a general misgiving about American health care across the ideological spectrum that the Canadian comparison highlights, it is around the failure to achieve universal access. Universal access to health care exists when all citizens, regardless of their socio-economic class, race, or gender, are assured access to a certain set of basic or 'medically necessary' health care services and products. In the United States, after the Second World War, there was, in Paul Starr's influential description, a shift from mass inequality in medical care – divergence of broad segments of American society from the medical care provided to the middle and upper classes – to marginal inequality – exclusion from this standard of access for poor Americans.[8] In Canada, every Canadian has been assured health care coverage since 1971. Coverage is said to be universal, as opposed to selective. Nobody is denied coverage because of (1) his or her inability to pay an insurance premium, (2) high risk, or (3) failure to meet a means test. The 1984 Canada Health Act provides the legislative guarantee of this level of coverage. Among health care reformers in the United States, the platitude of 'universal access' has dominated initiatives now for a decade. Important developments

---

[8] Paul Starr, 'Medical Care and the Pursuit of Equality in America' *in Securing Access to Health Care, Vol. 2* (Washington, DC: President's Commission for the Study of Ethical Problems in Medicine and Biomedical and Behavioral Research, 1983), pp. 3–22.

such as the Children's Health Insurance Program, passed by Congress in 1997, which seeks universal access for every child in America, illustrate the power of that platitude.

But, as is often the case with platitudes, the substance of the commitment to universal access to health care is less than clear. Certainly, it has long been recognized that universal access is not the same as equal access.[9] It is nonsense in Canada to allege that, by comparison with residents of large urban centers, there exists equal access to health care for those in rural and geographically remote areas. Likewise, although there is a consensus in Canada around universal access, there is no parallel agreement about what that access is to. Does it include home care and prescription drugs? One way to view the current crisis in health care in Canada is in terms of universal access to what.[10] Similar points can be made about universal access for whom. The lack of health care insurance in the United States is not uniform across ethnic and racial groups. In California, for example, while roughly similar percentages of whites (23 percent), Asian Americans (22 percent), and African Americans (22 percent) are uninsured, Latinos are nearly twice as likely to be uninsured (42 percent).[11] This means that extending access will have a disproportionate impact upon these different groups. What role do factors such as illegal immigration play? Should social benefits such as health care be accessible without regard to such considerations?

It is not possible to resolve these issues about universal access without exposing the deeper normative principle upon which that level of access is based. What underlies universal access to health care? What justifies making health care accessible to everyone? Perhaps the most familiar answer is that access to health care should not be based on ability to pay. This answer is in effect the one that unifies the views of Williams,

---

[9] According to Amy Gutmann, "A principle of equal access to health care demands that every person who shares the same type and degree of health need must be given an equally effective chance of receiving appropriate treatment of equal quality so long as that treatment is available to anyone." See 'For and Against Equal Access to Health Care' in S. Gorovitz, R. Macklin, A. Jameton, J. O'Connor, and S. Sherwin, editors, *Moral Problems in Medicine, 2nd edition* (Englewood Cliffs, NJ: Prentice-Hall, 1983), p. 558.

[10] See Margaret A. Somerville, editor, *Do We Care? Renewing Canada's Commitment to Health* (Montreal: McGill-Queen's University Press, 1999), and Lesley Jacobs, 'Universal Access to Health Care: For Whom? To What?,' *Literary Review of Canada* (November 1999), pp. 24–26.

[11] Dwayne Banks, Kimberly Kunz, and Tracy Macdonald, *Health Care Reform* (Berkeley, CA: Institute of Governmental Studies Press, University of California, Berkeley, 1994), p. 23.

Walzer, and Radin noted earlier. And since markets for goods are often structured on ability to pay, the markets for health care each rejects makes sense in that light. Their point, it seems, is that an individual should have access to health care, regardless of his or her socio-economic class, no matter whether the individual is rich or poor. Whatever its intuitive appeal, however, marginalizing ability to pay seems incapable of explaining universal access. Health care systems such as Canada's or Great Britain's, which achieve universal access, also retain ability-to-pay features. In Britain, there is of course a two-tier system in which the wealthier and those with private health care insurance can pay for health care outside the National Health Service. This certainly translates into quicker treatment, and quite likely better treatment. In Canada, this sort of two-tier system is forbidden by the Canada Health Act. But ability to pay plays a major role in goods and services not covered by the act such as prescription drugs, home care, and dental care. For instance, public spending accounts for only 35 percent of the total spent in Canada on drugs; the other 65 percent is paid for out-of-pocket by individuals or through private insurance plans.[12] Who enjoys access to these goods and services is therefore very much a matter of what particular individuals can afford to pay or what is covered by their private health care plan. Yet, despite the role ability to pay has in this system, there still seems to be no hesitation describing it as having achieved universal access.

My suggestion instead is that at its base, universal access to health care reflects the belief that individuals should not be in competition with each other for health care. What universal access to health care does is deny that health care is a prize for winners. Since everyone has access, nobody can be said to be a loser. By relying on the use of in-kind health care benefits that cannot be traded for cash or other goods, a scheme of universal access does not allow individual citizens to compete against each other for health care services and products. The broad non-partisan support for universal access to health care is evidence of how intuitively powerful is the view that health care is unsuitable for competition.[13]

The principle that health care should not be subject to competition is ironically both broader and more precise than the claim that health

---

[12] Armstrong, *Universal Health Care*, p. 100.

[13] In this chapter, I do not explain the normative foundations of universal access to health care; that is the topic of a different book. See my forthcoming book, *Canadian Health Care: Values, Rights, Law* (Vancouver, BC: University of British Columbia Press, Law & Society Series). My task here is merely to show that competitive models of equal opportunities cannot provide those foundations.

care allocation should not be subject to market forces. It provides a better explanation for why ability to pay is wrong. What is morally problematic about ability to pay is not the implied commodification of health care but rather the standard context in which ability to pay operates – for example, where prices are set so that buyers bid competitively against each other until the markets clear. This insight has significant implications for most public-supported health care systems. A standard debate is around the introduction of user-fees for some or all services. In Canada, for instance, under the terms of the Canada Health Act, user-fees for medically necessary services are illegal. Proponents of user-fees argue, however, that the legislation should be changed to allow for user-fees in order to increase funding in the system and reduce frivolous use of medical services. The main challenge they see is how to design user-fees so that the poor do not suffer disproportionately because of their inability to pay. Some defenders of the status quo, especially health care economists, have persuasively questioned the alleged beneficial effects of user-fees in health care.[14] Other defenders of the status quo have appealed, however, to a moral argument, saying that even with provisions to insulate the poor, user-fees require the commodification of health care, and for that reason are objectionable. My approach suggests that as long as user-fees do not entail competition for health care, they are not problematic on moral grounds. And it is that competition, as opposed to the commodification of health care, that should be avoided in reforms involving user fees.

7.3 TWO EGALITARIAN STRATEGIES

Thus far, I have tried to justify my view that health care should not be subject to competition by pointing out that it makes sense of the widespread commitment to universal access only if that view is assumed. The conclusion that health care is not to be distributed in competition is important because it means that the concept of equality of opportunity offers no insight into the regulation of a mechanism for allocating scarce health care goods and services between individuals.

The position I am taking may appear especially surprising because it is widely assumed that the commitment to universal access to health

---

[14] For a recent summary, see Rachel Grad, 'Health Care Reform in Canada: Is There Room for Efficiency?,' *Health Law in Canada, Vol. 20, no. 2* (November 1999), pp. 17–30.

care rests on egalitarian foundations. As Robert Veatch has put it, universal coverage "reflects egalitarian moral commitments that are deeply rooted in the American ethos no matter how unsuccessful efforts have been to operationalize that ethos."[15] Indeed, it is common sense to think that universal access to health care flows from some theory or other of distributional equality. And there have been some important attempts by philosophers to show this. I shall argue here that these attempts fail and that the common sense belief that universal access rests on egalitarian foundations is mistaken. This argument is structured to vindicate my general contention in this chapter that there are principled boundaries to the application of the three-dimensional model of equal opportunities as a regulative ideal. For if universal access to health care is a requirement of egalitarian justice, then it would be nonsense to insist, as I have, that that model of equality of opportunity should not be used to regulate health care allocation.

Broadly speaking, it is possible to distinguish two basic strategies that egalitarians have used to defend universal access to health care.[16] The first strategy (which I shall refer to as the *comprehensive strategy*) argues that distributional equality requires that each individual command an equal share of the resources in society, and included in that share is access to some minimal standard of health care. A proponent of this strategy must first offer a compelling general theory about what constitutes an equal share of the resources in a society and then show why universal access to health care flows from that general theory. The second strategy (the *restricted egalitarian strategy*) is not predicated on a general theory of distributional equality. It maintains instead that universal access to

---

[15] Robert Veatch, 'Single Payers and Multiple Lists: Must Everyone Get the Same Coverage on a Universal Health Plan?,' *Kennedy Institute of Ethics Journal*, Vol. 17, no. 2 (1997), p. 154.
[16] It could be said here that I ignore a third type of egalitarian strategy, one that appeals to some sort of Pareto principle. A powerful statement of this type of defence of universal access is made by Allan Gibbard, 'Health Care and the Prospective Pareto Principle' *Ethics* 94 (1984): 261–82. The pivotal question is whether a Pareto principle is in fact egalitarian. I shall not here answer that question in any serious sense. However, I am obviously sceptical that it is. And Gibbard, for example, assumes that the appropriate association is with utilitarianism, not egalitarianism. I suspect that the principal reason for associating Paretian principles with egalitarianism stems from Rawls' formulation and defence of the difference principle in *A Theory of Justice* (Cambridge, MA: Harvard University Press, 1971). Derek Parfit has put significant pressure on the close identification between distributional equality and giving priority to the least advantaged in his paper, 'Equality and Priority' in Andrew Mason, editor, *Ideals of Equality* (Oxford: Blackwell, 1998).

health care can be justified in a more restricted fashion on the grounds that it is necessary for equality of opportunity. This second strategy is especially relevant because of my efforts in this book to retrieve equal opportunities as a serious theory of egalitarian justice.

The main objection I shall press against both the comprehensive and the restricted egalitarian strategy for justifying universal access to health care is quite simple. The policy of universal access to health care involves providing people with health care coverage even if they would prefer that the money required to provide that coverage be spent on something else. In the terms I introduce later, the policy relies on in-kind benefits and does not allow citizens to sell or trade those benefits to others. This feature of the policy is difficult for egalitarians to justify. When they pursue a comprehensive strategy, egalitarians are hard pressed to explain why, when an individual would prefer something else of similar value, health care coverage should be part of his equal share of society's resources. When they pursue a restricted strategy, egalitarians cannot explain why equality of opportunity doesn't hold when every individual has the money to buy adequate health care insurance coverage; this scenario raises a problem because some individuals will in fact decide not to buy insurance, in which case there would not be universal access. In effect, what egalitarians can justify is making health care (insurance) affordable for all to buy if they want to, not making health care universally accessible.[17]

7.3.1 The Comprehensive Egalitarian Strategy

The comprehensive strategy for justifying universal access to health care on egalitarian grounds is predicated on a general theory of distributional equality. What is the best account of what constitutes for an individual an equal share of the advantages of social life? There is a wide range of competing theories that purport to answer this question. For our present purposes, I will concentrate on the prospects for justifying universal access to health care under Ronald Dworkin's general theory of distributional equality (which he calls "equality of resources") and try to draw from this analysis some general conclusions about the

---

[17] In this chapter, I ignore the complex issue of whether universal access is even compatible with a completely private health insurance market. For an argument that it is not, see Allen Buchanan, 'Privatization and Just Healthcare,' *Bioethics*, Vol. 9, no. 3/4 (1995), pp. 220–39.

likely prospects for any comprehensive strategy. Dworkin's theory, as we shall see, is similar to competitive theories of equality of opportunity insofar as it incorporates the idea of individuals' competing for scarce resources. It is singled out as important both because of its extraordinary influence in the past ten years and because recently Dworkin has brought his general insights on distributive justice to bear on questions about the distribution of health care. Keep in mind that I have already in Chapter 2 expressed my scepticism about comprehensive approaches to equality; I have suspended that scepticism here to pursue the more limited agenda of assessing the prospects for justifying universal access to health care.

Although Dworkin's work on political morality has been innovative in many different respects, there are two claims that he has advanced that are especially important and central to his egalitarian vision of a just society. The first claim is that despite many deeply rooted disagreements among contemporary political philosophers, there is nonetheless a consensus around the principle that is foundational to all political morality in a democratic society. This principle, which Dworkin calls the abstract egalitarian principle, says: "Government must act to make the lives of those it governs better lives, and it must show equal concern for the life of each."[18] For Dworkin, this abstract egalitarian principle reflects a platitude among philosophers and public officials, and disagreements arise principally over how to interpret it. The second claim has a central place in his particular interpretation of the abstract egalitarian principle. Specifically, Dworkin maintains that in order for a government to show equal concern for the life of each of those it governs, it must design a mechanism that distributes privately owned resources in a manner that treats each individual as an equal, and to do so it must be sensitive to the different ambitions, goals, and choices of each individual. This requirement, which I will explain in more depth later, Dworkin terms "ambition-sensitivity." I will show that Dworkin's interpretation of the abstract egalitarian principle, and especially the requirement of ambition-sensitivity, is incompatible with a policy of universal access to health care. After arguing that Dworkin is unable to justify universal access to health care, I shall suggest why his failure may have important

---

[18] Ronald Dworkin, 'What Is Equality? Part 3: The Place of Liberty,' *Iowa Law Review*, Vol. 72 (1987), p. 7. For similar statements, see *Taking Rights Seriously* (Cambridge, MA: Harvard University Press, 1978), pp. 182–83, and especially his essay 'Liberalism' in *A Matter of Principle*, pp. 191–92.

implications for any comprehensive egalitarian strategy for justifying universal access.

7.3.2 *Equality of Resources*

For Dworkin, the primacy of the abstract egalitarian principle is significant because it narrows in an important respect the scope of competing theories of distributive justice. It suggests that the central feature of a mechanism for distributing privately held resources in a just society is that it treat all individuals as equals. An individual has command over an equal share of the advantages of social life precisely when a distributional scheme treats him or her as an equal. Equality of resources is Dworkin's particular theory about when a distributional scheme treats an individual as an equal. The issue that concerns me is how well Dworkin's theory of equality of resources can accommodate a policy of universal access to health care. Before turning to that issue, however, it is necessary first to explain briefly the main ideas of his theory of equality of resources, including especially the requirement of ambition-sensitivity.[19]

At the core of Dworkin's theory of distributive justice is the distinction between an individual's personality and his or her circumstances. Among the features of an individual's personality, Dworkin includes those such as convictions, ambitions, tastes, and preferences. An individual's circumstances include his or her resources, talents and skills, and physical and mental capacities.[20] The peculiarity of including talents, skills, and capacities among an individual's circumstances rather

---

[19] For a much more detailed critical examination of Dworkin's theory of distributional justice, see Lesley Jacobs, *Rights and Deprivation* (Oxford: Oxford University Press, 1993), ch. 5.

[20] R. Dworkin, 'What Is Equality? Part 2: Equality of Resources,' *Philosophy & Public-Affairs* 10 (1981): 283–345, p. 302, and 'What Is Equality? Part 3: The Place of Liberty,' pp. 18–19. Both of these papers have been reprinted in Ronald Dworkin, *Sovereign Virtue: The Theory and Practice of Equality* (Cambridge, MA: Harvard University Press, 2000). Page references are to the original. Note that Dworkin sometimes expresses this distinction in terms of the contrast between a person and his or her circumstances. G.A. Cohen in 'On the Currency of Egalitarian Justice' argues that Dworkin has misdescribed this crucial cut, and that the correct one should be between choices and brute bad luck [*Ethics* 99 (1989): 906–944; see especially pp. 916–44]. This relocation does not have any serious implications for my later argument. For Dworkin's responses to this criticism, see 'Foundations of Liberal Equality,' *The Tanner Lectures on Human Values* 11 (1991): 106–10, and especially *Sovereign Virtue*, pp. 287–99.

than as features of his or her personality will be discussed later. According to Dworkin, a distributional scheme treats an individual as an equal when no further economic transfer would leave him or her with circumstances more equal to those of any other individual. Equality of resources says, in others words, that shares are equal when people's circumstances are equal.

But this raises, in turn, the question of just when people's circumstances are equal. A basic axiom of Dworkin's position is this: Equality of resources is concerned fundamentally with the share of resources devoted to the whole life of an individual.[21] People are treated as equals when their share of resources across their lives as a whole is equal. The guiding principle for determining what constitutes equal circumstances builds on this basic axiom. It requires that any distributive scheme be sensitive to the cost of each person's life to other people. That cost is to be measured by how valuable the resources and other elements of circumstances consumed – interpreted broadly to suggest also use, and so on – by that person are to those other people. Dworkin terms this cost the "opportunity cost" of one's life. Clearly, though, people will choose to do different things with their initial circumstances. These differences will reflect their personalities. One person might prefer to use his or her resources to produce something; someone else might prefer only to consume. The first person will over time come to have more resources than the second. But this does not mean that he or she would have been treated as less than an equal. Provided that each is equal in the circumstances devoted to the whole of their lives, the differences resulting from differences in personality do not undermine their having equal shares. It is in this sense that we might say that equality of resources is "personality-sensitive," or, to use Dworkin's preferred expression, "ambition-sensitive."[22]

If we accept, as Dworkin suggests, that distributional equality be ambition-sensitive, what then is the best way to distribute resources? What is the best way to measure opportunity costs? This role is assigned, in the first instance, to the economic market for goods. An illustration of how it determines opportunity costs is provided by Dworkin. Imagine the situation of a group of shipwrecked survivors washed up on a desert island with an abundance of resources. The issue is how to distribute equally those resources that are to be privately owned. Some form of

---

[21] Dworkin, 'Equality of Resources,' p. 310.
[22] *Ibid.*, pp. 333, 338.

auction or market is proposed. (This demonstrates clearly Dworkin's commitment to utilizing competition to achieve egalitarian justice.) One basic requirement is that all of the shipwrecked immigrants enter the market on equal terms.[23] This requirement is met, in the first instance, if everyone has the same number of "counters" to be used for bidding in the auction. The most difficult task is proposing a set of prices at which the resources will be sold. The person who has this task must post a set of prices that "clear the markets." Technically, this requires that only one person among the bidders be willing to pay the price for each resource, and that all resources are sold. The importance of price-setting in this way is that it determines how valuable each resource is to other people. We have, then, a way of measuring opportunity costs. Of course, if one is the buyer of a resource at the price of x counters, this means that one has fewer counters to buy other resources. The consequent bundle of resources each person has after the successful run of the auction where everyone has spent all of his or her counters would constitute an equal share.[24]

After the initial auction, the markets will stay open. This presents a problem for Dworkin's ideal of distributional equality. Everyone, it was presumed, entered the auction as equals if each had the same number of counters. Clearly, however, people do not have identical endowments and capacities; some will have physical or mental handicaps; others will have highly valued talents and skills. Recall that Dworkin includes talents and capacities among the circumstances that equality of resources seeks to equalize. Wouldn't this mean that people would not be entering the market as equals? The problem is that because talents and handicaps cannot be transferred among persons, they cannot be bid for in the auction like other sorts of more contingent goods.[25]

How then can the compensation paid to those who suffer from handicaps and other forms of under-endowment be "ambition-sensitive"? Dworkin's innovative solution to this problem is to have, operating alongside the economic market for transferable goods, a progressive income tax scheme modelled on a hypothetical insurance market, in which people are imagined to have insured themselves against being

---

[23] *Ibid.*, p. 289.
[24] This is a slight over-simplification, since it downplays Dworkin's emphasis on the "Envy Test." For a criticism of Dworkin's reliance on (Walrusian) market theory in this context, see Jonathan Bennett, 'Ethics and Markets,' *Philosophy & PublicAffairs* 14 (1985), especially pp. 199–204.
[25] Dworkin, "The Place of Liberty," p. 18n19.

handicapped or untalented. Although Dworkin's sketch of this insurance market is very complex, the basic idea that informs it is simple. Imagine that people pay an insurance premium against being handicapped or untalented based on how much each disvalues suffering from a specific handicap or being untalented in some respect. If a person turns out to suffer from a disadvantage that he or she would have been insured against, then the insurance scheme will compensate him or her accordingly, although at a level that reflects how many other people are also entitled to compensation. The device is "ambition-sensitive" because the coverage provided by the hypothetical insurance market is supposed to reflect the actual value each person places on not having a certain talent or suffering from a certain handicap in view of the opportunity costs to others.

7.3.3 *The Place of Health Care*

We are now in a position to focus our attention on Dworkin's comprehensive egalitarian strategy for justifying universal access to health care. Can his theory of equality of resources provide the normative foundations for such a policy? Dworkin has in fact written a pair of articles that explicitly address problems about justice in the distribution of health care from the perspective of equality of resources.[26] Specifically, Dworkin tries to show how the main ideas of that general theory of distributive justice, and especially the idea of ambition-sensitivity, shine light on two pressing issues about health care distribution in countries such as the United States, Canada, and Britain. How much should a society as a whole spend on health care? How, in turn, should the amount to be spent on health care be rationed in terms of who should receive health care and what forms of health care should be provided?

Dworkin defends what he calls the "prudent insurance" approach to health care distribution. The core of this approach is the following principle:

A just distribution [of health care] is one that well-informed people create for themselves by individual choices, provided that the economic system and the

---

[26] Ronald Dworkin, 'Justice in the Distribution of Health Care,' *McGill Law Journal* 38 (1993): 883–98, and 'Will Clinton's Plan Be Fair?,' *New York Review of Books*, 13 January 1994, pp. 20–25. The latter has been reprinted with slight revisions in *Sovereign Virtue*, ch. 8.

distribution of health in the community in which these choices are made are themselves just.[27]

What Dworkin is getting at is that how much a just society should spend on health care is simply an aggregate of what individuals in that society would spend. In other words, social decisions about health care spending should be a function of what individuals would in just circumstances spend. The point is that because spending on health care means that there is less money to spend on other valuable goods, the decision about exactly how much should be spent on health care ought to reflect how important health care is to particular individuals. The main idea is that health care spending is principally a matter of individual responsibility. Against a background where there is a fair initial distribution of resources, and information about the effectiveness and costs of particular health care procedures is widely known, each individual should be responsible for deciding how much to spend on health care based on how important he or she considers health care by comparison with other goods that he or she might acquire.

The prudent insurance approach to justice in the distribution of health care is entirely consistent with, and indeed flows from, Dworkin's more comprehensive theory of equality of resources. The basic theme is that the distribution of health care must be ambition-sensitive in the sense that how much we spend on health care and which medical procedures we pay for must be sensitive to the particular ambitions, preference orderings, lifeplans, tastes, and commitments of each person. Introducing ambition-sensitivity into the distribution of health care is significant not only because it allows us to treat social choices about health care spending as an aggregate of individual choices, but also because it makes individuals directly responsible for the cost of the health care they receive.

The approach Dworkin takes to justice in the distribution of health care is especially insightful when it comes to hard choices about rationing health care spending – that is to say, deciding which medical procedures should be funded and which should not. His view is that

---

[27] Dworkin, 'Will Clinton's Plan Be Fair?,' p. 23. Note, however, that Dworkin qualifies this principle in what he regards as two minors respects: (1) Some measures may be necessary to protect people from making imprudent choices, especially when they are young, and (2) measures may be necessary to protect future generations. See 'Will Clinton's Plan Be Fair?,' p. 23 n. 12, and 'Justice in the Distribution of Health Care,' p. 889–90n3.

these choices are best made when individuals are required to bear the true costs of their choices in the sense that when individuals are choosing whether or not a particular medical procedure should be funded, their choice is going to affect their access to other valuable goods and opportunities, such as, for example, going on a particular holiday or acquiring a new car.

In my view, Dworkin's discussion of health care distribution is noteworthy not only because it makes the case for applying the idea of ambition-sensitivity to problems having to do with just health care, but also because it fails to extend his innovative idea of hypothetical insurance markets in skills and handicaps to the realm of health care distribution.[28] This latter feature is surprising because differences between individuals in terms of ill health would seem to pose a threat to equal circumstances in exactly the same way that differences in skills and handicaps do, since they too seem to be in most cases instances of brute bad luck.[29] Hence the case for redistribution to mitigate for this threat would seem to be identical. Moreover, it seems that this kind of extension of his argument is essential to explain any sort of health care policy that has a redistributive character.

Recall that for Dworkin, equality of resources requires that people be equal in their circumstances, and that an individual's circumstances include talents and skills, and physical and mental capacities. Presumably, too, the logic of Dworkin's distinction between personality and circumstances is such that ill health not engendered by personal choice would also be included in an individual's circumstances. In other words, the state of an individual's health should be taken seriously in the effort to make people equal in their circumstances. The practical difficulty is that, like skills and handicaps, health is a nontransferable resource – it cannot be bought and sold in a market.

How should an egalitarian respond to the unequal circumstances that arise because of ill health? Presumably, for Dworkin, the best way to approach the problem is through his device of hypothetical insurance

---

[28] He indicates sympathy with this idea, however, on p. 43 of 'What Is Equality?, Part 3: The Place of Liberty.'

[29] Whilst it seems obvious that there is a parallel in terms of brute luck between, on the one hand the allocation of talents and skills, and health, on the other hand, it has sometimes been suggested that there is some sort of relevant moral difference. For example, Thomas Nagel in *Equality and Impartiality* (New York: Oxford University Press, 1991), pp. 103–4, maintains such a view, but it is a mystery to me what his grounds are for the distinction.

markets. Imagine that people pay an insurance premium against the costs of health care based on how much each disvalues suffering specific forms of ill health, where everyone is uncertain about the particular details of his health over his lifetime. If an individual turns out to suffer from a form of ill health that he or she would have insured against, then the insurance scheme will in theory compensate him or her accordingly. This approach to the problem of health distribution is "ambition-sensitive" because the coverage provided by the hypothetical insurance market is supposed to reflect the actual value each person places on not suffering from a particular form of ill health by comparison with other goods and opportunities he or she values.

How would this hypothetical insurance market approach to addressing the unequal circumstances created by ill health translate into a concrete health care program? What would such a program look like? Certainly, such a program would necessarily be redistributive in the sense that some people would have to pay more towards the funding of such a health care program than they would require in actual health care, and others less. In other words, implementing a health care scheme modelled on Dworkin's hypothetical insurance markets requires (indirect) redistributive transfers from certain individuals to other individuals. This is not a surprising conclusion, since Dworkin has shown how the use of hypothetical insurance markets in skills and handicaps can be translated into a progressive income tax system that is redistributive in character. The relevant issue for our purposes is whether or not this health care program will guarantee universal access to health care.

I shall now introduce a distinction that must be given careful attention in an examination of the problem of justifying universal access to health care. Recall from the previous chapter that redistribution is ordinarily pursued through what economists and public policy analysts call "redistributive transfers." Redistributive transfers can be either in-kind or cash. Benefits, as I shall use the term, denote particular *in-kind* or *cash* transfers. In-kind redistributive transfers involve the transfer of specific goods in some form or another. The central point is that a policy of universal access to health care involves the use of in-kind transfers and does not allow citizens to trade-off health care benefits for cash or other goods. In-kind benefits other than health care include education, housing, and food stamps. These differ from benefits in cash. Typical cash benefits are child benefits, tax credits, social assistance, unemployment insurance, disability insurance, and social security pensions. This type of benefit leaves it up to the recipient to decide what to spend the cash on. For the operation of cash redistributive transfers, it is obviously necessary for there to be economic markets that allow people to buy goods with their cash benefits.[30]

It is my view that most discussions of justice in the distribution of health care have paid insufficient attention to the fact that a successful justification of universal access to health care must make the case not just for a redistributive health care policy, but more specifically for the use of in-kind rather than cash transfers with their attendant restrictions on trading the benefit for cash or some other benefit. The relevant questions for our purposes are: Can Dworkin's hypothetical insurance market in health care justify the use of in-kind redistributive transfers? Can his approach to justice in health care be translated into a system in which everyone will be guaranteed some minimal standard of health care?

My argument that Dworkin is unable to justify universal access to health care will now proceed through two steps. First, I will advance the claim that Dworkin's theory of equality of resources – because of its insistence on the requirement of ambition-sensitivity – is compatible with the use of cash transfers but is generally incompatible with the use of in-kind transfers. This is what can be described as Dworkin's *prima facie* case for the use of cash transfers. Second, I will examine three cases in which there appear to be good grounds within Dworkin's theory of distributive justice for using in-kind transfers, and show why they do not have any bearing on the problem of justifying universal access to health care. The upshot of this argument is that Dworkin's comprehensive egalitarian strategy is unable to justify the existence of a policy of universal access to health care.

The main pillar of Dworkin's theory of equality of resources is this: The determination of equal shares requires that all people be treated as equals, and as such be ambition-sensitive. In other words, a person's share of resources must reflect his or her personality-preferences, goals, ambitions, and the cost to others. I have emphasized earlier how, for Dworkin, the market is the distributional mechanism that meets these requirements. In the desert island example, each person was provided with some counters with which he or she could bid for the various resources on offer. In actual markets, cash has very much the same function

---

[30] To sustain the distinction between *cash* and *in-kind* transfers, it is absolutely essential that in-kind benefits not be exchangeable. See R.A. Musgrave and P.B. Musgrave, *Public Finance in Theory and Practice, 3rd edition* (New York: McGraw-Hill, 1980), p. 103n19.

as Dworkin's counters. We can use it to buy goods in those markets. In effect, then, the initial allocation of counters on the desert island is like a cash transfer in the real world.

The *prima facie* case for cash redistributive transfers rests on the claim that any other type of transfer would result in not everyone's being treated as an equal. The virtue of cash is that it is able to track the relative value each person places on having command over some resources rather than others. Cash transfers are inherently ambition-sensitive. To put it another way, cash benefits conform to what Dworkin calls "the principle of abstraction." The principle of abstraction holds that any distributive scheme that purports to treat individuals as equals must maximize the freedom individuals have to do what they wish.[31] The attraction of cash for Dworkin is precisely that it allows people to buy whatever they want. The relevant contrast is with in-kind benefits, which do set considerable constraints on how they can be used.

The general incompatibility I am suggesting between Dworkin's requirement of ambition-sensitivity and the use of in-kind transfers can be illustrated more clearly through an example. Consider the case of someone who has, through bad luck, contracted a serious illness. An operation can be performed that will treat this illness. Suppose that the patient is a citizen in a state that operates a health care scheme that guarantees universal access and that the operation in question will be covered under this scheme. But the ill person is peculiar because he says that he would spend the money on something else, some good he values more than health care. (It is easy to imagine, at present, an AIDS patient saying precisely this sort of thing – he would prefer to have certain resources in cash so that he could use it to do things in life he had always wanted to do instead of spending it on expensive medical equipment designed to prolong his life.) Why shouldn't the health care scheme compensate him in this form rather than by paying for the operation? For an egalitarian concerned with the requirement of ambition-sensitivity, it seems only logical that if the normative foundations for the health care scheme rest on distributional equality, then it does make sense to compensate the patient with whatever he values the most, whether that be health care or some other good with the equivalent cash value.[32] In that case,

---

[31] Dworkin, 'The Place of Liberty,' pp. 25, 28.

[32] It is interesting to note here that Dworkin himself makes a similar argument in *Sovereign Virtue* as to why a scheme of universal access should provide a minimal rather than an expansive amount of coverage for medical services and products.

however, the health care scheme should cease to operate through an in-kind transfer. Instead, it should compensate with cash transfers that would allow recipients to make their own choices about the value of health care relative to other goods. But then we would no longer have a health care scheme that guarantees universal access.[33]

My analysis so far has been designed to establish, on the one hand, that a *prima facie* commitment to cash transfers flows from the requirement of ambition-sensitivity and, on the other hand, that there is a general incompatibility between the requirement of ambition-sensitivity and the use of in-kind transfers. While Dworkin might concede that this analysis of his theory of distributional equality reveals a *prima facie* commitment to cash transfers, he might nevertheless resist the conclusion that equality of resources never allows for the use of in-kind transfers. It seems that equality of resources can make room for three possible egalitarian grounds for in-kind transfers: (1) efficiency, (2) externalities, (3) superficial paternalism. While considering these grounds in turn, the issue I want to keep in clear sight is whether any of these is capable of justifying the sort of in-kind redistribution involved in the provision of universal access to health care.

Unlike many of those who are committed to equality, Dworkin denies that this commitment requires a trade-off between equality and efficiency. His argument can be summarized briefly.[34] The basic metric for measuring when individuals each have an equal share of resources is, as we saw earlier, what Dworkin terms "opportunity costs." Opportunity costs reflect how much others value a resource that someone else

In his view, a more expansive scheme would be imposed on some people who might not want it, and this would be unjust. Instead, he says, "it seems fair to construct a mandatory coverage scheme on the basis of assumptions about what all but a small number of people would think appropriate, allowing those few who would be willing to spend more on special care to do so, they can afford it, through supplemental insurance," p. 315.

[33] This also holds against other versions of the comprehensive strategy such as that pursued by Eric Rakowski in *Equal Justice* (Oxford: Oxford University Press, 1991). Rakowski, unlike Dworkin, is explicit that his main commitment as an egalitarian is to making health care affordable for all, not universally accessible: "So long as people had an equal opportunity and the rational capacity to devote some portion of their personal holdings to measures designed to allay possible misfortunes [of illness and injury], they could not later complain, if they neglected to look ahead, that they were treated unjustly if equality were not restored once the lightning had struck," p. 89.

[34] Dworkin, 'Why Efficiency'?,' in *A Matter of Principle*, pp. 267–73. This view is also defended in a different way by Julian Le Grand, 'Equity versus Efficiency: The Elusive Trade-off,' *Ethics* 100 (1990): 554–68.

has. Efficiency is principally a matter of maximizing social wealth or the total resources available in a society. It follows that the value of efficiency can be measured in terms of opportunity costs. Greater efficiency may have a detrimental effect on some people by, for example, denying to them certain resources that would otherwise have been available. But improved efficiency would increase the total resources available in society and, as a result, make bigger the resource shares of others. The point is that deciding whether or not to promote efficiency in a particular instance requires the balancing of these opportunity costs. Although in some cases, this balancing might work against efficiency, it is likely that in most cases, the opportunity costs of those who benefit from efficiency will outweigh those who lose from it. Therefore, equality of resources will favor improved efficiency in those cases. There is not, then, an inevitable trade-off between distributional equality and efficiency.

The fact that Dworkin is able to defend improved efficiency on egalitarian grounds may seem directly relevant to the provision of health care. After all, many of the debates over the provision of health care revolve around issues of efficiency. There is at present, for example, some powerful evidence to suggest that the Canadian system of health care provision is much more efficient than the existing American model.[35] But for our purposes it is important to note that these efficiency arguments generally only establish a case for why the state should coordinate the delivery of health care; they do not directly establish the efficiency of universal access. The basic argument noted here for cash benefits is that they are the only sort of transfer that treats people as equals. The idea is that a health care benefit, for example, does not treat as an equal someone who would prefer something else over health care. Logically it would make sense under equality of resources to provide all people with cash benefits that they could then at their own discretion use to buy health care insurance coverage, perhaps from an HMO or the state.

Efficiency considerations would enter into the debate when determining how much cash would be involved in such a transfer. If, for example, the state was able to provide coverage at a premium of $1,200 compared with $2,000 by private firms, the appropriate level of cash benefit would seem to be $1,200. Indeed, assuming that the preference structure of individuals such as our AIDS patient is an exception, it might even make

[35] See, e.g., Theodore L. Marmor, Jerry L. Mashaw, and Philip L. Harvey, *America's Misunderstood Welfare State: Persistent Myths, Enduring Realities* (New York: Basic Books, 1990), ch. 6, and Armstrong, *Universal Health Care*, ch. 6.

sense to provide everyone, in the first instance, with health care benefits under a state-administered scheme with an opting-out clause that allows an individual to withdraw from the scheme and receive instead the cash equivalent of that benefit. Of course, given the effects that his or her opting out may have on the economies-of-scale benefits that derive from a state-administered health care scheme, it might even be the case that the cash benefit ends up being slightly less than the market exchange value of the health care coverage from which he or she opts out. The important point is that an argument for providing universal health care benefits cannot be based on weighing up the opportunity costs of this sort of benefit by comparison with cash benefits, since the level of cash benefits can be set so as to offset any costs of providing them rather than in-kind benefits.

Another way Dworkin might try to defend universal access to health care is on the grounds that when it comes to the provision of health care, market pricing mechanisms are inadequate because of the externalities that occur because of imperfect information or knowledge. And Dworkin maintains that the freedom of choice required by the principle of abstraction can be limited in such a case.[36] The point is that given the existence of externalities in the case of health care, it might be appropriate to make distributive transfers less ambition-sensitive and provide individuals with in-kind health benefits instead of cash. The classical argument against having markets in health care has been made by Kenneth Arrow.[37] As Arrow points out, prospective patients do not have sufficient knowledge to make decisions about treatment, referral, or hospitalization and thus to judge between competing sellers of health care services. This means that the market-pricing mechanism ceases to be an accurate way to track how people would prefer to have health care resources allocated. Arrow's concern is with people who want health care but lack the knowledge required to make informed choices about the type of health care they want. Nonetheless, while it might make sense to have experts making decisions about the sort of health care a patient should receive, it goes against the very core of Dworkin's egalitarianism to say that individuals are not their own best judges of whether or

---

[36] Dworkin, 'The Place of Liberty,' pp. 32–33, Note too that an important part of Dworkin's introduction of the idea of prudent insurers into the health care distribution debate is conditional on individual insurers' not suffering from imperfect information or knowledge.

[37] Kenneth Arrow, 'Uncertainty and the Welfare Economics of Medical Care,' *American Economic Review* 53 (1963), pp. 946, 951n, and esp. 965–66.

not they value health care over other non-medical goods. My point is that while individuals may lack the knowledge to make an informed choice between competing health care providers, there is not a parallel information problem when we are considering whether an individual values health care more or less than other (non-medical) goods that he or she could buy with the same amount of cash. Yet it is precisely this sort of information problem that is required to warrant, on egalitarian grounds, an in-kind health care benefit rather than a cash one.

The final way in which Dworkin might try to defend in-kind health care benefits and therefore universal access to health care is on the grounds of what he calls "superficial" paternalism – "forcing people to take precautions that are reasonable within their own structure of preferences."[38] It might be argued that many of the people who will choose to spend their cash on something other than health care are experiencing some form of *akrasis*, or weakness of will. And in these cases, the superficial paternalism involved in providing an in-kind health care benefit instead of simply cash is warranted: Quite clearly, such transfers would treat people as equals, since by definition they are "ambition-sensitive." The problem is that in the case of the AIDS patient who would prefer some resource other than health care, we cannot justify providing him or her with health care on the grounds of superficial paternalism, since the provision of health care does not reflect his or her own structure of preferences – he or she is not suffering from *akrasis*. In other words, while superficial paternalism might warrant providing health care benefits in some instances, it is unable to justify the use of in-kind health care benefits in all instances – which is what is presupposed by universal access to health care.

7.3.4 *The General Prospects for the Comprehensive Strategy*

So far, I have shown that it is not possible for Dworkin to reconcile a commitment to ambition-sensitivity with the necessary use of in-kind benefits under a policy of universal access to health care. The upshot is that his comprehensive egalitarian strategy for justifying universal access to health care is a failure. What does this failure suggest for the prospects of other egalitarians who might pursue the comprehensive strategy? It depends on just how central the requirement of ambition-sensitivity is to a general theory of distributional equality. There have been certain very

---

[38] Dworkin, 'Foundations of Liberal Equality,' p. 85.

influential general theories of distributional equality that have not emphasized the importance of ambition-sensitivity. Presumably, for these theories, it may not be that difficult to justify universal access to health care. But, as I have indicated in Chapter 2, general egalitarian theories that neglect ambition-sensitivity and individual responsibility are now often dismissed for precisely that reason. The power and influence of Dworkin's theory of equality of resources derives in large part from the fact that it demands that equal shares be determined in a manner that is ambition-sensitive. And the important role Dworkin assigns to competition, especially in auctions, is closely linked to his concern with ambition-sensitivity and individual responsibility. What I am getting at is that there is a dilemma facing egalitarians attracted to the comprehensive strategy: On the one hand, the requirement of ambition-sensitivity makes it difficult to justify universal access to health care; on the other hand, a general theory of distributional equality seems to have to take seriously the requirement of ambition-sensitivity. My view is that we should avoid the dilemma altogether by turning to a model of equality of opportunity that is not comprehensive and general but instead functions as a regulative ideal on competitions for scarce resources while recognizing the pluralist character of social justice.

7.3.5 The Restricted Egalitarian Strategy

We have just seen that Dworkin's comprehensive egalitarian strategy for justifying universal access to health care fails because the requirement of ambition-sensitivity generally demands the use of cash transfers rather than in-kind transfers. As I noted, however, the comprehensive strategy is not the only one that has been employed by egalitarians concerned to justify universal access to health care. What I described as the restricted strategy is an alternative egalitarian strategy that defends universal access to health care on the grounds that this degree of access is a requirement of equality of opportunity.

It is important to distinguish between at least two different versions of the restricted egalitarian strategy. One version (the *equal benefit* version), which has been advanced in different ways by John Harris,[39]

---

[39] John Harris, 'What Is the Good of Health Care?,' *Bioethics*, Vol. 10, no. 4 (1996), 269–91, and 'Justice and Equal Opportunities in Health Care,' *Bioethics*, Vol. 13, no. 5 (1999), pp. 392–413.

Thomas Pogge,[40] and Robert Veatch,[41] says in effect that every individual should have the same amount of money to spend on insurance coverage for health care, and provided that this holds, then equality of opportunity for health care holds. The other version of the restricted egalitarian strategy that concerns me has been elaborated with considerable care and sophistication by Norman Daniels.[42] This version begins with John Rawls' idea of fair equality of opportunity, as discussed in Chapter 2, and its application to education and extends the insight to health care. Neither version of the restricted egalitarian strategy can in the end justify universal access to health care.

7.3.6 The Equal Benefit Version of the Restricted Strategy

For many egalitarians, a just health care system should provide equal benefits for all, and in this way guarantee universal access. This strategy for justifying universal access is restricted because, unlike Dworkin, who envisions equality of all resources, its proponents do not commit themselves to any sort of comprehensive view of distributional equality.

Consider, for instance, the approach taken by Robert Veatch. He claims:

In the case of a universal, single-payer health care system, it seems that the reasonable and appropriate goal should be to give everyone access to benefits that the average consumer of health care could purchase for a fixed dollar amount. Thus, in our present health care climate, a fixed premium of $3000–$4000 per family per year would probably constitute a decent basic level of coverage.[43]

The important innovation Veatch introduces is that a single-payer system such as this could allow for a multitude of lists of basic covered services rather than the commonly assumed single list of covered services. His point is that individuals could use the fixed dollar amount – the

---

[40] Thomas Pogge, *Realizing Rawls* (Ithaca: Cornell University Press, 1989), pp. 181–96. I have criticized Pogge in considerable depth elsewhere; my criticisms of his position are tangential to the main theme of this chapter. See Lesley Jacobs, 'Can an Egalitarian Justify Universal Access to Health Care?,' *Social Theory and Practice*, Vol. 22, no. 3 (Fall 1996), pp. 338–44.

[41] Robert Veatch, 'Single Payers and Multiple Lists: Must Everyone Get the Same Coverage on a Universal Health Plan?,' pp. 153–69.

[42] Norman Daniels, *Just Health Care* (New York: Cambridge University Press, 1985); *Am I My Parents' Keeper* (New York: Oxford University Press, 1988); and *Justice and Justification: Reflective Equilibrium in Theory and Practice* (New York: Cambridge University Press, 1996).

[43] Veatch, 'Single Payers and Multiple Lists,' p. 160.

$3,000–$4,000 per family – to choose between the different lists. Although Veatch identifies some core services on all of the lists, he envisions considerable differences between them, especially regarding controversial services or those targeted only at certain groups of people. Some lists would include, for instance, chiropractor services or blood transfusions; others might include abortions or prenatal care. Veatch argues that egalitarians should favour multiple lists rather than a single list under a policy of universal access on the grounds that only in this way will everyone be treated as an equal. In his view, any attempt to draw a list of basic covered medical services will rely on a normative judgement about what is important and valuable. In a society where people hold to diverse and pluralistic values, it seems inevitable that a single list will favour some people over others. "[A]ny single list of basic covered services cannot," reasons Veatch, "provide equal treatment if equality is somehow related to opportunities to obtain benefit. Such a list will give those closest to the list makers the most value they could get from the funds invested in health care."[44] And those at the margins will get much less value and benefit from a single list. Only by allowing multiple lists of basic covered medical services that reflect the diverse normative judgements of all can unequal treatment be avoided.

The problem with Veatch's argument is that the same reasoning undermines the very policy of universal access to health care. His concern is with those individuals who will suffer unequal treatment because of single lists of covered services. His prescription is for individuals or households to have the choice to use their fixed dollar benefit to buy a level of health care coverage from a multitude of lists that reflect the diverse normative views of one's society. Yet, as I stressed in my criticism of the comprehensive strategy, it is likely that there will be some individuals who would prefer that the benefit be spent on something other than health care entirely. Wouldn't Veatch have to concede that forcing them to use the fixed dollar benefit to purchase health care coverage, even when there are multiple lists, constitutes unequal treatment?

A similar problem arises for the egalitarian approach to health care defended by John Harris. Harris is an advocate of what he calls equal opportunities in health care, which holds that

any system of prioritisation of the resources available for healthcare or for rationing such resources must be governed by . . . the principle that each individual

44 Veatch, 'Single Payers and Multiple Lists,' p. 159.

is entitled to an equal opportunity to benefit from any public health care system, and that this entitlement is proportionate neither to the size or their chance of benefitting, nor to the quality of the benefit, nor to the length of lifetime remaining in which that benefit may be enjoyed.[45]

The provocative implication of Harris's principle is that two of the standard bases for rationing health care – age and the likelihood of success of treatment – are unfair. Decision-making processes that rely on these bases are, in his view, practicing *de facto discrimination*.[46] They deny equal opportunities to health care to older patients and those with poor prospects. "A denial of equal opportunities is *a slap in the face*," charges Harris. "It is an existential rejection disproportionate to the value of the good or welfare that the opportunity might have afforded."[47] Thus, he urges, "the keeping open of opportunities is expressive of, and recognises that the person's objectives (whatever they are – however trivial or important) matter . . . the denial of them is a rejection of equality and therefore an affront to human dignity."[48] As with the theories of Dworkin and Veatch, the puzzle is how Harris, as an egalitarian, can then try to justify to the individual who would prefer the cash to spend on something why he or she must receive the in-kind benefit required by a policy of universal access to health care. Isn't this requirement, by Harris's own reasoning, a slap in the face of the hypothetical AIDS patient, considered above, who would rather go to Paris?

7.3.7 *Daniels's Version of the Restricted Strategy*

The most sophisticated and elaborate account of how equality of opportunity can be utilized in accounts of health care allocation has been developed by Norman Daniels. The account Daniels defends is multifaced and involves complex dimensions that are far outside the reach of the present discussion. My description of that account is necessarily selective in its emphasis but nonetheless accurate.

The central insight Daniels builds upon is that the logic of John Rawls's argument for fair equality of opportunity over formal equality of opportunity, as it was discussed in Chapter 2, entails not simply

---

[45] Harris, 'Justice and Equal Opportunities in Health Care,' pp. 392–93.
[46] John Harris, 'What Is the Good of Health Care?,' *Bioethics*, Vol. 10, no. 4 (1996), pp. 281–82.
[47] Harris, 'Justice and Equal Opportunities in Health Care,' p. 399. Emphasis added.
[48] *Ibid.*, pp. 399–400.

a concern for mitigating against the influence of socio-economic class on one's chances of success, but also a concern for those who suffer the bad luck of ill health. The basic idea is that since ill health is as arbitrary as the socio-economic class into which one is born, and also can have a major effect on one's life chances, it too should be remedied for as a background condition for fair equality of opportunity. "The moral *function* of the health care system must be," says Daniels, "to help guarantee fair equality of opportunity."[49] Rawls himself (prior to his recent death) endorsed Daniels's reasoning.[50]

In his development of a theory of just health care based on this insight, Daniels appeals to two fundamental ideas. The first is a biomedical model of health that identifies disease and illness as deviations from what he terms "species-typical normal functioning."[51] This model assumes some sort of theoretical account of what is normal human functioning, and makes health contingent on that account. That level of functioning forms a baseline for people to function as human beings abstracted from their individual differences. For Daniels, "A central, unifying function of health care is to maintain and restore functioning that is typical or normal for our species."[52] Health care services to treat or prevent illness and disease can thus be viewed as keeping people functioning normally. The other idea is the "normal opportunity range." This, explains Daniels, "for a given society is the array of life plans reasonable persons in it are likely to construct for themselves."[53] The particular make-up of this range will depend on historical factors such as the technical development of the society, its wealth, culture, and so on.

Daniels links these two idea in the following way:

Normal species functioning provides us with one clear parameter affecting the share of the normal range open to a given individual. It is this parameter which the distribution of health care affects. The share of the normal range open to an individual is also determined in a fundamental way by his talents and skills. Fair equality of opportunity does not require that opportunity be equal for all persons. It requires only that it be equal for persons with similar skills and

---

[49] Daniels, *Just Health Care*, p. 41.
[50] Rawls, *Political Liberalism, paperback edition* (New York: Columbia University Press, 1996), p. 184n, and *Justice as Fairness: A Restatement* (Cambridge MA: Harvard University Press, 2001), pp. 174–75.
[51] Daniels, *Just Health Care*, pp. 26–28, 32–33.
[52] Daniels, *Justice and Justification*, p. 269.
[53] Daniels, *Justice and Justification*, p. 214.

talents. . . . What is important here, however, is that impairment of normal functioning through disease and disability restricts an individual's opportunity relative to that portion of the normal range his skills and talents would have made available to him were he healthy . . . restoring normal functioning through health care . . . lets him enjoy that portion of the range to which his full array of talents and skills would give him access.[54]

The structure of the argument is, then, to say that (1) health care matters because it contributes to normal species functioning, (2) normal species functioning matters because it affects a person's opportunity range, and (3) a person's opportunity range matters because, for egalitarians at least, there is a commitment to equal opportunity. Thus, Daniels concludes, "Because we have obligations to ensure people of fair equality of opportunity, we have social obligations to provide health-care services that protect and restore normal functioning."[55]

So far, I have criticized egalitarians because they have justified the policy of making health care (insurance) affordable for all, rather than universally accessible. The two policies diverge when we think about individuals who could afford to buy health care insurance but choose not to; this is not allowable under a policy of universal access. Is Daniels's theory of just health care susceptible to a similar objection?

In certain respects, Daniels is better positioned to handle this criticism than the other egalitarians we have been discussing. This is because he presents health care as a concern about background fairness within a framework of equality of opportunity. As we have seen, Veatch and Harris are susceptible to the criticism I have been pressing because for them health care is an 'opportunity,' in which case it is puzzling why someone should have to forego some other opportunity he would prefer more, as is entailed by a policy of universal access to health care. Daniels does not treat health care simply as an opportunity. Health care makes a contribution to guaranteeing equality of opportunity. Health care institutions are among the background institutions that, for Daniels, "provide a framework of liberties and opportunities within which individuals can use fair income shares to pursue their own conceptions of the good."[56] They have, in his terms, a great "strategic" importance.

The most instructive parallel is with education. Like health care, educational institutions are also significant background institutions that

---

[54] Daniels, *Justice and Justification*, pp. 214–15.
[55] Daniels, *Justice and Justification*, pp. 269–70.
[56] Daniels, *Justice and Justification*, p. 192.

need to be utilized to guarantee equality of opportunity. Education is also therefore of great strategic importance. The added problem for Daniels is that in terms of needs, education and health care seem no more urgent than things such as food and clothing. But food and clothing are clear examples where an egalitarian policy aims at guaranteeing affordability for all, rather than universal access. Why is having universal access to health care and education justified but not food and clothing? Health care and educational needs are, according to Daniels, distributed unequally among persons; some people have much greater needs than others. Someone with breast cancer, for instance, has much greater health care needs than someone suffering from a simple cold. The need for food and clothing, by contrast, is said to be more equally distributed among individuals. "The combination of unequal distribution and the great strategic importance of the opportunity to have health care and education," argues Daniels, "puts these needs in a separate category from those basic needs we can expect people to purchase from their fair income shares."[57]

Even though Daniels makes an interesting case for why health care is special, his argument does not succeed at justifying universal access.[58] He fails to make a case for a policy that uses in-kind benefits to compensate people with illnesses or diseases that affect their species-typical normal functioning rather than cash. Consider, first, the analogy he draws between health care and education. Education, because of its background importance, is not an opportunity like any other, and therefore has a sense of urgency that is independent of what subjectively someone might prefer. But suppose that the cost of, say, attending university was escalating dramatically. (This isn't at all difficult in the present climate of higher education.) Should the cost reach a certain point, it is reasonable to begin to weigh up the other opportunities that are going to be waived in order to pay the price of attending university, while still acknowledging that education is special in the way that Daniels claims it is. Say the cost were $50,000 per year, and there were a public policy in place that provided individuals with a transfer to cover

---

[57] Daniels, *Justice and Justification*, p. 193.
[58] Others have pointed out other shortcomings in Daniels's theory with regard to universal access. See, e.g., Allen Buchanan, 'The Right to a Decent Minimum of Health Care,' *Philosophy & Public Affairs*, Vol. 13 (1984), p. 65, and Einer Elhauge, 'Allocating Health Care Morally,' *California Law Review*, Vol. 82 (1994), p. 1469. See also my very different criticism of Daniels in 'Can an Egalitarian Justify Universal Access to Health Care?,' *Social Theory and Practice*, Vol. 22 (1996), pp. 334–38.

that cost. I don't find in Daniels any basis for objecting to an individual who would say that he or she should have the cash to spend on something other than university on the grounds that, given the large amount of money involved, by doing so he or she could enhance his or her opportunity range more than by attending university.

Exactly the same point can be made about health care on Daniels's account, in which case he is unable to justify universal access. Daniels succeeds at showing that health (and education) are special because of their relation to opportunities in the normal range, but he does not insulate them completely from the sort of trade-off considerations that undermine the use of in-kind benefits. Being special may raise the threshold for when to undertake this sort of consideration, but so long as health care is viewed through the lens of equalizing opportunities, there is some point at which it is no longer justified to provide expensive health care on egalitarian grounds when the beneficiary would prefer to have his or her opportunity set enhanced in other ways. In other words, the example of the AIDS patient I pressed against Dworkin's comprehensive strategy has as much force against Daniels's restricted egalitarian strategy for justifying universal access to health care.

7.4 CONCLUSION

The purpose of this chapter has been to illustrate the limitations on the three-dimensional model of equal opportunities as a regulative ideal. From the beginning, I have insisted that that model is applicable only when a competition is at stake. Rather than envisioning a theory of egalitarian justice that is applicable to each and every social policy issue, I have proposed a more restricted model. This modesty means that I think the three-dimensional model is silent if competition is inappropriate or out of place. Being silent is not necessarily a vice; in conversation, as we all know, knowing when to be silent is a great virtue and a sign of genuine civility and respect. Precisely the same point can be made about theories of egalitarian justice.

I have illustrated the force of this approach to egalitarian justice here by focussing on health care. I have argued in Section 7.2 that health care should not be allocated on a competitive basis. For this reason, health care is outside the regulative scope of all equal opportunity models; it involves non-competitive opportunities. I have also shown the folly of those who have sought to apply to health care competitive models of equal opportunity or other egalitarian theories that emphasize competition. For most people, including committed egalitarians, it is a platitude that whatever else might characterize a health care system, it should include the policy of universal access. We would expect, therefore, that any reasonable theory of health care allocation should be able to explain or justify the policy of universal access. My analysis found that neither comprehensive nor restricted egalitarian strategies succeed at meeting this challenge, and thus are inadequate for the task of allocating health care justly. This reinforces my overall claim that social justice is a complex business and that the three-dimensional model of equal opportunities as a regulative ideal is to be viewed as only part of the whole picture.

PART IV

Gender

Chapter 8

Gender Inequalities in the Workplace

8.1 INTRODUCTION

The final two chapters of this book are concerned with pursuing equality between men and women. It is this egalitarian pursuit through legislation and the courts that has probably resulted in the most visible social change in modern industrial societies over the past twenty-five years. Restrictions and barriers for women that a mere fifty years ago were thought unassailable have crumbled in recent times. Women have to some degree gained access to practically all of the principal social institutions of civil society. Perhaps the most important change has been in the labour market. In Canada, for example, 22 percent of women were in the labour force in 1931 compared with 54.8 percent in 1998. Similarly, in the United States, labour market participation increased from 30 percent to 55 percent from 1950 to 1998. These statistics mask some of the complex differences among women. Women of colour, for instance, have a much longer history of high rates of labour market participation, as have women heading single-parent households.[1] But the dramatic increase in labour market participation by women in general revealed by these numbers suggests why, from a social justice perspective, the labour market emerged thirty years ago as a major site for regulating inequalities between men and women.

Much of the first wave of legal reforms was directed at removing undeniable barriers for women participating in the labour market. These

---

[1] The significance of this observation is succinctly argued by Julianne Malveaux, 'Gender Difference and Beyond: An Economic Perspective on Diversity and Commonality among Women,' in Deborah Rhode, editor, *Theoretical Perspectives on Sexual Difference* (New Haven: Yale University Press, 1990).

Gender

reforms were typically preceded by influential public enquiries. In the United States, for example, President Kennedy established the Presidential Commission on the Status of Women in the early 1960s. Canada followed suit in 1967 with the Royal Commission on the Status of Women. Britain established the Royal Commission on the Distribution of Income and Wealth in 1974. The main tenor of these reforms was the end of formal measures that excluded women. In the public sector, except for the military, all jobs and positions became open to men and women. In the private sector, hiring and promotion practices became subject to civil rights or human rights legislation intended to protect women from discrimination.

The next wave of legal reforms was likewise designed to remove barriers, but the view of what constituted a barrier for women in the labour market was much more robust. A clear illustration is the recognition of sexual harassment as sex discrimination in the workplace.[2] *Quid quo pro* sexual harassment is now uncontroversially viewed as a barrier to equality. "Chilly climates," on the other hand, remain contested, even though the courts and human rights tribunals have shown considerable sympathy for the idea. Another example of a barrier under assault during this second wave of reform was the so-called glass ceiling. Whatever one's views on particular issues, however, there is an indisputable conceptual connection suggested by the focus on barriers. The pursuit of equality for working women in this regard is largely *negative*, a task in demolition.

Distinct from this task in demolition are those *positive* measures undertaken to combat gender inequality in the workplace. This chapter focusses on the two most significant positive measures undertaken by governments to address workplace gender inequalities – (1) affirmative action in the hiring and promotion of women, and (2) pay equity, or comparable worth. While it is generally accepted that equal opportunity models are capable of explaining the importance of the removal of barriers faced by women in the workplace, there is a great deal of scepticism about their capacity to provide the normative foundations for these sorts of positive measures by government. And, indeed, conservative critics of such policies often insist that they are inconsistent with the very idea of equality of opportunity. My goal in this chapter is to show how affirmative action and pay equity flow

[2] The classic analysis is Catharine A. MacKinnon, *Sexual Harassment of Working Women* (New Haven: Yale University Press, 1979).

206

from the three-dimensional model of equal opportunities as a regulative ideal.

Rather than discussing these policies in abstract form, I shall use two Canadian examples to situate my analysis, although my argument is designed to have a general application. The first is an example of affirmative action undertaken by the Federal Government of Canada. The program at issue has two components – the 1986 Employment Equity Act, which mandated affirmative action in the federal civil service, and the 1986 federal Contractor's Program, which imposed similar affirmative action requirements on all public agencies or private firms holding a major contract with the Federal Government. The significant point is that the programme in question was intended to regulate not just the public sector but also part of the private sector of the Canadian economy. In 1992, in an assessment of the programme, a House of Commons Committee reported that the programme affected at least 1.5 million Canadians, more than 10 percent of the entire Canadian work force.[3] Unlike in the United States, where affirmative action is widely and almost immediately associated with race-conscious programmes, this policy was directed principally (some would say exclusively) at women, as opposed to visible minorities or indigenous peoples. Indeed, following the recommendation of a Royal Commission report two years earlier, the Federal Government in 1986 relabelled its affirmative action policy as "employment equity" in order to avoid the negative connotations of the terms "affirmative action" and "reverse discrimination" that spilled over from the United States. (For this reason, throughout this chapter, I use the terms "affirmative action" and "employment equity" more or less interchangeably.)

The second example is the Ontario Pay Equity Act, which institutionalized the principle of equal pay for work of equal value, or as it is often referred to in the United States, the principle of comparable worth. (Throughout this chapter, I use "pay equity" and "comparable worth" interchangeably.) This legislation introduced by the Government of Ontario was viewed at the time it was passed as the most far-reaching attempt made anywhere in the world to legislate on women's wages, and remains more than a decade later among the most ambitious pay equity laws anywhere. This is because it applied the principle of comparable worth to both the public and private sectors of the Ontario economy

---

[3] Government of Canada, *A Matter of Fairness: Report of the Special Committee on the Review of the Employment Equity Act* (Ottawa: House of Commons, 1992), p. 1.

and required a gender-neutral baseline for assessing women's wages.[4] The intention of the legislation was to identify female-dominated occupations in the private and public sectors and mandate wage increases so that they eventually move into line with comparable male-dominated occupations.

Affirmative action and pay equity are both controversial because they appear to give special consideration to individual women simply because they are women.[5] For critics, these policies of employment and pay equity are therefore in tension with the core idea of equality of opportunity, which forbids both privileges and barriers to opportunities based on sex.[6] In response to this concern, I shall show why the three-dimensional model of equal opportunities as a regulative ideal requires both of these policies – affirmative action, because it remedies a form of background unfairness women face in the workplace, and pay equity, because it remedies a form of stakes unfairness women experience in the labour market. My defence of these two sorts of policies relies on a particular analysis of gender disadvantage in the workplace that has become widely accepted in the past ten years. At the centre of that analysis is the claim that many of the disadvantages women suffer in the workplace have their origins in the unfair burden women carry within families. In other words, injustices within families generate injustices within the labour market. Although egalitarian defences of affirmative action and comparable worth based on this sort of analysis are now commonplace, I shall show in this chapter that the three-dimensional model of equal opportunities as a regulative ideal is innovative in its explanation as to why legislators are justified in developing policies that target workplace inequalities but not inequalities within families.

---

[4] The innovative features of the Act are discussed in Carolyn P. Ergi and W.T. Stanbury, 'How Pay Equity Came to Ontario,' *Canadian Public Administration*, Vol. 32 (1989), p. 274, and Judy Fudge and Patricia McDermott, 'Introduction: Putting Feminism to Work' in J. Fudge and P. McDermott, editors, *Just Wages: A Feminist Assessment of Pay Equity* (Toronto: University of Toronto Press, 1991), p. 8.

[5] These policies are also controversial in their implementation, for instance, with regard to establishing a gender-neutral baseline for assessing women's wages for pay equity. My concern in this chapter, in keeping with the rest of the book, is with the broader normative controversies.

[6] See, e.g., Martha Minow, 'Partial Justice: Law and Minorities' in Austin Sarat and Thomas R. Kerans, editors, *The Fate of Law* (Ann Arbor: University of Michigan Press, 1993), pp. 24–26.

8.2 UNDERSTANDING GENDER GAPS IN THE WORKPLACE

There is a series of well-known economic indicators that reveal important gaps – the gender wage gap and the senior hiring and promotion gap – between men and women in the workplace. These indicators show that in North America, women working full-time earn considerably less than men working full-time. Although this so-called gender wage gap varies from year to year and has narrowed slightly over the past twenty years, women continue to earn roughly 70 percent of what men earn. Likewise, the senior hiring and promotion gap is evident if one looks through the notices of senior promotions and hirings in the pages of major financial newspapers such as *The Wall Street Journal* or *The Financial Times*, for it is notable that men far outnumber women, even though the firms in question often have as many, or more, female employees than male. Within professions such as law and medicine, similarly, even though women have been graduating at levels on a par with men for more than a decade, it is still the case that in the prestigious specialties, in senior administration, and as a proportion of the highest earners, men continue to overwhelm women.

Prior to the waves of legal reform noted in the introduction to this chapter, it was plausible to attribute these two gaps to the presence of formal barriers for women in the labour market. Women, it might be said, experienced overt discrimination at the hands of men in terms of hirings, promotions, and the wages they received. Although this was certainly true in the past, and there remains a certain degree of overt discrimination, for this to be an adequate explanation of phenomena such as the gender wage gap at present, it would mean that laws against discrimination on the basis of sex are being completely disregarded in the workplace and that formal barriers to access for women remain in place. There is in fact little evidence to support the claim that undisputed legal rights of women against discrimination in hirings, promotions, or pay are being systematically violated. (I leave aside controversies about legal rights that are in dispute.) Even those most critical of the initial waves of legal reform concede that the civil rights initiative has succeeded in demolishing some of the formal barriers faced by women in the workplace. Conservatives typically lament the integration of women into the workplace, which they see as the result of such reforms. Feminist critics argue typically that the targetted barriers are only part of the problem, and that more needs to be done to achieve equality for men and women in the workplace.

A different explanation is that the gender gaps noted earlier reveal a "backlash" against women.[7] This view holds that the legal reforms of the past thirty years directed at barriers for women, such as civil rights or human rights that protect women from discrimination, are a significant achievement, and ultimately will result in the closing of the gender wage gap and in parity for women in terms of hirings and promotions. But in reaction to this achievement, there was said to have been a backlash against pursuing equality for women since the mid-1980s, accented by a successful effort by the media and public officials to portray the legal reforms designed to demolish barriers for women as having made women worse off. The findings that the gender wage gap has failed to narrow, and that women continue to not enjoy a greater share of privileged positions in business and the professions, are said to be the effect of this backlash. The main problem with this view is that it assumes that prior to the backlash, legal reforms that extended rights against discrimination to women were resulting in the closing of these two gender gaps. This assumption was, however, already being challenged in the early 1980s.[8] In other words, even before the alleged backlash, the removal of barriers for women was not having a significant effect on the wage gap or on the senior hiring and promotion gap.

My view is that, historically, the gaps we are examining between men and women in the workplace have a variety of sources. Some of the disadvantages stem from the legacy of formal barriers of access faced by women intended to promote what was then perceived to be in the best interests of society. These include provisions that excluded women from professions, hiring and promotion policies that gave preference to men over women, and practices that paid men more than women for performing the same job. Such blatant acts of discrimination are now generally forbidden by law. Distinct from these disadvantages is the legacy of those barriers intended to promote what was then thought to be in the best interests of individual women. These sorts of measures are classic illustrations of paternalistic social policies – policies that re-stricted the choices of women on the grounds that, even though women may not appreciate it, such restrictions best serve the interests of those

---

[7] The most influential statement of this view is, of course, Susan Faludi, *Backlash: The Undeclared War Against American Women* (New York: Anchor Books, 1991).

[8] See, e.g., Deborah Rhode, *Justice and Gender* (Cambridge, MA: Harvard University Press, 1989), ch. 8.

women.[9] Examples include restrictions on the number of hours women (but not men) could work, the requirement that women, when they marry, must quit their jobs, and prohibitions on women undertaking certain dangerous jobs. Most of these paternalistic disadvantages are also now prohibited by anti-discrimination law.

What then explains the persistent gap between men and women in terms of wages and senior hirings and promotions? A major part of the answer can be found by looking at the family – in particular, families with children. Although we have witnessed a dramatic increase in the participation of women in the labour market over the past fifty years, labour burdens within families have not changed at the same pace. Historically, women throughout the twentieth century have carried a much greater responsibility for domestic labour, especially relating to raising children, than men. The statistics are familiar enough. In the early 1990s, women were found to perform at least 70 percent of the domestic labour in American families.[10] And despite some anecdotal evidence that there might be a major shift from women to men in taking responsibility for young children, this is not supported by an examination of the concrete data on social policy. In Canada, for instance, since October 1990, a national government-funded paid parental leave of ten weeks (raised to thirty-five weeks beginning in 2001) had been available for one of the parents of a newborn baby or newly adopted child. This leave is available to men or women, and guarantees the leave holder his or her position upon returning to work as well as 55 percent of his or her regular earnings up to a set weekly maximum. (It exists in addition to state-funded maternity leave available to women having a new baby.) Even though this parental leave is available to both men and women, 96 percent of the beneficiaries of the programme were women, and only 3 to 4 percent men, in its first eight years.[11] In other words, although

---

[9] The classic attack on this sort of paternalistic treatment of women is John Stuart Mill's 'The Subjection of Women' [1869], reprinted in Lesley Jacobs and Richard Vandewetering, editors, *John Stuart Mill's 'The Subjection of Women': His Contemporary and Modern Critics* (Delmar, NY: Caravan Books, 1999). See also the introduction by the editors. For some modern criticisms of this sort of legal paternalism, see Catherine A. MacKinnon, *Toward a Feminist Theory of the State* (Cambridge, MA: Harvard University Press, 1989), pp. 165–67, and Drucilla Cornell, *At The Heart of Freedom: Feminism, Sex, and Equality* (Princeton: Princeton University Press, 1998), pp. 72–81.

[10] Faludi, *Backlash*, p. xiv.

[11] Statistics Canada, *Stay-at-Home Dads* (Ottawa: Government of Canada, 1998).

Canadian men do sometimes take paid leaves from work to take care of young children, women are *thirty* times more likely to do so. The general point is that even though families have evolved in countless ways, women continue to carry a disproportionately larger burden of the domestic labour within families than men.

The added complication here is the dramatic increase in labour market participation by women over the past fifty years, as noted at the beginning of this chapter. If labour market participation for women was low, the uneven allocation of domestic labour between men and women may not be surprising, or even worrisome. The problem arises because many women who perform large amounts of domestic labour also hold full-time positions in the workplace. As the sociologist Arlie Hochschild has described it, working women with families, when they go home, work "the second shift."[12] These women, by comparison with their husbands, are much more likely to take days off when children are sick, drop off and pick up children from school or daycare, refuse offers to work overtime for additional pay, and assume responsibilities such as dentist and doctor appointments. Hochschild's point is that while competing in the labour market with men, women also carry the heavier burden of domestic labour.

This "second shift" phenomenon is capable of explaining to a significant degree both the gender wage gap and the senior hiring and promotion gap between men and women. In a careful government study of the gender wage gap that preceded the introduction of pay equity in Ontario, it was found that the wage gap between men and women working full-time had three major contributors: (1) men worked more hours than women, (2) men were more likely to be unionized than women, and (3) female-dominated jobs are lower paid on average than male-dominated jobs.[13] (Intentional discrimination by employees was found to have only a small effect overall on women's wages.) The second-shift perspective readily explains why women work fewer hours than men; they do so in order to accommodate the demands of childcare and other demands of domestic labour. Why, if there are no formal barriers to access, don't more women choose unionized jobs or higher paying male dominated jobs? A plausible answer is that female-dominated jobs are

---

[12] Arlie Hochschild with Anne Machung, *The Second Shift* (New York: Viking Penguin, 1989), p. 4.

[13] Ian Scott, Minister Responsible for Women's Issues, *Green Paper on Pay Equity* (Toronto: Government of Ontario, November 1985), pp. 2–3.

better structured to accommodate women working a second shift. And standard features of unionized workplaces, such as the significance of seniority, often do not reflect the reality of women's patterns of work. Women are, for instance, much more likely to have interrupted work histories because of having and taking care of children. The well-known cliche is "last hired, first fired."

A similar story can be told about the senior hiring and promotions gap. In effect, the second shift that women work at home hinders their prospects for promotion. The legal profession is often used as an illustration of this point. For associates in law firms, promotion to partner is ordinarily contingent on a sustained record of billing hours built up over a number of years. The norm in the legal profession is set by what is an outstanding record for a male lawyer, a record that is characterized by a career that has followed a direct path from university through law school into the bar and so on. The point is that the normal career path of a lawyer is taken to be that of men. This reflects bias against women in the legal profession insofar as there is little flexibility in career paths.[14] Female lawyers with young children, however, often don't follow straight linear career paths, and the sustained record of billing hours required for a partnership is often incompatible with their second shift at home.

8.3 IS THE SECOND SHIFT UNFAIR TO WOMEN?

The foregoing analysis of the gender wage gap and the senior hiring and promotion gap has attributed these gaps in large part to the unequal burdens of domestic labour that men and women carry. The gaps reflect the fact that women's behaviour in the labour market is affected by their heavier burden of domestic labour, especially when their families include young children.

Are these gender gaps, then, unfair to women? Any adequate answer to this question presupposes a discussion of why something is unfair. Two views are prevalent. On the one hand, there are those who maintain that the gaps are not unfair, provided that individual women have chosen to assume the second shift. Here, the gaps appear to reflect merely

---

[14] This is emphasized in the report of the Canadian Bar Association, Task Force on Gender Equality in the Legal Profession, Justice Bertha Wilson, Chair, 'Touchstones for Change: Equality, Diversity and Accountability' (Ottawa, 1993), reprinted in Donald Buckingham, Jerome Bickenbach, Richard Bronaugh, and Bertha Wilson, editors, *Legal Ethics in Canada* (Toronto: Harcourt Brace, 1996), p. 269.

the costs women must bear for their choices. On the other hand, many feminists have argued that any sort of gap between men and women is, at least *prima facie*, unfair. As Catharine MacKinnon has put it, "All that is required are comparatively unequal results."[15] This perspective assumes that gender equality requires equal results. Consider the role this perspective has assumed in the debate around pay equity. There was initially considerable optimism about the potential of pay equity to narrow the gender wage gap. One economist, for example, projected in 1987 that the Ontario Pay Equity Law could reduce the gap by 10 to 15 percentage points in Ontario.[16] The rationale for pay equity was thought to rest on its effectiveness at achieving a particular result – the closing of the wage gap.

The perspective I shall advance as an alternative to these two prevalent views is informed by the three-dimensional model of equal opportunities as a regulative ideal. The immediate context is set by women and men in competition in the labour market. The analysis in Section 8.2 suggests that this competition is tainted by injustices within families seeping into it. In other words, an unfair practice in one sphere of civil society – the family – makes such waves that it upsets the prospects of fair competition in another – the labour market. (In Section 8.4, I defend with some care the assumption here that the family and the labour market are, from a normative perspective, distinct.) A concern for equal opportunities for women and men alike would seem to warrant a public policy response.

Analytically, it is possible to divide public policies that might be motivated by this concern into two broad classes – *family-based* policies and *workplace-based* policies. Including housewives in existing pension schemes, and having the state collect child-support payments from absent fathers, might be examples of family-based policies. Employment and pay equity legislation should be regarded as workplace-based policies designed to promote equal opportunities as a regulative ideal. Logically, family-based policies seem preferable because they address the problem at its roots. I argue later on, however, that the three-dimensional model cannot be applied to problems of injustice within families. Families and family-based policies, while not outside the scope of social justice, should not be subject to the

---

[15] MacKinnon, *Sexual Harassment of Working Women*, p. 118.
[16] Roberta Edgecombe Robb, 'Equal Pay for Work of Equal Value: Issues and Policies,' *Canadian Public Policy*, Vol. VIII (1987), p. 455.

regulative ideal of equal opportunities. This leaves only workplace-based policies – in particular, affirmative action and comparable worth.

Affirmative action for women in the workplace should be understood as an effort to remedy for the background unfairness in labour market competition caused by women's carrying a greater burden of domestic labor than men. Recall from Chapter 2 that at the core of background fairness is the ideal of individuals all competing on a level playing field. The principle of status equality identifies a starting position – the same moral status for each, and no higher moral standing possible – in a competition that all individuals should enjoy. The elementary problem with the second-shift phenomenon is that it means that men and women are often not competing in the labour market on a level playing field. Some women carry a burden that hinders their standing from the beginning of the competition. That this favours men is reinforced by the example of the law profession discussed earlier. Many opportunities in the labour market are structured around the assumption that the 'normal' competitor for the position is not an employee committed to working 'the second shift.' For women, the second shift is normal. Yet, what counts as normal in the integrated workplace is what is normal for men – for example, no second shift or a lighter load of domestic labour. What we have, in other words, is women in the labour market entering competitions with a lower status. From the perspective of background fairness, there is a sort of double disadvantage to this lower status: the disadvantage of working the second shift and the disadvantage that in the workplace, that second shift is invisible, unrecognized, and unacknowledged.[17] The first disadvantage falls mainly on women with children, but the second is faced by all women.

In labour market competitions, it is reasonable to assume that the choices women make are sensitive to this double disadvantage. Women, either because they work the second shift or they anticipate in the future assuming the second shift (more than 80 percent of women in North America have children eventually), choose jobs and career paths that accommodate the demands of domestic labour.[18] What we find here is

---

[17] I do not mean to imply that this second form of disadvantage is imposed on women intentionally by employers. Indeed, part of the disturbing aspect of the second shift is precisely its covert role in the labour market.

[18] It must be acknowledged here that the process of socialization and education for girls and young women with regard to familial expectations plays a role in these choices, and there are compelling grounds to challenge the justice of this process.

an example of the phenomenon of adaptation, where individual women adapt their desires and choices about work in anticipation of the way of life they expect with regard to domestic labour.[19] There is no similar adaptation by men in the labour market.

Affirmative action is designed to neutralize the effects of the second shift on background fairness without directly ending the actual practice of the second shift for working women. (Family-based reforms, in contrast, often address the second shift head-on.) An important consequence of the second-shift phenomenon is that many women choose positions in female-segregated occupations such as secretarial work and child care because those jobs are structured to accommodate their second shift, allowing them flexibility in terms of hours worked as well as the possibility of entering and leaving the labour market frequently. The role of affirmative action or employment equity is to give women more opportunities to pursue job prospects in occupations other than those traditionally dominated by women. It seeks to ensure that hiring and promotion practices do not reflect engendered disadvantage stemming from the second shift. Timetables and quotas for the hiring of women serve this function by compensating women for the disadvantage this phenomenon places on the initial starting position of women in a competitive labour market. The issue is, of course, more complicated than this because women are not the only participants in the labour market to face background unfairness.[20] Persons with disabilities, indigenous

This raises questions for example, about, educational reform that are beyond the scope of this chapter.

[19] For a careful survey of the complex literature on adaptation, see Martha Nussbaum, *Women and Human Development: The Capabilities Approach* (Cambridge, UK: Cambridge University Press, 2000), ch. 2.

[20] An important difference between gender-based affirmative action and race-conscious affirmative action concerns the status equality of members of groups not targeted by affirmative action. In Section 4.5, I insisted that the status equality of white applicants to selective universities is not jeopardized by affirmative action programs targetted at African Americans and Latinos. Affirmative action targetted at women has greater potential to threaten the standing of at least some men in the labor market. (More specifically, unlike in the case of race, I am simply less sure that the status equality of all men is being fully respected without qualification.) This difference underlies why race-conscious and gender-based affirmative action are treated separately in this book and warrant different justifications within the three-dimensional model of equal opportunities as a regulative ideal. In the case of race-based affirmative action, I have defended that policy on the grounds of stakes fairness. Here I have grounded gender-based affirmative action on an analysis of background unfairness, allowing that in order to enhance the standing of women in labor market competitions, it may be inevitable that the standing of

peoples, and certain other minorities face disadvantages in the labour market that can also be viewed in terms of background fairness. The inevitable consequence of an employment equity program that only focusses on gender as a form of disadvantage is that it is likely to benefit principally white women from well-off family backgrounds. For this reason, it makes sense to have an integrated affirmative action program such as the Canadian Federal Employment Equity Plan, which addresses not only gender as a form of disadvantage in labour market competition but also the social status of disability, nationality, sexual orientation, and so on.

Pay equity, likewise, is designed to neutralize the effects of the second shift on the stakes fairness of labour market competition without ending the actual practice of the second shift for women. Pay equity ideally functions to correct market-determined wages in female-segregated occupations. From the perspective of the three-dimensional model of equal opportunities as a regulative ideal, the principal problem with relying solely on the market to determine wages in female-segregated occupations is that those wages inevitably reflect the unequal starting positions experienced by women in the workplace. The market is by its very nature unable to correct for unequal starting positions. It is, to use an analogy, like a black box with inputs and outputs – the character of outputs is a function of the inputs. It doesn't follow, of course, that the market is necessarily inegalitarian. Indeed, logically, if the inputs into the market are egalitarian, so too will be the outputs.[21] What constitutes fair stakes for women in the labour market? Pay equity answers this question by aiming to make wages in female-dominated occupations equal to market-determined wages earned by men in occupations of comparable worth. In this sense, pay equity is predicated on the notion that the market should determine wages. Any pay equity settlement operates in the shadow of the market; all that any such policy purports to do is correct the wage outcomes of markets when those outcomes are tainted by the second shift and other injustices within families.

My treatment of pay equity differs significantly from the view that gender wage gaps are not unfair, provided individual women have

---

some men may be diminished. Ultimately, although this involves the trading-off of the standing of some for the sake of others, this does not violate the equal status of men and women.
[21] This is the fundamental insight of Ronald Dworkin's seminal paper, 'What Is Equality? Part 2: Equality of Resources,' *Philosophy & Public Affairs*, Vol. 10 (1981), pp. 283–345.

chosen to assume their domestic burdens. I have suggested here that although women do often freely choose lower paying occupations with fewer opportunities for promotion, their choices should be viewed within the context of the phenomenon of adaptation. They make their choices in anticipation of the second-shift responsibility. This doesn't make those choices less valid or unauthentic, but it does seem disingenuous to insist that pay equity is misconceived either because wage gaps can be traced to women's choices about where and when to work[22] or that it entails a form of social engineering that undermines the legitimate choices of individuals.[23] The inference I draw from the phenomenon of adaptation is not that the choices women make are bad – how can it be bad that a new mother chooses to take a leave from her job to spend time with her baby? – but that there is something circular about arguments that validate the status quo by appealing to choices that have been made in response to the status quo. Furthermore, there is now considerable evidence showing that market forces often play only a marginal role in employers' wage assessments of male- and female-dominated occupations.[24]

I have also not insisted, as some legal feminists demand, that workplace-based policies be judged by their effectiveness at bringing about equal results in terms of wages for men and women. Earlier, I noted that some of the initial proponents of the Ontario Pay Equity Act defended the act because they thought it would narrow significantly the gender wage gap. It is now unclear what effect pay equity has had or will have on the gender wage gap because that law is directed at equalizing salaries between job types, whereas the wage gap is a function of the wages of individual men and women.[25] This

[22] See, e.g., Ellen Frankel Paul, *Equity and Gender: The Comparable Worth Debate* (New Brunswick, NJ: Transaction Publishers, 1989), pp. 121–22, and Thomas Flanagan, 'Equal Pay for Work of Equal Value: Some Theoretical Criticisms,' *Canadian Public Policy, Vol. 13* (1987), p. 66.

[23] Rainer Knopf with Thomas Flanagan, *Human Rights and Social Technology: The New War on Discrimination* (Ottawa: Carlton University Press, 1990).

[24] This is carefully argued in William Bridges and Robert Nelson, *Legalizing Gender Inequality: Courts, Markets, and Unequal Pay for Women in America* (New York: Cambridge University Press, 1999).

[25] Nan Weiner and Morley Gunderson, *Pay Equity: Issues, Options, and Experiences* (Toronto: Butterworths, 1990, p. 11); and Morley Gunderson, Leon Muszynski, and Jennifer Keck, *Women and Labour Market Poverty* (Ottawa: Canadian Advisory Council on the Status of Women, 1990), pp. 159–61. For an argument to the same effect in an American context, see Paul Weiler, 'The Wages of Sex: The Uses and Limits of Comparable Worth,' *Harvard Law Review, Vol. 100* (1986), p. 1728.

means, ironically, that for those who demand equal results, there may not be a good case for pay equity or comparable worth laws.[26] I have staunchly defended pay equity laws because I judge that they help to offset the effects of the second shift on women competing in the labour market. They do so even if they do not help to narrow the gender wage gap.

8.4 WHY FAMILIES ARE BEYOND EQUAL OPPORTUNITY REGULATION

The core insight of the preceding argument for employment and pay equity has been to view these controversial public policies as measures that address the effects of an injustice within families – the second shift – on women competing in the labour market. They are designed to provide normative regulation of the labour market, not to bring about a particular outcome in labour market competition. Rather than advocating undoing the second shift directly through family-based legal reforms, I have argued that the three-dimensional model of equal opportunities as a regulative ideal entails mitigating only for the effects of the second shift on labour market competition. Injustices within families *per se*, as distinct from their effects on labour market competitions or when marriages break up, are outside the scope of regulation by that equal opportunities model. For this reason, egalitarians concerned with injustices within families must concentrate their efforts on refinements to workplace-based policies based on principles such as affirmative action and comparable worth.

My position here can be subject to three distinct lines of criticism. The first questions my refusal to apply an equal opportunities model to injustices within families. Susan Moller Okin, for example, shares with me the view that what I have been calling the second-shift phenomenon is a major explanatory factor for gender disadvantages in the workplace. But Okin thinks that logically therefore it is also appropriate to pursue equal opportunity within families.[27] I have endorsed, from an equal opportunities perspective, only workplace-based public policies. Hence, Caroline Andrew has characterized my position as the "politics

---

[26] Patricia McDermott, 'Pay Equity in Canada: Assessing the Commitment to Reducing the Wage Gap' in *Just Wages*, p. 31.
[27] Susan Moller Okin, *Justice, Gender, and the Family* (New York: Basic Books, 1989), pp. 16–17.

of mainstreaming," in effect because it does not propose to restructure the family.[28]

It is important to recognize that I am not saying that the family is outside the scope of justice. What I am insisting upon rather is that equal opportunities is not the appropriate principle of justice for regulating families. In the last chapter, I argued that social justice involves a plurality of principles, and that because health care should not be subject to competition, it is a category mistake to utilize an equal opportunities model for thinking about allocating health care. A parallel point is being made here about families. Families are not best thought of as a forum for competition among members (although, unfortunately, *de facto* within some families there is intense competition.) Since equal opportunities models are intended to regulate only competitions, they are therefore inappropriate for providing insight into how to pursue justice within families. As in the case of health care, egalitarians seem overzealous in their efforts to apply equality of opportunity to the family, and risk failing to find the right principle of family justice.

I suspect that a concern about the economic and social consequences of marital breakdown for women underlies much of the effort to apply equality of opportunities to families. As Okin has put it, "The impact of the unequal distribution of benefits and burdens between husbands and wives is hardest and most directly felt by the increasing numbers of women and children whose families are no longer intact."[29] My view, which is explained in depth in the next chapter, is although it cannot be applied to the family, the three-dimensional model of equal opportunities as a regulative ideal can be applied to divorce settlements. The reason is that divorces and separations can be viewed as competitive processes.

The contrast I am emphasizing here between families – outside the scope of equal opportunities – and divorce settlements – a valid subject of the regulative ideal of equal opportunities – is reinforced by an insightful discussion of Kant and Hegel by Jeremy Waldron. Around the issue of marriage, Kant and Hegel offered sharply contrasting images. Kant insisted on a contractual model in which partners in a marriage are equals in sacrifices to the marriage and the benefits they draw from it.

---

[28] Caroline Strange, 'The Fine Line – Strategies for Change' in Francois Gingras, editor, *Gender and Politics in Contemporary Canada* (Toronto: Oxford University Press, 1995), pp. 249, 253.
[29] Okin, *Justice, Gender, and the Family*, p. 160.

Hegel famously attacked this contractual approach, insisting that marriage at its foundation is about love, trust, and sharing. While Kant adopted a view of marriage that highlights rights and duties, Hegel's view is less about individuals in competition and more about relationships and community. Although Waldron is sympathetic to Kant, he makes a fundamental concession to Hegel: "Few of us disagree with Hegel's basic point: claims of rights should have little part to play in the context of a normal loving marriage."[30] However, the need for rights arises, according to Waldron, when the love or trust of a marriage fades or fails. Kant's view anticipates this as a real possibility in a way that Hegel's does not. The relevant point for us is that even on Waldron's account, equal opportunities should be applied at the point of marital breakdown, not during, in his words, "a normal loving marriage."

Iris Marion Young also raises an important objection to readily applying equality of opportunity to the family. She charges that this reduces the complex injustices within families to mainly distributive injustices.[31] She thinks that this obscures issues such as sexuality and reproduction within the family that are not easily thought about in a distributive paradigm. This reinforces my claim that some principle of justice other than equal opportunities should regulate the family.

The second line of criticism against my justification for employment and pay equity is that because of the emphasis on the second shift, there is too narrow a concentration on the traditional heterosexual family with children. This feeds the neglect of non-traditional families such as those of gays and lesbians as well as single-parent families. Okin's work has been criticized in a similar way.

In reply to this criticism, it should be emphasized that in North America, heterosexual families with children prevail; there certainly are other family types, but in terms of sheer numbers they remain marginal.[32] Notice, too, that the second-shift phenomenon is not just insightful for thinking about the fairness of traditional families. Consider, for instance, single-parent families. When those single parents work, they all face the second shift at home. Indeed, that second shift necessarily falls on their shoulders. This analysis applies regardless of

---

[30] Jeremy Waldron, 'When Justice Replaces Affection: The Need for Rights' in *Liberal Rights* (New York: Cambridge University Press, 1993), p. 372.

[31] Iris Marion Young, *Intersecting Voices* (Princeton: Princeton University Press, 1998), pp. 98–99.

[32] A classic illustration of this point remains Mary Jo Bane, *Here to Stay: American Families in the Twentieth Century* (New York: Basic Books, 1976).

whether these single parents are men or women. But, given that more than 80 percent of single-parent households are female-headed, it is predominantly women in this type of family who face the unfair burden of the second shift in labour market competition. And this clearly crosses lines based on both class and race.

This concern about privileging a particular type of family is an additional reason for rejecting the simple application of the equal opportunities model to injustices within families. Part of the philosophical challenge of thinking about justice within families is precisely respecting the diversity of family types. As Will Kymlicka has perceptively put it, "To assume that justice requires fairness between *mothers* and *fathers* in the raising of *their* children is to have already assumed much of what a theory of family justice needs to determine."[33] Drucilla Cornell rejects Okin's application of equal opportunity to the family for much the same reason. Cornell says, "My central difference with Okin is that whereas my program of legal reform emphasizes our equal standing as free persons, her program emphasizes reforms that would make women more equal to men within heterosexual marriage."[34] Her main objection to Okin's approach is that in order to promote fair equality of opportunity within families, it is necessary to have a state-imposed definition of the normal or ideal family.[35]

This problem will loom large for any embrace of home-based policies for addressing the unfairness of the second shift for women. Consider, for instance, Martha Fineman's argument that legal reform of family law should be focussed on displacing marriage as its core and replacing it with "the mother-child formation."[36] Her call is for feminists to reclaim 'motherhood' and mothering. Fineman's view is that this will lead to the valuing of women's work, especially caretaking, and ground women's claims in family law disputes such as custody and financial support. What has worried even sympathetic critics of Fineman is that, in Molly Shanley and Diane Harriford's words, "her approach runs the risks both of essentializing *Mother* and of limiting the number of persons who feel themselves to have, and are regarded by the law as having, permanent

---

[33] Will Kymlicka, 'Rethinking the Family,' *Philosophy & Public Affairs*, Vol. 20 (1991), p. 97.

[34] Drucilla Cornell, *At the Heart of Freedom: Feminism, Sex, and Equality* (Princeton: Princeton University Press, 1998), p. 67.

[35] Cornell, *At the Heart of Freedom*, pp. 26, 90–91.

[36] Martha Fineman, *The Neutered Mother, the Sexual Family, and Other Twentieth Century Tragedies* (London: Routledge, 1995), pp. 6–12.

responsibility for a child or other dependent person."[37] It seems hard for any home-based approach to avoid this charge of essentializing some aspect of the home and family.

The third line of criticism is that my approach assumes far too rigid a distinction between the family and the labour market.[38] The two, it might be said, cannot be separated; the structure of the labour market reflects the structure of the family. Hence, it is impossible to limit, as I propose, the three-dimensional model of equal opportunities as a regulative ideal to the labour market.

While I agree that the labour market and the family cannot be separated – indeed my analysis here relies on the claim that family structure effects the behaviour of women in the labour market – it is still plausible to insist that they are distinct for the purposes of law and policymaking. This is clearest when one thinks about constraints on legislation. When regulating the workplace or the labour market, the sorts of limitations that have currency are typically those that appeal to economic efficiency and similar such notions. The family, on the other hand, generates concerns about intimacy, personal affairs, and so on. Take the example of cigarette smoking. Laws against smoking in the workplace are widespread, and the main sticking points – for example, restaurants and bars – focus on the economic consequences of such bans. In contrast, to the best of my knowledge, at least in North America, there are no legal bans on smoking in family homes even though there may well be justifications for such bans that parallel those appealed to in the case of workplaces. Notice, too, that given this close symbiotic relationship between the family and the labour market, it is reasonable to assume that changes in the latter will seep eventually into the former. This means that policies such as affirmative action and comparable worth will eventually bring about changes to the family. The substantive question is whether or not those changes lessen the burden of the second shift on women.

Ultimately, the distinction I am drawing is not between public and private institutions. As I have insisted throughout this book, the labour market and the family are both institutions of civil society. They are part of neither the government nor the private sphere. Hence, I am not suggesting that the three-dimensional model of equal opportunities

---

[37] Diane Harriford and Mary L. Shanley, 'Revisioning Family Law,' *Law & Society Review, Vol. 30, No. 2* (1996), pp. 437–38.
[38] I owe this objection to Martha Fineman.

should regulate only public institutions. My claim is simply that that model is designed to regulate allocation when there is competition for opportunities. And the family, whatever the particular form it might take – traditional, gay, lesbian, single parent, extended, polygamous, and so on – is not a competitive forum.

8.5 CONCLUSION

My line of argument in this chapter is a simple one. First, I presented an analysis of two well-known gender gaps – the wage gap and the senior hirings and promotions gap – that traces these gaps to the fact that women competing in the labour market also work a second shift at home, especially when they have children. Next, I argued that this second shift is unfair to women because it is inconsistent with the requirements of stakes fairness and background fairness set out in the three-dimensional model of equal opportunities as a regulative ideal. Third, I presented employment and pay equity based on the principles of affirmative action and comparable worth as correctives for this unfairness in the labour market. Finally, I defended this indirect attack on the second shift through workplace-based policies rather than through direct measures to regulate the division of domestic labour between men and women within families by insisting that families are not forums for competition and therefore should not be regulated by the model of equal opportunities.

This last point is worth elaborating upon in yet another way. Hochschild, in her research on the second shift, found that twenty percent of American dual-career families do share housework equally between men and women. This led her to speculate on what makes these families different.[39] The standard answer she received is that women who have husbands who share the housework are "lucky." But Hochschild found a worrisome asymmetry to the extent that in the other 80 percent of families where women did much more housework, men with these wives were not said to be lucky. This was simply normal and typical. An important inference Hochschild makes is that among the institutions of civil society, families have been much more resistant to change than the labour market, which adapted very quickly to accommodate the participation of huge numbers of women. The conclusion I want to draw from this is that once the second shift is identified as

---

[39] Hochschild, *The Second Shift*, pp. xi–xiii.

disadvantaging women in competition for opportunities such as jobs, it is much more promising to pursue change through policies in the workplace such as affirmative action and comparable worth that remedy for the effects of the second shift than to seek reform of the family directly.

Chapter 9

Equal Opportunities after Divorce

9.1 INTRODUCTION

Among liberal egalitarian feminists, few issues in the past twenty years have more starkly raised questions about gender inequalities and legal institutions than the economic and social consequences of divorce law reforms since the early 1970s. These reforms, which began in California in 1970 and were adopted virtually throughout Canada and the United States over the subsequent decade, allowed for easier divorce, ending the legal requirement that one of the parties be found at fault.[1] The initial effect of these reforms was a significant acceleration in the divorce rate. The extent to which the divorce rate has stabilized remains unclear. While some conservatives attacked easier divorce because they viewed it as a threat to the traditional institution of the family, many egalitarians viewed it as progressive, especially from the perspective of women, because it offered the opportunity to lift the yoke of unhappy and repressive marriages.[2] Women continue to petition for divorces at much higher rates than men; these legal reforms make those applications easier, and increase their likelihood of success.

Parallel to these developments were discoveries about the changing face of poverty. In the early 1970s, poverty rates in both the United States and Canada were at record lows. However, beginning in the mid-1970s,

---

[1] California in 1970 famously abolished all fault-based grounds for divorce. Many other legal jurisdictions, whilst following California in allowing for no-fault divorce, retained fault-based grounds. But in practice those grounds are now rarely relied upon in petitions for divorce.

[2] This is well described by Lisa C. Bower, 'Unsettling "Woman": Competing Subjectivities in No-Fault Divorce and Divorce Mediation' in Leslie Friedman Goldstein, editor, *Feminist Jurisprudence: The Difference Debate* (NJ: Rowman & Littlefield, 1992), pp. 213–217.

poverty rates on most standard indices began to climb, and despite an often-booming economy, have not declined significantly. Poverty was said to have a new face because women and children made up a much greater portion of the poor than before. In the United States, about 40 percent of the poor are children.[3] And at least two-thirds of the adults living in poverty are women. A similar trend was found in Canada.[4] This new face of poverty was quickly labelled "the feminization of poverty."[5]

In the mid-1980s, several scholars, most notably Lenore Weitzman, linked these two developments – the onslaught of no-fault divorce law reforms and the feminization of poverty. The observation that there is some connection between the feminization of poverty and the liberalization of divorce laws in Canada and the United States was commonplace at that time.[6] The reason was that almost every careful analysis revealed that poverty rates among single-parent households were high, and appeared to be accelerating. Hence, since divorce generates single-parent households, poverty levels are likely to be influenced by divorce rates. The innovative argument that Weitzman made in her 1985 book, *The Divorce Revolution: The Unexpected Social and Economic Consequences for Women and Children in America*, was that post-divorce economic settlements are a major cause of the feminization of poverty. Weitzman claimed that in no-fault divorces in California, there are significant asymmetrical economic consequences for men and women. She appeared to have found "that the standard of living of divorced women and their children dropped 73 percent in the first year after divorce, while that of divorced men increased 42 percent."[7] Whilst this specific finding by Weitzman is widely disputed, and she herself has apparently conceded that it may be inaccurate, there does now seem to be

---

[3] See Rebecca Blank, *It Takes a Nation, paperback edition* (Princeton, Russell Sage/Princeton University Press, 1997), pp. 16–17.

[4] E.g., the annual report cards on child poverty in Canada by the Toronto-based Campaign 2000.

[5] Barbara and Frances Fox Piven, 'The Feminization of Poverty,' *Dissent* (Spring 1984), pp. 162–170.

[6] See, e.g., Mary Jane Mossman and Morag MacLean, 'Family Law and Social Welfare: Toward a New Equality,' *Canadian Journal of Family Law*, Vol. 5 (1986), pp. 81–89; Terry Arendell, 'Women and the Economics of Divorce in the Contemporary United States,' *Signs*, Vol. 13 (1987), pp. 121–23; and Janice Peterson, 'The Feminization of Poverty,' *Journal of Economic Issues*, Vol. 21 (1987), pp. 331–32.

[7] Lenore Weitzman, *The Divorce Revolution* (New York: The Free Press, 1985), p. 362.

general agreement that no-fault divorce does have considerable asymmetrical economic effects on men and women.[8] The distinctive feature of Weitzman's work is that she attributes this asymmetry to the design and implementation of no-fault divorce laws. As she puts it, "The laws regulating divorce exert a powerful independent force in shaping the social and economic consequences of divorce,"[9] and that therefore it is not surprising to find that no-fault divorce law reform is in large part to blame for "impoverishing divorced women and their children."[10] The challenge she poses is her proposal that by altering the laws governing post-divorce economic settlements, the feminization of poverty will be lessened.

This challenge has engendered many different sorts of responses. Some, such as Herma Hill Kay and Herbert Jacob, questioned any generalizations about the negative effects of no-fault divorce law because of the diversity of no-fault divorce law provisions in the United States.[11] This diversity makes it difficult, if not impossible, to attribute the alleged ill-effects of divorce on women and children to the legal reforms of the 1970s.[12] Others found in this challenge to no-fault divorce law a nostalgic view of divorce law based exclusively on fault.[13] Many others have proposed specific changes and additions to existing no-fault laws regulating economic settlements. These include a wide range of

---

[8] The following are among the most cogent such challenges: Saul D. Hoffman and Greg J. Duncan, 'What Are the Economic Consequences of Divorce?,' *Demography, Vol. 25* (1988), pp. 641–45; Herbert Jacob, 'Another Look at No-Fault Divorce and the Post-Divorce Finances of Women,' *Law & Society Review, Vol. 23* (1989), pp. 95–116; Gene E. Pollock and Atlee L. Stroup, 'Economic Consequences of Marital Dissolution for Blacks,' *Journal of Divroce & Remarriage, Vol. 26* (1996), pp. 49–67; and Stephen Sugarman, 'Dividing Interests on Divorce' in Stephen Sugarman & Herma Hill Kay, editors, *Divorce Reform at the Crossroads* (New Haven: Yale University Press, 1990), pp. 131–35. For an analysis that emphasizes the political dimension of this debate, see Susan Faludi, *Backlash* (New York: Doubleday, 1991), pp. 19–25.

[9] Lenore Weitzman, 'Bringing the Law Back In,' *American Bar Foundation Research Journal, Vol. 4* (1986), p. 791.

[10] Weitzman, *The Divorce Revolution*, p. xi.

[11] Herma Hill Kay, 'Equality and Difference: A Perspective on No-Fault Divorce and Its Aftermath,' *University of Cincinnati Law Review, Vol. 56* (1987), pp. 55–77; Herbert Jacob, 'Faulting No-Fault,' *American Bar Foundation Association, Vol. 4* (1986), pp. 773–80.

[12] The diverse character of no-fault divorce law is transparent in, for instance, Brett R. Turner, *Equitable Distribution of Property, 2nd edition* (Colorado Springs: Shepard's/McGraw-Hill, 1994).

[13] Marsha Garrison, 'The Economics of Divorce' *in Divorce Reform at the Crossroads*, pp. 75–101.

suggestions falling under the general rough rubric of marital property such as expanding the definition to include career assets, degrees, professional status, and goodwill; revising alimony; and altering what is community property. Others have emphasized judicial reform, seeking stricter guidelines for judges and curtailing their discretion. Still others have sought increases in the level and enforcement of child support payments by non-custodial parents, typically men. More ambitious proposals have revolved around the idea of compensating stay-at-home parents for loss of earning potential, placing the mother-child relationship at the centre of family law, and income-sharing between divorced parties.[14] The impact of these suggestions has been mixed, varying widely from legal jurisdiction to legal jurisdiction. The diversity of family law regimes makes it hard to identify any specific legal prescription that is a remedy for the ills of the current systems.

My intention in this chapter is to step back initially from these fundamental questions about divorce law reform and attempt to rethink the broader normative question of what is a fair post-divorce economic settlement. This normative question has been neglected in the rush to undertake 'empirical' research and prescribe legal reforms.[15] My view is, however, that only with a firm answer to this question can we propose sound, constructive reforms to existing divorce law with an eye to promoting greater gender equality.

After providing some preliminary comments on fault-based divorce settlements, I sketch the three dominant accounts of a fair post-divorce economic settlement and their inadequacies. Then I utilize the three-dimensional model of equal opportunities as a regulative ideal advanced earlier in this book to provide an alternative account of a fair post-divorce economic settlement, an account that better fits with a range of considerations that influence our normative views of divorce. Finally, I strengthen the case for this account of equal opportunities after divorce by considering the implications of this account for two central

[14] See, e.g., C. Funder, 'Australia: A Proposal for Reform' in Maclean and Weitzman, *Economic Consequences of Divorce*; Martha Fineman, *The Neutred Mother, the Sexual Family, and Other Twentieth Century Tragedies* (London: Routledge, 1995); June Carbone, 'Income Sharing: Redefining the Family in Terms of Community,' *Houston Law Review*, Vol. 31 (1994); J. Thomas Oldham, 'The Economic Consequences of Divorce in the United States in A. Bainham, D. Pearl, & Ros Pickford, editors, *Frontiers of Family Law* (Chichester, UK: John Wiley, 1995).

[15] Representative here is Mavis Maclean and Lenore Weitzman, 'Introduction to the Issues' in Mavis Maclean & Lenore Weitzman, editors, *Economic Consequences of Divorce* (Oxford: Clarendon Press, 1992), p. 3.

issues in the division of marital property – dealing with the family home and assessing career assets.

9.2 WHAT'S WRONG WITH FAULT-BASED DIVORCE LAW?

The fundamental characteristic of the liberalization of divorce law throughout North America during the 1970s was the introduction of no-fault grounds for divorce. Prior to this reform, divorce law required that at least one of the parties be found at fault in order for the marriage to be dissolved. It is now reasonably clear that a major impetus for this reform was the widespread perception and practice of deception and perjury in order to establish fault in divorce cases.[16] Most legal reform led to the establishment of either pure no-fault divorce systems, such as California's, or mixed systems, such as Canada's, which retained fault as a basis for divorce but also allowed for no-fault grounds.[17] In practice, no-fault grounds quickly emerged as the dominant basis for the dissolution of marriages in all jurisdictions.

From the perspective of post-divorce economic settlements, the introduction of no-fault grounds posed an interesting problem. Historically, finding one of the parties to the divorce at fault had important implications for the economic settlement because the actual settlement could have a punitive function – in effect, who was at fault and the character of the fault helped to determine the nature of the settlement. For instance, alimony was not generally awarded to a spouse at fault.[18] There is an obvious parallel here with the role fault can play in auto insurance.[19] Under a fault-based auto insurance system, financial responsibility for an accident can be assigned based on who was at fault for the accident. No-fault auto insurance clearly requires some sort of different standard for assigning financial responsibility in the case of an accident. Similarly, no-fault divorce requires some sort of other basis for reaching an economic settlement between the parties.

The normative argument at stake here is often obscured by the historical debate around whether allowing fault to determine post-divorce

---

[16] Herbert Jacob, *Silent Revolution: The Transformation of Divorce Law in the United States* (Chicago: University of Chicago Press, 1988), chs. 3–4.
[17] For this distinction between pure and mixed systems of divorce, see Kay, 'Equality and Difference,' pp. 55–77.
[18] Oldham, 'The Economic Consequences of Divorce in the United States,' p. 107.
[19] Despite the conceptual similarities between no-fault divorce and no-fault auto insurance, their origins in the policymaking process are very different. See Jacob, *Silent Revolution*, p. 64.

economic settlements had good economic consequences for women. In some instances, women did very poorly under a fault-based system. For example, adultery by the wife was often a bar to any amount of alimony or financial support. However, according to Lenore Weitzman, in California when women were not at fault, they did quite well:

In 1968, under the old fault-based law, the wife, as the "innocent" plaintiff, was typically awarded the lion's share of the property. She received more than half (i.e., 60 percent or more) in four out of five divorce cases in San Francisco, and in three out of five cases in Los Angeles... In 1968 the property was divided equally in only 12 percent of the cases in San Francisco, and 26 percent of the cases in Los Angeles. Under the no-fault law, the percentage of cases in which the property was divided equally increased from 12 to 59 percent in San Francisco between 1968 and 1972, and from 26 to 64 percent in Los Angeles.[20]

In general, although it is doubtful that there is a simple answer to the question of whether women's interests were well served by fault-based economic settlements, when it comes to the normative question of what is a just or fair settlement, considerations of fault no longer play a primary role. In effect, there is now a broad consensus among policymakers and in legal circles that a sustainable theory of what is a just or fair post-divorce economic settlement must appeal to a principle other than fault. And it is in this context that I defend the principle of equalizing opportunities after divorce.

9.2.1 Three Dominant Approaches to Divorce Settlements

In response to the end of fault-based post-divorce economic settlements, it is important to distinguish between three distinct answers to the question of what is a fair settlement that have prevailed in the courts and legislatures as well as in academic discussions of this issue. Each offers an account of what the primary objective of the economic settlement should be, and treats the issue of legal reform as a matter of finding the appropriate means to promote this objective. These three approaches I label, respectively, the *clean break* approach, the *dissolving partnership* approach, and the *equal living standards* approach. I shall show that none of these approaches can withstand careful scrutiny and that therefore there is a real need for an alternative approach to what is a fair economic settlement after divorce.

---

[20] Weitzman, *The Divorce Revolution*, pp. 73–74.

9.2.2 *The 'Clean Break' Approach*

From the perspective of society in general, it might seem that the primary objective in a divorce is simply a clean break between the parties. Each party should be able to start fresh, free to enter into another relationship, and perhaps remarry. A just economic settlement after divorce would therefore be one that assumes and promotes self-reliance and self-sufficiency for each of the parties. As Claire L'Heureux-Dube, a recently retired judge on Canada's Supreme Court, explains it, "A 'clean break' between divorcees may be the ideal solution when it can be achieved, as it enables each party to go on with their separate lives, unburdened by financial responsibilities toward the former family unit."[21]

A major theme among a diverse group of feminist legal and political theorists including Martha Fineman, Martha Minow, Susan Moller Okin, Deborah Rhode, and Lenore Weitzman is that this approach rests on a misconception – they reject the view that a just economic settlement after divorce is one that assumes and promotes self-reliance for each of the parties.[22] The fundamental problem with the clean break approach to a fair economic settlement after divorce is that it mistakenly assumes that divorced women are similarly situated to divorced men. As Martha Fineman puts it:

Under such [sic] laws, divorced women are to assume sole economic responsibility for themselves and joint economic responsibility for their children. Theoretically, the requirement is fair because divorced women will assume this responsibility under the same terms and conditions as their ex-spouses. Equal treatment in divorce, however, can only be fair if spouses have access to equivalent resources. Realistically, many women do not have such economic advantages.[23]

---

[21] Claire L'Heureux-Dube, 'Economic Consequences of Divorce: A View from Canada,' *Houston Law Review*, Vol. 31 (1994), pp. 479–80.

[22] Martha Fineman, 'Implementing Equality: Ideology, Contradiction and Social Change,' *Wisconsin Law Review*, no. 4 (1983), pp. 790–886; Fineman, 'Illusive Equality,' *American Bar Foundation Research Journal*, Vol. 4 (1986), pp. 781–90; Fineman, *The Illusion of Equality* (Chicago: University of Chicago Press, 1991), ch. 3; Deborah Rhode, *Justice and Gender* (Cambridge: Harvard University Press, 1989), pp. 149–50; Deborah Rhode and Martha Minow, 'Reforming the Questions, Questioning the Reforms: Feminist Perspectives on Divorce Law' in *Divorce Reform at the Crossroads*; Okin, 'Economic Equality After Divorce,' *Dissent* (Summer 1991), pp. 383–87; *Justice, Gender, and the Family* (New York: Basic Books, 1989), ch. 7; and Weitzman, *The Divorce Revolution*, esp. chs. 4, 6, 7.

[23] Fineman, 'Implementing Equality,' p. 830.

In a similar vein, Weitzman says, "divorce laws that treat women 'equally' and assume that all women are equally equipped to survive the breakup of their families without support from their ex-husbands or society, only serve to enlarge the gap between men and women and create even greater inequalities."[24]

With divorces involving children and those following marriages of a long duration in mind, these critics of the clean break approach argue that the differences in circumstances between divorced women and divorced men follow two trajectories. One trajectory is specific to the divorce context. Two considerations are especially important. The first is that women typically retain custody of the children of the marriage and therefore bear many of the indirect costs of child rearing that may affect how well they can easily perform jobs that enable them to become self-sufficient. (There are also the direct costs of child-rearing, which are rarely adequately covered by child support payments by the non-custodial parent.) The second consideration is that in marriages with children couples typically invest more human capital in the husband than in the wife, thus giving men greater earning potential in the labour market.[25] The other trajectory emphasizes the broader context of gender inequalities in society. These include the sorts of gaps between men and women in the workplace discussed in the previous chapter, such as the gender wage gap. Given these differences in circumstances, a clean break approach seems unfair because it imposes on women the overwhelming costs of marital breakdown.

The clean break approach also seems inconsistent with trends in child custody provisions, in particular in the increase in joint or shared custody arrangements, since such arrangements presuppose an on-going relationship between the former spouses. Of course, while it remains unclear whether or not joint custody is in the best interests of the child, such child-care arrangements do seem to promote gender equality insofar as they challenge conventional views of the roles that women and men can assume.[26]

---

[24] Weitzman, *The Divorce Revolution*, p. 362.

[25] Oldham in 'Economic Consequences of Divorce in the United States' cites evidence that "a person who stays out of the work-force incurs an annual loss of approximately 2 percent in seniority rights and pay raises, as well as .5 percent in human capital depreciation,' p. 113.

[26] Diane Harriford and Mary J. Shanley, 'Revisioning Family Law,' *Law & Society Review*, Vol. 30 (1996), pp. 437–45.

9.2.3 Partnership Analogies

A popular alternative to the clean break approach to just economic set-tlements after divorce relies on drawing an analogy between a marriage and a business partnership. This approach treats the question of what is a fair post-divorce economic settlement as secondary to the more ba-sic problem of correctly characterizing an equal relationship between men and women in marriage. The underlying strategy is to identify *a priori* what sort of relationship marriage ought to be, and infer from that what is a fair settlement upon its dissolution. Especially among socio-legal scholars, it is common to argue that properly understood, a marriage should be considered a legal partnership between equals analogous to a legal partnership in business. The general point is that if marriage is so considered, a just economic settlement is a function of the rules that regulate the termination of a partnership. Since the legal rules that regulate the termination of a business partnership are well established, and a marriage is an analogous type of partnership, then those same rules should be readily applied to the dissolution of marriage.

An important presumption that underlies this claim that marriage should be regarded as a type of partnership between equals is that many of the asymmetrical economic consequences of divorce for men and women stem from the failure to recognize the marriage as a partnership of this kind. The logic is that if marriage on dissolution is treated by the courts as a partnership of equals, many of the unfair asymmetrical eco-nomic consequences of divorce emphasized by Weitzman and others will disappear. James McLindon, for example, argues that marriage "should be considered a partnership from which, upon its dissolution, each spouse and the children deserve to withdraw with an equal stan-dard of living."[27] Others, such as Jana Singer, advance "an investment model of marriage" and infer from it the principle that post-divorce in-come should be divided equally for a time period equal to the length of the marriage.[28] Still others, such as Joan Krauskopf, characterize mar-riage as a type of partnership such that "the purpose of economic set-tlement is to assure that, at the conclusion of the marriage, one party does not suffer unduly while the other gains because of the marriage

[27] James McLindon, 'Separate but Equal: The Economic Disaster of Divorce for Women,' *Family Law Quarterly*, Vol. 21 (1987), p. 396.
[28] Jana Singer, 'Divorce Reform and Gender Justice,' *North Carolina Law Review*, Vol. 67 (1989), pp. 1114–1118.

experience."[29] Thus, in appearance, the implications of the view that marriage should be regarded as a partnership of equals seem to be significant for the normative issue of what constitutes a fair economic settlement upon divorce.

However, on closer inspection, I think that these sorts of partnership analogies are problematic and ultimately question-begging. My disagreement is not with the characterization of marriage in its normative ideal as a partnership of equals. This ideal is indeed a powerful one with a long history, dating back more than a century to the liberal feminism of John Stuart Mill.[30] However, the strategy of identifying *a priori* the character of marriage seems to be an extreme type of essentialism; it presupposes that all marriages share a common essence. But in practice, as in the case of essentialist strategies for defining what constitutes a family,[31] it is very doubtful that all marriages share a common essence.[32] Ironically, Mill introduced the analogy between marriage and a business partnership precisely to illustrate the absurdity of the law's trying to define precisely the rights and duties of the parties in a marriage. Like business partnerships, every marriage, Mill reasoned, is different and there is no division of powers pre-established by law.[33] Ultimately, however, I find any sort of partnership analogy to be unhelpful because it is question-begging to assume any obligations between partners after the dissolution of the partnership. Certainly, most business partnerships do not. As Ira Mark Ellman has stressed in his critique of this analogy, "Once the partnership liquidation is completed, the partners have no further continuing obligations to one another."[34] Yet this would seem to reinforce the clean break approach rather than serve as an alternative vision of just economic settlements after divorce.

---

[29] Joan Krauskopf, 'Theories of Property Division/Spousal Support: Searching for Solutions to the Mystery,' *Family Law Quarterly, Vol. 23* (1989), p. 256.
[30] John Stuart Mill, The Subjection of Women [1869], reprinted in Lesley Jacobs and Richard Vandewetering, editors, *John Stuart Mill's 'The Subjection of Women': His Contemporary and Modern Critics* (Delmar, NY: Caravan Press, 1999), pp. 94– 96.
[31] Will Kymlicka, 'Rethinking the Family,' *Philosophy & Public Affairs, Vol. 20* (1991), pp. 83–86.
[32] For an excellent discussion of the diversity of marriage and the problems with assuming a singular model, see June Carbone and Margaret Brinig, 'Rethinking Marriage: Feminist Ideology, Economic Change, and Divorce Reform,' *Tulane Law Review, Vol. 65* (1991), pp. 953–1010.
[33] Mill, *The Subjection of Women*, p. 95.
[34] Ira Mark Ellman, 'The Theory of Alimony,' *California Law Review, Vol. 77* (1989), p. 35. See also Sugarman, 'Dividing Financial Interests on Divorce,' p. 140.

9.2.4 Equalizing Post-Divorce Standards of Living

Amongst feminist legal and political philosophers, the most attractive approach to the normative question of what is a fair economic settlement after divorce has been to insist on equalizing standards of living between parties for a length of time after divorce.[35] This reflects, especially, the influence of Susan Okin, who has argued that "arrangements after divorce should aim to equalize the standards of living of both postdivorce households."[36] More recently, Drucilla Cornell has reiterated equalizing standards of living after divorce as a fundamental component of an agenda to achieve sex equality.[37] Among lawyers concerned with divorce law reform, this approach is also prevalent. For instance, during public consultations in 1996 regarding amendments to the child support sections of the Canadian Divorce Law Act, the Canadian Bar Association also appealed explicitly to the normative ideal of equalizing standards of living between households after divorce, calling for legal changes "to ensure there is no discrepancy in the standard of living of custodial and non-custodial parents."[38]

The preoccupation with equalizing standards of living is a clear illustration of the profound impact Weitzman's empirical work has had on theorizing fair economic settlements after divorce. As I noted at the beginning of this chapter, Weitzman found that after divorce, there is a significant difference in the standard of living of men and women. Whilst men enjoy a significant increase in their standard of living, women and children suffer a significant decline. Weitzman maintains that this consequence is unjust because it deviates from the requirement of justice that an economic settlement after divorce achieve equal living standards for the principal parties. And she appears to be the first person to articulate this view, saying in 1985, "What we need is a new standard [for economic settlements] based on equality of results for the two spouses ... i.e., equality in the postdivorce standards of living of the two spouses."[39]

---

[35] The claim that this is the dominant approach is also made by June Carbone, 'Income Sharing: Redefining the Family in Terms of Community,' *Houston Law Review*, Vol. 31 (1994), p. 372.

[36] Okin, 'Economic Equality after Divorce,' p. 386. See also *Justice, Gender, and the Family*, pp. 179, 83.

[37] Drucilla Cornell, *At the Heart of Freedom: Feminism, Sex, and Equality* (Princeton: Princeton University Press, 1998), p. 93.

[38] 'Change Support Formula, CBA urges,' *The Globe and Mail* (Toronto), October 25, 1996.

[39] Weitzman, *The Divorce Revolution*, pp. 104–105.

What is striking, however, from a philosophical perspective is the lack of critical engagement with the very concept of equalizing standards of living between households after divorce. While people certainly have rejected this standard for divorce settlements and favoured others, it is surprising that the very idea of equalizing standards of living has not been scrutinized carefully, especially given the huge amount of relevant literature written by philosophers and economists over the past thirty years on the nature of economic justice.

An elementary feature of this approach is that insisting on the comparison between households entails a comparative standard of fairness when assessing the standards of living rather than an absolute or basic minimum standard. This is contrary to the most familiar usages of standard-of-living criteria in assessing economic justice. For example, Article 25 of the 1948 Universal Declaration of Human Rights states, "Everyone has the right to a standard of living *adequate* for the health and well-being of himself and of his family, including food, clothing, housing and medical care and necessary social services."[40] Weitzman, Okin, and others are not simply calling for "adequate" standards of living in both households after divorce; their focus is on equalizing those standards. The transparent reason is that the asymmetries between the post-divorce standards of living of men and women and children Weitzman found are disturbing when we assume a comparative perspective. The tragedy is that often in the years immediately following divorce, neither household can achieve an adequate standard of living without some measure of public support. Highlighting the asymmetries between men and women, as Weitzman does, generally obscures this tragedy.[41]

Part of the reason for being uneasy about talking about comparable standards of living rather than about an adequate standard of living derives from semi-technical debates among economists and philosophers. One such debate is around the very possibility of making inter-personal comparisons of standards of living. Scepticism among economists about

---

[40] Emphasis added. See David Copp, 'The Right to an Adequate Standard of Living' in Ellen Fankel Paul, Fred Miller, and Jeffrey Paul, editors, *Economic Rights* (New York: Cambridge University Press, 1992).

[41] This is well argued by Jane Pulkingham, 'Private Troubles, Private Solutions: Poverty among Divorced Women and the Politics of Support Enforcement and Child Custody Determination,' *Canadian Journal of Law & Society*, Vol. 9 (1994), pp. 73–97, and 'Investigating the Financial Circumstances of Separated and Divorced Parents: Implications for Family Law Reform,' *Canadian Public Policy*, Vol. 21 (1995), pp. 1–19.

making such comparisons is widespread.[42] Yet, being able to make such comparisons, and indeed having a legal mechanism that can do so, is a basic requirement of any defensible proposal that equalizing living standards is the appropriate objective of fair divorce settlements.

A related debate revolves around the question of how one measures the standard of living. Is the appropriate form of measurement a subjective yardstick such as preference-satisfaction or happiness or a more objective yardstick such as income, goods, and resources? Often, Weitzman simply equates income and standard of living.[43] But others, such as Okin, who otherwise follow Weitzman, reject this equivocation since it does not adequately capture the effects of being the custodial parent of children on a person's standard of living.[44] The idea is more complex than simply the observation that raising children has both direct and indirect costs and that the latter are often neglected. It also involves the observation that some of the work of raising children is under-valued precisely because it is done predominantly by women.[45] Amartya Sen has pointed out a number of other important considerations for many women that are also not captured by a focus on income, including

the capability of being nourished (e.g. because of the demands of pregnancy and neonatal care), achieving security (e.g. in single-parent families), having fulfilling work (e.g. because of stereotyping of 'women's jobs'), establishing one's professional reputation early on in one's career (e.g. because of the asymmetric demands of family life).[46]

If an objective yardstick other than income is used, however, it becomes difficult to identify a particular good or a bundle of goods without engaging in the moral basis for invoking those goods rather than others.[47]

---

[42] Amartya Sen in *Choice, Welfare and Measurement* (Oxford: Basil Blackwell, 1982), chs. 9, 12, provides an accessible review of the standard problems with making these comparisons, and some possible replies. See also the range of papers in Jon Elster and John Roemer, editors, *Interpersonal Comparisons of Well-Being* (Cambridge: Cambridge University Press, 1991).

[43] Sugarman, 'Dividing Financial Interests on Divorce,' p. 150.

[44] Okin, 'Economic Equality after Divorce,' p. 384.

[45] L'Heureux-Dube, 'Economic Consequences of Divorce,' pp. 470–71.

[46] Amartya Sen, *Inequality Reexamined* (Cambridge, MA: Harvard University Press, 1992), p. 113.

[47] Thomas M. Scanlon, 'The Moral Basis of Interpersonal Comparisons' in Jon Elster and John Roemer, editors, *Interpersonal Comparisons of Well-Being* (Cambridge: Cambridge University Press, 1991).

Subjective yardsticks for measuring standards of living are also controversial, especially when the underlying concern is with equality for men and women. Developmental economists studying severe deprivation and famine in the developing world have found that subjective yardsticks for measuring standards of living contain gender bias. In effect, women in developing countries are typically satisfied with less food, fewer calories, and so on than their male counterparts.[48] The implication is that this is the result of adaptive preference formation, famously illustrated by Aesop's tale about the fox and the grapes. The unsavoury upshot is that using a subjective standard of living yardstick such as preference-satisfaction or happiness may justify women's receiving fewer resources than similarly situated men.

From a more general philosophical perspective, what is especially problematic about equalizing standards of living after divorce is the equality of results framework within which it is situated. Weitzman, in the passage quoted earlier, is explicit about this framework. Political and legal philosophers such as Okin and Cornell seem to ignore this point. In philosophical debates around egalitarian justice, as we saw in Chapter 2, considerable pressure has been put on the alleged fairness of an equal-results principle such as this one that sets the equalizing of standards of living as the paramount aim of economic justice. Such a principle does not seem capable of distinguishing between negative effects on a person's standard of living caused by, on the one hand, a disability or handicap and, on the other hand, expensive tastes or preferences. Yet such a distinction is of fundamental importance to discussions of the fairness of post-divorce settlements. Feminist critics of the clean break approach often say that what that approach fails to appreciate is the extent to which women are handicapped by marriage. The intended contrast is with the disadvantage that women incur because of their preferences about marriage. Whilst men, like women, can suffer disadvantage because of their preferences about marriage, they cannot be handicapped by marriage.

Furthermore, there is an important sense in which equalizing standards of living between households after divorce might not be sufficiently sensitive to variations in ambitions among individuals and hence may lead to perverse conclusions to the extent that it might punish those with greater ambition. Consider, for example, the case of someone who

---

[48] Jean Dreze and Amartya Sen, *Hunger and Public Action* (Oxford: Clarendon Press, 1989), ch. 4.3.

Gender

after divorce chooses to work very hard and, as a result, increases significantly his or her income. Under the norm of equalizing standards of living, any such gains in income should be redistributed between the two households, even though the increased income has its origins in something that followed the divorce.[49] Conversely, imagine someone who after divorce makes choices that decrease significantly his or her income. Under the norm of equalizing standards of living, it is justified for the 'innocent' household to suffer a decline in its standard of living.

9.2.5 An Equal Opportunities Approach

As an alternative to the three dominant approaches not based on fault just reviewed, I now advance and defend the view that a fair economic settlement after divorce is one that provides equal opportunities for both parties. Underlying this equal opportunities approach is the belief that divorces can be regarded as competitions between the parties. Unlike in families, therefore, it is justified to utilize the three-dimensional model of equal opportunities as a regulative ideal in post-divorce economic settlements. Just as in the other applications of this model discussed throughout this book, the core idea is that post-divorce settlements should be regulated by three dimensions of fairness – procedural fairness, stakes fairness, background fairness – to ensure equal opportunities for both of the parties at the time of divorce.

There are many points of contrast between an equal opportunities approach to post-divorce settlements and the traditional fault-based one. The most significant turn on issues of stakes fairness. Fault-based settlements often made the stakes in the divorce competition simply too high. This is evident in the practice, already noted earlier, of never awarding alimony to a woman in a fault system if she were at fault for the dissolution of the marriage. Even more stark are child custody decisions based on fault. Rather than assuming a balanced approach, fault divorce frequently relies on a winner-take-all punitive mentality. An equal opportunities approach envisions economic settlements more consistent with the ideals of stakes fairness.

This also means an equal opportunities approach takes seriously some of the concerns that are sometimes raised about post-divorce economic settlements being unfair to men, especially when they are the

[49] Carbone, 'Income Sharing,' p. 388.

non-custodial parents. Two issues are especially instructive to illustrate the point. The first concerns access to children by non-custodial parents. It is now often claimed that custodial parents (read women) punish their ex-spouses by restricting or denying access to their children. This has led to calls for divorce law reform that better guarantees access. While these concerns have not always been well received, especially when the proposals entail linking access and child support payments, it seems to me that from the perspective of fair stakes, putting access by a non-custodial parent to his or her children on the table in a post-divorce settlement is unacceptable. There are certain things, such as access to children, that are simply too important to subject to a competitive divorce process with winners and losers. The second issue involves men's opportunities to remarry or form new families – straight, gay, and so on – after divorce. Women's opportunities to remarry have been widely discussed; a common criticism of the status quo is that remarriage is often the best way for women and children to escape poverty after divorce. And indeed it sometimes seems that they are 'forced' into remarrying. There has been little doubt that women have considerable opportunities to remarry; the doubts revolve around whether they can chose not to remarry. A concern can be raised about the effects of post-divorce economic settlements on men's opportunities to remarry, especially when courts order them to make substantial child support and spousal maintenance payments.[50] Pursuing equal opportunities after divorce validates this concern, requiring that a fair economic settlement must also be sensitive to the opportunities of men to remarry by comparison with women.

The most insightful contribution to theorizing a fair post-divorce economic settlement comes, however, from the background fairness dimension of the equal opportunities approach. Although it is not ordinarily characterized in this way, at the center of most feminist critiques of what constitutes a just post-divorce economic settlement is a concern

---

[50] This concern has also been expressed by others, including Oldham, 'Economic Consequences of Divorce in the United States,' p. 117; Martha Minow and Mary Lyndon Shanley, 'Relational Rights and Responsibilities: Revisioning the Family in Liberal Political Theory and Law,' *Hypatia*, Vol. 11 (1996), p. 22; and Iris Marion Young, *Intersecting Voices* (Princeton: Princeton University Press, 1998), who comments, "If courts consistently ruled for child-support awards that put the needs of children first, however, they might sometimes unfairly burden parents who have left a household, most often men, who would because of these constraints be unable to form or enter new families or make other life choices," p. 111.

for background fairness. The principle of status equality requires that in the competitive divorce process, men and women enjoy the same standing. There are at least three distinct respects in which background fairness and standing arises in the context of divorce: (1) How was domestic labour divided within the family during the marriage? (2) Who is the custodial parent after divorce? (3) What effect does gender disadvantage in the labour market have on the initial starting positions of the two parties after divorce? All three are central in most analyses of gender inequality in Canada and the United States. I shall discuss each in turn.

The first was highlighted earlier in the critique of the 'clean break' approach. It revolves around the fact that women are much more likely to sacrifice their opportunities in the labour market during the marriage for gains within the family. This was illustrated in the previous chapter by reference to the so-called second-shift phenomenon. Moreover, families with young children are much more likely to invest in the man's 'human capital.' The upshot is that upon divorce, men and women rarely enter the labour market at the same starting position. In accordance with an equal opportunities approach, post-divorce economic settlements should be designed to provide for some degree of income sharing to offset this type of background unfairness between the two parties. Obviously, the presence of children and the longer the duration of the marriage, the greater will be the extent of the income sharing. It is significant, however, that the purpose of the income sharing is clearly defined – namely, to remedy for disadvantages in initial starting positions.[51] The point of income sharing, on this account, is not punitive nor is it designed to achieve equal standards of living between households.

The costs of being the custodial parent after divorce raise the second distinct issue of background fairness.[52] The costs of being the custodial parent are both *direct* for goods such as food, housing, and clothing, and *indirect* insofar as a person's availability in the labour market – for

---

[51] An important upshot of this analysis is that in some cases, such as a short marriage, the best strategy for pursuing equal opportunities after divorce might be a clean break. The difference between the *clean break* approach and the *equal opportunities* approach in these cases concerns why, not how.

[52] The focus of this chapter is on post-divorce economic settlements, not all aspects of divorce. Custody decisions may in themselves raise distinct questions about background fairness – e.g., is a bias in favour of the primary caregiver unfair to men? – quite independently of the economic questions.

example, with respect to accepting overtime – is curtailed because of child custody responsibilities. Given the fact that women are in most instances the custodial parent, failure to remedy for these costs constitutes a form of systemic gender disadvantage. Child support payments are obviously designed to offset some of the direct costs of child care incurred by the custodial parent. But they do not address the respects in which the responsibilities of being the custodial parent after divorce handicap him or her in terms of initial starting position or standing in a competitive race for scarce resources and other sorts of opportunities. A fair economic settlement that aims for equal opportunities after divorce would also have to take this kind of background unfairness into consideration.

It might seem that the significance of this sort of background fairness in fair post-divorce economic settlements will diminish as the practice of divorcing parents' jointly sharing custody of their children increases. After all, joint custody would seem to distribute the direct and indirect costs of child care more equally between the two parents. It is of course an empirical question as to whether in practice joint custody genuinely has this effect. It is, however, important not to exaggerate the impact of joint custody. In Canada in 1986, 11.6 percent of child custody awards were joint, compared with 14.3 percent in 1990. Women were awarded sole custody in 72 percent of cases in 1986 and 73.3 percent in 1990. Men were awarded sole custody in 15.3 percent in 1986, but only 12.2 percent in 1990. Hence, Jane Pulkingham comments, "While there does appear to be a small upward trend in the award of joint legal custody, this increase is at the expense of sole paternal custody, not sole maternal custody. What appears to be happening is that fathers who may have previously been awarded sole custody are now being awarded joint legal custody. The proportion of mothers receiving sole maternal custody is not on the decline."[53] In other words, if this trend continues, joint custody is unlikely to make much of a mark on this second type of background unfairness raised by divorce.

The third type of background fairness that the equal-opportunities-after-divorce approach is concerned to address has to do with more general gender inequalities in the labour market discussed in Chapter 8. The upshot of the gender wage gap, for instance, is that after divorce, female-headed households will likely have considerably lower employment incomes than male-headed households. In effect, upon the

[53] Pulkingham, 'Private Troubles, Private Solutions,' pp. 90–99.

dissolution of their marriages, women as a group in their initial starting positions are more likely to face financial hardship than men.

What is noteworthy is that the equal opportunities approach is able, because of its emphasis on background fairness, to explain the moral significance of this type of gender disadvantage. Unlike the two other issues of background fairness discussed here, the appropriate remedy is not individual 'private law' post-divorce economic settlements, but rather public policies such as employment and pay equity defended in Chapter 8. What the equal-opportunities-after-divorce approach captures is the continuity between these public policy initiatives to address gender inequalities and the use of family law to reform post-divorce economic settlements. Here, the contrast with the model of equalizing standards of living is striking. A common theme among critics of Weitzman's is that her proposals seem to rely on the use of private means, such as the increased enforcement of child support payments, to address society's sex-based economic inequalities.[54] This follows logically from her findings because they imply, in effect, that the principal problem is the distribution of economic resources between post-divorce households. The problem can thus allegedly be solved by redistributing resources between households, and hence there seem to be no grounds here for initiating public policies oriented towards employment equity such as comparable worth and affirmative action.

There is one additional advantage of the equal opportunities approach that should be noted. Recall that one of the most serious difficulties with the equalizing-standards-of-living approach is the technical one of comparing standards of living. Why doesn't a similar difficulty arise for the equal opportunities approach? At issue here for egalitarian theories in general is the indexing problem described in Section 2.3. The indexing problem asks how we can aggregate diverse goods – standards of living, opportunities, or other measures – so that we have a complete measure of the share size for each individual. I argued that the three-dimensional model sidesteps the indexing problem by functioning as a regulative ideal for individual competitions and avoiding aggregating an individual's opportunities across competitions in civil society. In a divorce context, this means, in practice, selecting a certain limited set of opportunities – say, the labour market, moving on to new relationships, housing, and so on – and comparing the divorcing parties in each of these

---

[54] Lesley Jacobs, *Rights and Deprivation* (Oxford: Oxford University Press, 1993), pp. 206–211.

spheres one at a time. And the regulative role of the equal opportunities approach here is to assess whether differences in opportunities between the parties are in accordance with the three dimensions of procedural fairness, background fairness, and stakes fairness.

9.2.6 Dividing Marital Property Upon Divorce

The strengths of the equal opportunities approach and the contrasts with the three dominant approaches are clear when we examine the division of marital property. One of the familiar facts about divorce is how little property there is to divide. Often the most substantial piece of property is the (heavily mortgaged) marital home. The marital home has a unique place in divorce law practices with regard to economic settlements. In effect, while the home is technically no different from any other piece of marital property, its division is generally subject to certain special considerations that suggest that the home is in fact different from everything else. This is evident in Brett Turner's discussion of the marital home in his major law text, *Equitable Distribution of Property*. Turner insists:

Courts do not apply any special rules of law in classifying and valuing the marital home. Thus, marital homes are classified and valued under the same principles of law which apply to other assets.[55]

He then proceeds to emphasize that in certain situations, there is a *special need* for one spouse to remain in the home. The three cases Turner highlights are (1) when the spouse has custody of minor children, (2) is disabled, or (3) has been abused by the other spouse.[56] His point is that when these special needs exist, the court should either award ownership to the spouse or award that spouse exclusive use for a specified period of time – for example, until the minor children grow up. Leaving aside the puzzle of why Turner insists initially that the home is simply like all other marital property, the real question is why do these special needs have any normative purchase or sense of urgency in post-divorce settlements? Since I suspect that the second and third cases – the disabled spouse and the abused spouse – are a remnant of an earlier fault-based divorce system, I shall concentrate on the first case of the custodial parent with young children.

---

[55] Turner, *Equitable Distribution of Property*, p. 435.
[56] *Ibid.*, pp. 436–37.

The idea that the division of the marital home should be constrained by the special needs of one spouse enjoys considerable currency among those concerned with gender equality in economic settlements. Mavis Maclean and Weitzman, for instance, say, "The basic principle, if there are any children, is that the home should follow the children."[57] One of Weitzman's major criticisms of California's no-fault system is that the special needs of custodial parents do not have a place in the division of the marital home after divorce.[58] She found that there is a strong tendency for the courts to simply order the home sold and the assets divided equally between the parties. Weitzman is critical of this tendency because she believes it is especially harmful to children and their custodial parents, mostly women. Specifically, her view is that the living standards of women and children suffer significantly when the court simply orders the home sold. The contrast she draws is between California's no-fault law and English family law, where division of the marital home is much more likely to recognize the special needs of the spouse, especially when children are involved. At stake here, according to Weitzman, are competing views of a fair economic divorce settlement. "The English system tries," she writes, "to divide the family resources so as to provide roughly *equal standards of living* for husbands and wives after divorce. Justice in this system means that a mother with young children will typically remain in the family home."[59]

Weitzman here is attempting to show how the *special needs* consideration regarding the family home flow from her belief that a fair economic settlement after divorce should pursue equal standards of living between the parties. There are several major problems with this approach. The first concerns the accuracy of Weitzman's description of English family law. Rather than providing equal living standards, it seems much more accurate to say that the concern of English family law is with an adequate standard of living for all parties to the divorce.[60] (The appeal in English law is to what I characterized earlier as an absolute idea of living standards rather than an inter-personal comparative one.) The second major problem is that it is doubtful, from the perspective of equalizing living standards, that leaving the home in the possession of one of the

[57] Mavis Maclean and Lenore J. Weitzman, 'The Way Ahead: A Policy Agenda' in *Economic Consequences of Divorce*, p. 421.
[58] Weitzman, *The Divorce Revolution*, pp. 86–96.
[59] Weitzman, *The Divorce Revolution*, pp. 95–96.
[60] See, e.g., John Eekelaar and Mavis Maclean, *Maintenance after Divorce* (Oxford: Oxford University Press, 1986).

parties is ever fair. The reason is that the party who vacates the family home will very likely move (at least initially) into a smaller, less expensive home – for example, a small apartment. For that party, it would seem that this would constitute a significant decline in living standards; but for the party who remains in the family home, there is no parallel decline. Doesn't this suggest a significant inequality in living standards between households? Frankly, I think that this is not obvious, *only* when standard of living is equated with income. But, as I noted earlier, there are compelling reasons to rejection any such equivocation.

The equal opportunities approach to divorce settlements can better explain why the special needs of the spouse with custody of young children warrant the court's awarding either ownership to that spouse or exclusive use of the house to that spouse for a specified period of time. (Keep in mind that since the house is typically mortgaged, the custodial spouse generally assumes responsibility for the mortgage.) In effect, this case involves a situation where the background conditions affect the opportunities for the two divorcing parties to acquire a new home in the period after divorce. At issue here are both the direct and indirect costs of being the custodial parent. The direct costs include, most obviously, the need for more living space because of the number of persons in the household. The indirect costs of being a custodial parent are less often acknowledged. One such cost is well illustrated if one focusses on the requirements to secure a bank-approved mortgage to buy a new home. Most banks base their mortgage approval on earned income. The problem for many custodial parents, as we discussed in Chapter 8, is that they forgo earned income in order to fulfill their second-shift obligations. For divorced parties, payments such as child support and maintenance are intended to *partially* offset this loss of earned income as well as the direct costs of being the custodial parent. Banks generally don't want to include payments of this sort in their calculations for mortgage approval, presumably because they are well aware of the high rates of non-payment. The relevant point is this. By assuming custody for young children, one of the parties to the divorce sacrifices or diminishes his or her opportunity after divorce to buy a new home. The non-custodial parent makes no such sacrifice. (The one complication is the effect of child support payments on his or her earned income.) From an equal opportunities perspective, awarding the family home (even if heavily mortgaged) to the custodial parent as a component of the post-divorce economic settlement can be viewed as a form of regulative device to help equalize opportunities between the divorcing parties.

Aside from possession of the family home, the other major issue concerning the division of marital property is the treatment of so-called career assets. The career assets of individuals are "their earning capacities and the benefits and entitlements of their employment (such as their pensions, medical insurance, and social security)"[61] An important theme in studies of the economic consequences of no-fault divorce such as Weitzman's is that although in terms of traditional forms of wealth such as cash, divorcing couples appear to have little to divide, this is misleading because it neglects career assets. And it is in career assets – the earning capacities of the couple – that most marriages invest heavily. The upshot is that in the division of marital property, careful attention should be paid to career assets.

This prescription has gained considerable currency among both influential political philosophers[62] and advocates of divorce law reform. With regard to certain career assets, it is now the legal norm to include among marital property, for example, pensions acquired during a marriage.[63] Much more difficult is whether degrees and professional licences acquired during the marriage are marital property. Should, for instance, the law degree earned by one of the spouses during the marriage be included among the marital property? In practice, there are three distinct positions that can be taken on this issue. At one extreme is a complete rejection of any consideration of a degree among a divorcing couple's marital property. At the other extreme is the simple inclusion of all degrees acquired during the marriage among the marital property. An intermediate position recognizes the contribution of the other spouse to the earning of the degree and seeks some sort of remedial solution in the division of marital property.

What position does the equal living standards approach take? Weitzman certainly favours simply including degrees among the marital property.[64] This would mean, in effect, sharing the future earnings of one of the spouses between the two parties. And (it could be argued) by doing so, the standards of living of the two post-divorce households could be equalized. There are two major problems with this. The first is that by making an award based in part on the future earnings of the

---

[61] Lenore J. Weitzman, 'Marital Property: Its Transformation and Divsion in the United States' in *Economic Consequences of Divorce*, p. 85.
[62] John Rawls, *Justice as Fairness: A Restatement* (Cambridge MA: Harvard University Press, 2001), p. 167.
[63] Weitzman, 'Marital Property,' p. 112.
[64] *Ibid.*, p. 138.

spouse with the degree, there ceases to be a distinction between the division of marital property and maintenance or child support payments.[65] The second problem is that there is a clear sense in which making an award based on the future earnings of the spouse with the degree is a form of 'slavery' to the extent that that spouse is forced, in effect, to labour in the given occupation – for example, law – and therefore forgo the opportunity to quit or choose another less well paying job.[66] Suppose, for instance, that a spouse with a medical degree is projected to have an income of $500,000 over the next five years and that his or her ex-spouse is awarded a significant portion of that income because the degree was earned during the marriage. In that case, it would seem that he or she would not have the freedom to choose to do something else that would not generate such an income, be it working for a humanitarian group such as Doctors Without Borders, or outside medicine altogether as, say, a sidewalk artist.

The reaction of the legislatures in terms of statutory reforms and the courts has been overwhelmingly to adopt the intermediary position.[67] This position recognizes the significance in terms of enhanced career assets of a degree earned during a marriage, but does not entail any entitlement to the future earnings of the spouse who earned the degree. The main response has been to hold the spouse who earned the degree responsible for debts such as student loans incurred to earn the degree, even though those debts ordinarily constitute marital property. From the perspective of the three-dimensional model of equal opportunities as a regulative ideal, what is at stake in the post-divorce economic settlement is the lost opportunities of the spouse who did not earn the degree. It follows logically that the objective in a post-divorce economic settlement in which one of the parties earned a degree during the marriage is to provide a similar opportunity for the other party. This means, as when the one spouse earned the degree during the marriage, sharing the financial costs of exercising that opportunity – for example, tuition fees, books, living expenses. In practice, this may involve one party's making a lump sum payment to the other party as part of the divorce settlement. But this award is not a claim against the future earnings of that party – this distinguishes it from maintenance and child support

---

[65] See, e.g., *Roberts v. Roberts*, 670 N.E. 2c 72 (Ind. App. 1996) at 75.
[66] The parallel here is with Ronald Dworkin's criticism of an auction of talents and skills amounting to "slavery of the talented" in 'What Is Equality? Part 2: Equality of Resources,' *Philosophy & Public Affairs*, Vol. 10 (1981), p. 312.
[67] See Weitzman, 'Marital Property,' p. 132.

payments – but rather an award designed to equalize the opportunities between the parties after divorce.

9.3 CONCLUSION

This final chapter, like the previous ones, has been designed to show the strengths and insights of the three-dimensional model of equal opportunities as a regulative ideal. I have argued that the fairest economic settlement upon the dissolution of a marriage is one that promotes equal opportunities for the parties after divorce. This approach seeks not equal results in standards of living between post-divorce households but rather fairness along the three dimensions emphasized by the equal opportunities model – procedural fairness, stakes fairness, and background fairness. Many of the concerns that have motivated feminist critiques of existing divorce law are in fact issues of background fairness and can therefore be readily incorporated into the equal opportunities approach to divorce. The broader point is to illustrate the dynamic potential of this model of equality of opportunity, showing, on the one hand, how it can be nuanced enough to address the specific issues in a law reform issue such as divorce and, on the other hand, how it is possible for an egalitarian to have a consistent view on a range of social policy issues organized around race, class, and gender that arise in the diverse institutions of civil society affirmative action and standardized tests, welfare reform and universal health care, pay and employment equity, and divorce law.

Bibliography (including cases cited)

Altman, Andrew. 'Race and Democracy: The Controversy Over Racial Vote Dilution,' *Philosophy & Public Affairs, Vol. 27* (Summer 1998).

Ambert, Anne-Marie. *Divorce: Facts, Figures and Consequences.* Ottawa: Vanier Institute of the Family, 2000.

Anderson, Elizabeth. *Value in Ethics and Economics.* Cambridge, MA: Harvard University Press, 1993.

Andrews, Caroline. 'The Fine Line – Strategies for Change' in Francois-Pierre Gingras, editor, *Gender and Politics in Contemporary Canada.* Toronto: Oxford University Press, 1995.

Arendell Terry. 'Women and the Economics of Divorce in the Contemporary United States,' *Signs, Vol. 13* (1987).

Armstrong, Pat and Hugh, with Claudia Fegan. *Universal Health Care: What the United States Can Learn From the Canadian Experience.* New York: The New Press, 1998.

Arneson, Richard. 'A Defense of Equal Opportunity for Welfare,' *Philosophical Studies, Vol. 62* (1991), 187–95.

Arneson, Richard. 'Equality and Equal Opportunity for Welfare,' *Philosophical Studies, Vol. 56* (1989), 77–93.

Arneson, Richard. 'Liberalism, Distributive Subjectivism, and Equal Opportunity of Welfare,' *Philosophy & Public Affairs, Vol. 19* (1990), 158–94.

Arneson, Richard. 'Primary Goods Reconsidered,' *Nous, Vol. 24* (1990).

Arneson, Richard. 'Is Work Special? Justice and the Distribution of Employment,' *American Political Science Review, Vol. 84* (1990), 1127–1147.

Arrow, Kenneth. 'Uncertainty and the Welfare Economics of Medical Care,' *American Economic Review 53* (1963), 941–73.

Association of Mexican-American Educators ("AMAE") v. The State of California, 937 F.Supp. 1397 (9th Circuit, 1996).

Ayers v. Fordice 111 f.3d 1183 (5th Cir. 1997).

Ayers II, 879 F.Supp. 1434 (1995).

Backhouse, Constance. *Petticoats & Prejudice: Women and Law in Nineteenth Century Canada.* Toronto: Osgoode Society, 1991.

Bane, Mary Jo. *Here To Stay: American Families in the Twentieth Century*. New York: Basic Books, 1976.

Banks, Dwayne, Kimberly Kunz, & Tracy Macdonald. *Health Care Reform*. Berkeley, CA: Institute of Governmental Studies Press, University of California, Berkeley, 1994.

Barr, Nicholas. *The Economics of the Welfare State, New Edition*. London: Weidenfeld & Nicolson, 1993.

Barry, Brian. *Political Argument, reissue*. Brighton, UK: Harvester/Wheatsheaf, 1990.

Barry, Brian. 'Equal Opportunity and Moral Arbitrariness' in Norman Bowie, editor, *Equal Opportunity*. Boulder: Westview Press, 1988.

Bell, Derrick. *Faces at the Bottom of the Well: The Permanence of Racism*. New York: Basic Books, 1992.

Bell, Derrick. *And We Are Not Saved: The Elusive Quest for Racial Justice*. New York: Basic Books, 1987.

Bellah, Robert, et al. *Habits of the Heart: Individualism and Commitment in American Life*. New York: Harper and Row, 1985.

Bennett, Jonathan. 'Ethics and Markets,' *Philosophy & PublicAffairs, Vol. 14* (1985).

Berger, Peter. 'On the Obsolescence of the Concept of Honor' in Stanley Hauerwas & Alasdair MacIntyre, editors, *Revisions: Changing Perspectives in Moral Philosophy*. Notre Dame: University of Notre Dame Press, 1983.

Bickenbach, Jerome E. *Physical Disability and Social Policy*. Toronto: University of Toronto Press, 1993.

Blank, Rebecca M. *It Takes a Nation: A New Agenda for Fighting Poverty*, paperback edition. Princeton: Princeton University Press/Russell Sage Foundation, 1998.

Bowen, William, and Derek Bok. *The Shape of the River: Long-Term Consequences of Considering Race in College and University Admissions*. Princeton: Princeton University Press, 1998.

Bower, Lisa. '"Unsettling Women": Competing Subjectivities in No-Fault Divorce and Divorce Mediation' in Leslie Friedman Goldstein, editor, *Feminist Jurisprudence: The Difference Debate*. NJ: Rowman & Littlefield, 1992.

Boxill, Bernard R. 'Washington, Du Bois and Plessy V. Ferguson,' *Law and Philosophy, Vol. 16* (1997), 299–330.

Brest, Paul, and Miranda Oshige, 'Affirmative Action for Whom?,' *Stanford Law Review, Vol. 47* (1995).

Brest, Paul. 'Forward: In Defense of the Antidiscrmination Principle,' reprinted in Christopher McCrudden, editor, *Anti-Discrimination Law*. New York: New York University Press, 1991.

Bridges, William, and Robert Nelson, *Legalizing Gender Inequality: Courts, Markets, and Unequal Pay for Women in America*. New York: Cambridge University Press, 1999.

Brooks v. Canada Safeway Limited (1989) 1 S.C.R. 143.

Brown v. Board of Education of Topeka 347 U.S. 490 (1954).

Brown, Henry Phelps. *Egalitarianism and the Generation of Inequality*. Oxford: Oxford University Press, 1988.

Buchanan, Allen. 'The Right to a Decent Minimum of Health Care,' *Philosophy & Public Affiars, Vol. 13* (1984), 55–78.

Buchanan, Allen. 'Privatization and Just Healthcare,' *Bioethics, Vol. 9, No. 3/4* (1995), 220–39.

Buchanan, Allen, Dan Brock, Norman Daniels, and Daniel Wikler. *From Chance to Choice: Genetics and Justice.* New York: Cambridge University Press, 2000.

Burman, Patrick. *Killing Time, Losing Ground: Experiences of Unemployment* Toronto: Thompson, 1988.

Burstein, *Paul. Discrimination, Jobs, and Politics: The Struggle for Equal Employment Opportunity in the United States Since the New Deal, new edition.* Chicago: University of Chicago Press, 1998.

California Federal Savings and Loan Association v. Guerra, 479 U.S. 272 (1987)

Campaign 2000. *Chilld Poverty in Canada: Report Card 1999* (Toronto, November 1999).

Canadian Bar Association. Task Force on Gender Equality in the Legal Profession, Justice Bertha Wilson, Chair. 'Touchstones for Change: Equality, Diversity and Accountability' (Ottawa, 1993), reprinted in Donald Buckingham, Jerome Bickenbach, Richard Bronaugh, & Bertha Wilson, editors, *Legal Ethics in Canada.* Toronto: Harcourt Brace, 1996.

Carbone, June. 'Income Sharing: Redefining the Family in Terms of Community,' *Houston Law Review, Vol. 31* (1994).

Carbone, June and Margaret Brinig, 'Rethinking Marriage: Feminist Ideology, Economic Change, and Divorce Reform,' *Tulane Law Review, Vol. 65* (1991), 953–1010.

Carens, Joseph. 'Compensatory Justice and Social Institutions,' *Economics and Philosophy, Vol. 1, no. 1* (April 1985), 39–67.

Carens, Joseph. *Equality, Moral Incentives, and the Market.* Chicago: University of Chicago Press, 1981.

'Change Support Formula, CBA urges,' *The Globe and Mail* (Toronto), October 25, 1996.

Charles Murray, *Losing Ground: American Social Policy 1950–1980.* New York: Basic Books, 1984.

Christiano, Thomas. 'Difficulties with the Principle of Equal Opportunity for Welfare,' *Philosophical Studies, Vol. 62.*

Cohen, G.A. 'On the Currency of Egalitarian Justice,' *Ethics, Vol. 99* (1989), 906–44.

Cohen, G.A. 'Where the Action Is: The Site of Distributive Justice,' *Philosophy & Public Affairs, Vol. 26* (Winter 1997), 3–30.

Cohen, G.A. *History, Labour, and Freedom* (Oxford: Oxford University Press, 1988).

Constitution of the State of California. Article 1, § 31.

Cook, Fay Lomax, and Edith J. Barrett, *Support for the American Welfare State.* New York: Columbia University Press, 1992.

Copp, David. 'The Right to an Adequate Standard of Living' in Ellen Fankel Paul, Fred Miller, and Jeffrey Paul, editors, *Economic Rights.* New York: Cambridge University Press, 1992.

Cornell, Drucilla. *At the Heart of Freedom.* Princeton: Princeton University Press, 1998.

Cornell, Drucilla. *The Imaginary Domain.* New York: Routledge, 1995.

Cover, Robert. 'The Origins of Judicial Activism in the Protection of Minorities,' *Yale Law Journal, Vol. 91* (1982).

Daniels, Norman. 'IQ, Intelligence, and Educability,' *Philosophical Forum, Vol. 6* (1974–75).

Daniels, Norman. *Am I My Parents' Keeper* (New York: Oxford University Press, 1988).

Daniels, Norman. *Just Health Care*. New York: Cambridge University Press, 1985.

Daniels, Norman. *Justice and Justification*. New York: Cambridge University Press, 1996.

Day, J. P. 'Fairness and Fortune,' *Ratio, Vol. 19* (1977).

Delgado, Richard. 'Rodrigo's Tenth Chronicle: Merit and Affirmative Action,' *Georgetown Law Journal, Vol. 83* (1995), 1709–55.

Delgado, Richard. 'Why Universities Are Morally Obligated to Strive for Diversity: Restoring the Remedial Rationale for Affirmative Action,' *University of Colorado Law Review, Vol. 68* (1997), 1165–72.

Douglas, P. & Jon Nordheimer, 'Giant of Exam Business Keeps Quiet on Cheating,' *The New York Times* (Sunday, September 28, 1997).

Dreze, Jean, and Amartya Sen. *Hunger and Public Action*. Oxford: Oxford University Press, 1989.

Dupre, John. 'Global versus Local Perspectives on Sexual Difference' in Deborah Rhode, editor, *Theoretical Perspectives on Sexual Difference*. New Haven: Yale University Press, 1990.

Dworkin, Ronald. *Taking Rights Seriously, New Impression* (Cambridge, MA: Harvard University Press, 1978).

Dworkin, Ronald. 'What Is Equality? Part 3: The Place of Liberty,' *Iowa Law Review, Vol. 72* (1987), 1–54.

Dworkin, Ronald. 'Will Clinton's Plan Be Fair?,' *New York Review of Books*, 13 January 1994, 20–25.

Dworkin, Ronald. *Law's Empire*. Cambridge, MA: Harvard University Press, 1986.

Dworkin, Ronald. 'Justice in the Distribution of Health Care,' *McGill Law Journal 38* (1993), 883–98.

Dworkin, Ronald. 'What Is Equality? Part 2: Equality of Resources,' *Philosophy & Public Affairs, Vol. 10* (1981), 283–345.

Dworkin, Ronald. 'What is Equality? Part 1: Equality of Welfare,' *Philosophy & Public Affairs, Vol. 10* (1981), 185–246.

Dworkin, Ronald. *A Matter of Principle*. Cambridge, MA: Harvard University Press, 1985.

Dworkin, Ronald. 'Foundations of Liberal Equality,' *The Tanner Lectures on Human Values, Vol. 11*. Cambridge, UK: Cambridge University Press, 1991.

Dworkin, Ronald. *Sovereign Virtue*. Cambridge, MA: Harvard University Press, 2000.

Edley, Christopher. *Not All Black and White: Affirmative Action and American Values*. New York: Hill & Wang, 1996.

Eekelaar, John and Mavis Maclean. *Maintenance After Divorce*. Oxford: Oxford University Press, 1986.

Bibliography

Elhauge, Einer. 'Allocating Health Care Morally,' *California Law Review, Vol. 82* (1994).

Ellman, Mark. 'The Theory of Alimony,' *California Law Review, Vol. 77* (1989).

Ellwood, David T. *Poor Support: Poverty in the American Family.* New York: Basic Books, 1988.

Elster, Jon. 'Is There (or Should There Be) a Right to Work?' in Amy Gutmann, editor, *Democracy and the Welfare State.* Princeton: Princeton University Press, 1988.

Elster, Jon. 'Sour Grapes – Utilitarianism and the Genesis of Wants' in Amartya Sen & Bernard Williams, editors, *Utilitarianism and Beyond.* Cambridge, UK: Cambridge University Press, 1982.

Elster, Jon. *Sour Grapes.* Cambridge, UK: Cambridge University Press, 1983.

Ely, John Hart. *Democracy and Distrust.* Cambridge, MA: Harvard University Press, 1980.

Epstein, Richard. 'Two Conceptions of Civil Rights' in Ellen Paul, Fred Miller, & Jeffrey Paul, editors, *Reassessing Civil Rights.* Cambridge, MA: Blackwell, 1991.

Ergi, Carolyn P. and W. T. Stanbury, 'How Pay Equity Came to Ontario,' *Canadian Public Adminstration, Vol. 32* (1989).

Erickson, R. & J. H. Goldthorpe, *The Constraint Flux.* Oxford: Oxford University Press, 1992.

Evans, Patricia M., Lesley A. Jacobs, Alain Noel, and Elisabeth B. Reynolds. *Workfare: Does It Work? Is It Fair?* Montreal: Renouf/Institute for Research on Public Policy, 1995.

Faludi, Susan. *Backlash: The Undeclared War Against American Women.* New York: Anchor Books, 1991.

Feinberg, Joel. 'Justice and Personal Desert,' reprinted in Louis P. Pojman and Owen McLeod, editors, *What Do We Deserve?* New York: Oxford University Press, 1999.

Final Report of the Commission on Systemic Racism in the Ontario Criminal Justice System, Margaret Gittens and David Cole, Co-Chairs. Toronto: Queen's Printer for Ontario, 1995.

Fineman, Martha. 'Implementing Equality: Ideology, Contradiction and Social Change,' *Wisconsin Law Review, no. 4* (1983), 790–886.

Fineman, Martha. 'Illusive Equality,' *American Bar Foundation Research Journal, Vol. 4* (1986), 781–90.

Fineman, Martha. *The Illusion of Equality.* Chicago: University of Chicago Press, 1991.

Fineman, Martha. *The Neutered Mother, the Sexual Family, and Other Twentieth Century Tragedies.* London: Routledge, 1995.

Fischer, Claude S., Michael Hout, Martin Jankowski, Samuel Lucas, Ann Swidler, and Kim Voss. *Inequality by Design: Cracking the Bell Curve Myth.* Princeton: Princeton University Press, 1996.

Fiscus, Ronald J. *The Constitutional Logic of Affirmative Action.* Durham: Duke University Press, 1992.

Fishkin, James S. *Justice, Equal Opportunity, and the Family.* New Haven: Yale University Press, 1983.

Fiss, Owen. 'Groups and the Equal Protection Clause,' reprinted in Christopher McCrudden, editor, *Anti-Discrimination Law*. New York: New York University Press, 1991.

Flanagan, Thomas. 'Equal Pay for Work of Equal Value: Some Theoretical Criticisms,' *Canadian Public Policy, Vol. 13* (1987).

Foster, Cecil. *A Place Called Heaven: The Meaning of Being Black in Canada*. Toronto: HarperCollins, 1996.

Fox Piven, Barbara and Frances. 'The Feminization of Poverty,' *Dissent* (Spring 1984), 162–70.

Fraser, Nancy. *Justice Interruptus: Critical Reflections on the Postsocialist Condition*. New York: Routledge, 1997.

Fudge, Judy, and McDermott, Patricia. 'Introduction: Putting Feminism to Work' in J. Fudge and P. McDermott, editors, *Just Wages: A Feminist Assessment of Pay Equity*. Toronto: University of Toronto Press, 1991.

Funder, C. 'Australia: A Proposal For Reform' in Mavis Maclean and Lenore Weitzman, *Economic Consequences of Divorce*. Oxford: Oxford University Press, 1992.

Gardner, Howard. 'Scholarly Brinkmanship,' reprinted in Russell Jacoby & Naomi Glauberman, editors, *The Bell Curve Debate*. New York: Times Books, 1995.

Gardner, Howard. 'Who Owns Intelligence?,' *Atlantic Monthly* (February 1999).

Garrison, Marsha. 'The Economics of Divorce' in Stephen Shugarman and Herma Hill Kay, editors, *Divorce Reform at the Crossroads*. New Haven: Yale University Press, 1990.

Gates, Henry Louis Jr. 'The Two Nations of Black America,' *The Brookings Review, Vol. 16* (Spring 1998).

Gibbard, Allan. 'Health Care and the Prospective Pareto Principle,' *Ethics 94* (1984), 261–82.

Glazer, Nathan. 'In Defense of Preference,' *New Republic* (6 April 1998).

Glazer, Nathan. *The Limits of Social Policy*. Cambridge, MA: Harvard University Press, 1989.

Goldthorpe, J. H., with C. Llewellyn & C. Payne. *Social Mobility and Class Structure in Modern Britain, second edition*. Oxford: Oxford University Press, 1988.

Goodin, Robert, et al. *Not Only the Poor: The Middle Classes and the Welfare State*. London: Allen and Unwin, 1987.

Gould, Stephen Jay. *The Mismeasure of Man, expanded and revised edition*. New York: Norton, 1996.

Government of Canada. *A Matter of Fairness: Report of the Special Committee on the Review of the Employment Equity Act*. Ottawa: House of Commons, 1992.

Grad, Rachel. 'Health Care Reform in Canada: Is There Room for Efficiency?,' *Health Law in Canada, Vol. 20, no. 2* (November 1999), 17–30.

Green, S.J.D. 'Competitive Equality of Opportunity: A Defense,' *Ethics, Vol. 100* (1989), 5–32.

Griggs v. Duke Power Co., 401 U.S. 424 (1971)

Grofman, Bernard, et al., *Minority Representation and the Quest for Voting Equality*. New York: Cambridge University Press, 1992.

Bibliography

Grutter v. Bollinger, 2002 FED App. 0170 (6th Circuit).

Guinier, Lani. *The Tyranny of the Majority: Fundamental Fairness in Representative Democracy*. New York: Free Press, 1994.

Gunderson, Morley, Leion Muszynski, and Jennifer Keck, *Women and Labour Market Poverty*. Ottawa: Canadian Advisory Council on the Status of Women, 1990.

Gutmann, Amy. 'For and Against Equal Access to Health Care,' reprinted in S. Gorovitz, R. Macklin, A. Jameton, J. O'Connor, and S. Sherwin, editors, *Moral Problems in Medicine, 2nd edition*. Englewood Cliffs, NJ: Prentice-Hall, 1983.

Gutmann, Amy. 'Introduction' to Robert M. Solow, *Work and Welfare*. Princeton: Princeton University Press, 1998.

Gutmann, Amy. 'Responding to Racial Injustice' in David Wilkins, editor, *Color Conscious: The Political Morality of Race*. Princeton: Princeton University Press, 1996.

Hacker, Andrew. *Two Nations: Black and White, Separate, Hostile, Unequal*. New York: Ballantine, 1992.

Handler, Joel. 'Welfare Reform in the United States,' *Osgoode Hall Law Journal, Vol. 35* (1997), 289–308.

Harriford, Diane, and Mary L. Shanley, 'Revisioning Family Law,' *Law & Society Review, Vol. 30, no. 2* (1996), 437–445.

Harris, John. 'Justice and Equal Opportunities in Health Care,' *Bioethics, Vol. 13, No. 5* (1999), 392–413.

Harris, John. 'What Is the Good of Health Care?,' *Bioethics, Vol. 10, No. 4* (1996), 269–91.

Herrnstein, Richard, and Charles Murray, *The Bell Curve: Intelligence and Class Structure in American Life, paperback edition*. New York: Free Press, 1996.

Himmelfarb, Gertrude. "Comment' in Robert M. Solow, *Work and Welfare*. Princeton: Princeton University Press, 1998.

Hochschild, Arlie, with Anne Machung, *The Second Shift*. New York: Viking Penguin, 1989.

Hoffman, Saul D., and Greg J. Duncan. 'What Are the Economic Consequences of Divorce?,' *Demography, Vol. 25* (1988), 641–45.

Hopwood v. Texas, 78 F.3d 932 (5th Circuit, 1996), cert. denied, 116 S.Ct. 2582 (1996).

Hutchinson, Allan C. *Waiting for Coraf: A Critique of Law and Rights*. Toronto: University of Toronto Press, 1995.

Jacob, Herbert. 'Faulting No-Fault,' *American Bar Foundation Association, Vol. 4* (1986), 773–80.

Jacob, Herbert. *Silent Revolution: The Transformation of Divorce Law in the United States*. Chicago: University of Chicago Press, 1988.

Jacob, Herbert. 'Another Look at No-Fault Divorce and the Post-Divorce Finances of Women,' *Law & Society Review, Vol. 23* (1989), 95–116.

Jacobs, Lesley A., Evans, Patricia M., Alain Noel, and Elisabeth B. Reynolds. *Workfare: Does It Work? Is It Fair?* Montreal: Renouf/Institute for Research on Public Policy, 1995.

Jacobs, Lesley. 'Equity and Opportunity' in Francois Gingras, editor, *Gender and Politics in Contemporary Canada*. Toronto: Oxford University Press, 1995.

Jacobs, Lesley. Canadian Health Care: Values, Rights, Law. Vancouver: University of British Columbia Press, UBC Law & Society Series, forthcoming.

Jacobs, Lesley. 'Review of LaSelva's The Moral Foundations of Canadian Federalism: Federalism and National Minorities,' *University of Toronto Law Journal, Vol. 49* (1999), 295–304.

Jacobs, Lesley. 'Universal Access to Health Care: For Whom? To What?,' *Literary Review of Canada* (November 1999), 24–26.

Jacobs, Lesley. *Rights and Deprivation*. Oxford: Oxford University Press, 1993.

Jacobs, Lesley. 'Can an Egalitarian Justify Universal Access to Health Care?,' *Social Theory and Practice, Vol. 22* (1996), 315–48.

Jacobs, Lesley. 'Equal Opportunity and Gender Disadvantage,' *The Canadian Journal of Law and Jurisprudence, Vol. 7* (1994), 61–72.

Jacobs, Lesley. 'Integration, Diversity, and Affirmative Action,' *Law & Society Review, Vol. 32, No. 3* (1998), 725–46.

Jacobs, Lesley. 'Realizing Equal Life Prospects: The Case for a Perfectionist Theory of Equal Shares' in Glenn Drover & Patrick Kerans, editors, *New Approaches to Welfare Theory*. Aldershot: Edward Elgar, 1993.

Jacobs, Lesley. 'Replacing Welfare with Workfare,' *The Globe and Mail* (Toronto), April 29, 1994.

Jacobs, Lesley. 'The Second Wave of Analytical Marxism,' *Philosophy of the Social Sciences, Vol. 26, no. 2* (June 1996), 279–92.

Jacobs, Lesley. Review of Van Parijs in *Economics and Philosophy, Vol. 11, no. 1* (April 1995), 197–203.

Jacobs, Lesley. *An Introduction to Modern Political Philosophy: The Democratic Vision of Politics*. Upper Saddle River, NJ: Prentice-Hall, 1997.

Jacobs, Lesley. 'Equal Opportunity, Natural Inequalities, and Racial Disadvantage: The Bell Curve and Its Critics,' *Philosophy of the Social Sciences, Vol. 29, no. 1* (March 1999), 120–144.

Jencks, Christopher, and Meredith Phillips, 'The Black-White Test Score Gap,' *Brookings Review, vol. 16* (Spring 1998).

Jencks, Christopher. *Rethinking Social Policy*. New York: Harper Collins, 1992.

Johnson, Alex M. 'Bid Whist, Tonk, and United States v. Fordice: Why Integrationism Fails African-Americans Again,' *California Law Review, Vol. 81* (December 1993), 1401–74.

Johnson, Lyndon. Commencement address at Howard University, June 5, 1965. Excerpted in Neal Pierce, James Phillips, & Victoria Velsey, editors, *Revolution in Civil Rights*. Washington: Congressional Quarterly Service, 1965.

Kamm, Frances. *Morality, Mortality, Volume II: Rights, Duties, and Status*. Oxford: Oxford University Press, 1996.

Kaus, Mickey. *The End of Equality*. New York: Basic Books, 1992.

Kay, Herma Hill. 'Equality and Difference: A Perspective on No-Fault Divorce and Its Aftermath,' *University of Cincinnati Law Review, Vol. 56* (1987), 55–77.

Kennedy, Duncan. 'A Cultural Pluralist Case for Affirmative Action in Legal Academia,' *Duke Law Journal* (1990).

Bibliography

Kennedy, Duncan. *A Critique of Adjudication*. Cambridge, MA: Harvard University Press, 1998.

Kennedy, Randall. 'My Race Problem–and Ours,' *Atlantic Monthly* (May 1997).

Kesselman, Jonathan. 'Work Relief Programs in the Great Depression' in J. Palmer, editor, *Creating Jobs*. Washington: The Brookings Institution, 1978.

King, Desmond. *Separate and Unequal: Black Americans and the U.S. Federal Government*. Oxford: Oxford University Press, 1995.

King, Martin Luther. *Why We Can't Wait*. New York: Harper & Row, 1964.

Knopf, Rainer, with Thomas Flanagan, *Human Rights and Social Technology: The New War on Discrimination*. Ottawa: Carlton University Press, 1990.

Komaronmy, N. et al. 'The Role of Black and Hispanic Physicians in Providing Health Care for Underserviced Populations,' *The New England Journal of Medicine, Vol. 332, no. 20* (May 16, 1996).

Krauskopf, Joan. 'Theories of Property Division/Spousal Support: Searching for Solutions to the Mystery,' *Family Law Quarterly, Vol. 23* (1989).

Kymlicka, Will. 'Rethinking the Family,' *Philosophy & Public Affairs, Vol. 20* (1991), 77–97.

Kymlicka, Will. *Contemporary Political Philosophy*. Oxford: Oxford University Press, 1990.

Latinos Unidos De Chelsea En Acion v. Secretary of Housing and Urban Development, 799 F.2d 774 at 786 (1st Circuit, 1986).

Lamont, Julian. 'The Concept of Desert in Distributive Justice,' reprinted in Louis P. Pojman and Owen McLeod, editors, *What Do We Deserve?* New York: Oxford University Press, 1999.

Le Grand, Julian. 'Equity versus Efficiency: The Elusive Trade-off,' *Ethics 100* (1990), 554–68.

Lemann, Nicholas. 'The Great Sorting,' *Atlantic Monthly* (August 1995), 84–100.

Levine, Andrew. 'Fairness to Idleness: Is There a Right Not to Work?,' *Economics and Philosophy, Vol. 11* (1995).

L'Heureux-Dube, Claire. 'Economic Consequences of Divorce: A View from Canada,' *Houston Law Review, Vol. 31* (1994).

Lloyd-Thomas, David. 'Competitive Equality of Opportunity,' *Mind, Vol. 86* (1977), 288–304.

Loury, Glenn C. 'Is Affirmative Action on the Way Out? Should It Be?,' *Commentary* (March 1998), 38.

Loury, Glenn C. 'The Conservative Line on Race,' *Atlantic Monthly* (November 1997), 144–54.

Loving v. Virginia, 388 U.S. 1 (1967)

Lucas, John. *Responsibility*. Oxford: Oxford University Press, 1993.

Lukes, Steven. *Power: A Radical View*. London: Macmillan, 1974.

Lynch, Michael W. 'Affirmative Action at the University of California,' *Notre Dame Journal of Law, Ethics and Public Policy, Vol. XI* (1997).

MacIntyre, Alasdair. *After Virtue*. Notre Dame: University of Notre Dame Press, 1981.

Mackie, John. *Ethics: Inventing Right and Wrong*. Harmondsworth: Penguin Books, 1977.

MacKinnon, Catharine A. *Sexual Harassment of Working Women*. New Haven: Yale University Press, 1979.

MacKinnon, Catharine. *Feminism Unmodified*. Cambridge, MA: Harvard University Press, 1987,

MacKinnon, Catherine A. *Toward a Feminist Theory of the State*. Cambridge, MA: Harvard University Press, 1989.

Maclean, Mavis, and Lenore Weitzman. 'Introduction to the Issues' in Mavis Maclean & Lenore Weitzman, editors. *Economic Consequences of Divorce*. Oxford: Oxford University Press, 1992.

Maclean, Mavis, and Lenore Weitzman. 'The Way Ahead: A Policy Agenda' in Mavis Maclean & Lenore Weitzman, editors, *Economic Consequences of Divorce*. Oxford: Oxford University Press, 1992.

Macpherson, C. B. *Democratic Theory: Essays in Retrieval*. Oxford: Oxford University Press, 1973.

Malamud, Deborah C. 'Affirmative Action, Diversity, and the Black Middle Class,' *University of Colorado Law Review, Vol. 68* (1997).

Malveaux, Julianne. 'Gender Difference and Beyond: An Economic Perspective on Diversity and Commonality among Women' in Deborah Rhode, editor, *Theoretical Perspectives on Sexual Difference*. New Haven: Yale University Press, 1990.

Mandel, Michael. *The Charter of Rights and the Legalization of Politics in Canada, second edition*. Toronto: Thompson, 1994.

Marmor, Theodore L., Jerry L. Mashaw, and Philip L. Harvey. *America's Misunderstood Welfare State: Persistent Myths, Enduring Realities*. New York: Basic Books, 1990.

Marshall, Gordon, Adam Swift, and Stephen Roberts. *Against the Odds? Social Class and Social Justice in Industrial Societies*. Oxford: Oxford University Press, 1997.

Marshall, T. H. 'Citizenship and Social Class' (1949), reprinted in Robert Goodin and Philip Pettit, editors, *Contemporary Political Philosophy: An Anthology*. Oxford: Basil Blackwell, 1997.

Massey, Douglas, and Nancy Denton. *American Apartheid: Segregation and the Making of the Underclass*. Cambridge, MA: Harvard University Press, 1993.

Massing, Michael. 'The End of Welfare?,' *The New York Review of Books* (October 7, 1999), 22–26.

McAll, Christopher. 'Le Cercle Vicieux De L'Aide Sociale,' *Policy Options, Vol. 16, no. 4* (May 1995), 29–32.

McCormick, James. *Citizens' Service, The Commission on Social Justice Issue Paper, Vol. 10*. London: Institute for Public Policy Research, May 1994.

McDermott, Patricia. 'Pay Equity in Canada: Assessing the Commitment to Reducing the Wage Gap' in Patricia McDermott and Judy Fudge, editors, *Just Wages*. Toronto: University of Toronto Press, 1991.

McLeod, Owen. 'Contemporary Interpretations of Desert' in Louis P. Pojman and Owen McLeod, editors, *What Do We Deserve?* New York: Oxford University Press, 1999.

McLindon, James. 'Separate but Equal: The Economic Disaster of Divorce for Women,' *Family Law Quarterly, Vol. 21* (1987).

Mead, Lawrence. 'The New Welfare Debate: Workfare Will Transform Passive Recipients' in Beverly Fanning, editor, *Workfare vs. Welfare*. Hudson, WI: Gem Publications, 1989.

Mead, Lawrence. *The New Politics of Poverty*. New York: Basic Books, 1992.

Mead, Lawrence. *Beyond Entitlement: The Social Obligations of Citizenship*. New York: The Free Press, 1986.

Mezey, Susan Gluck. *In Pursuit of Equality: Women, Public Policy, and the Federal Courts*. New York: St. Martin's Press, 1992.

Mill, John Stuart. 'The Subjection of Women' (1869), reprinted in Lesley Jacobs and Richard Vandewetering, editors, *John Stuart Mill's 'The Subjection of Women': His Contemporary and Modern Critics*. Delmar, NY: Caravan Books, 1999.

Mill, John Stuart. (1873) *Autobiography*. Indianapolis: Bobbs-Merrill, 1957.

Miller, David. 'Desert and Determinism' reprinted in Louis P. Pojman and Owen McLeod, editors, *What Do We Deserve?* New York: Oxford University Press, 1999.

Miller, David. 'Equality and Justice' in Andrew Mason, editor, *Ideals of Equality*. Oxford: Blackwells, 1998.

Miller, David. *Social Justice*. Oxford: Oxford University Press, 1976.

Minow, Martha, and Mary Lyndon Shanley, 'Relational Rights and Responsibilities: Revisioning the Family in Liberal Political Theory and Law,' *Hypatia*, Vol. 11 (1996).

Minow, Martha. *Making All the Difference*. Ithaca: Cornell University Press, 1990.

Minow, Martha. 'Justice Engendered,' *Harvard Law Review* (1987), reprinted in Robert E. Goodin & Philip Pettit, editors, *Contemporary Political Philosophy: An Anthology*. Oxford: Basil Blackwell, 1997.

Minow, Martha. 'Partial Justice: Law and Minorities' in Austin Sarat & Thomas R. Kerans, editors, *The Fate of Law*. Ann Arbor: University of Michigan Press, 1993.

Moon, J. Donald. 'The Moral Basis of the Democratic Welfare State' in Amy Gutmann, editor, *Democracy and the Welfare State*. Princeton: Princeton University Press, 1988.

Mossman, Mary Jane, and Morag MacLean, 'Family Law and Social Welfare: Toward a New Equality,' *Canadian Journal of Family Law, Vol. 5* (1986), 81–89.

Murray, Charles. *Losing Ground*. New York: Basic Books, 1984.

Musgrave, R.A., and P.B. Musgrave. *Public Finance in Theory and Practice, 3rd edition*. New York: McGraw-Hill, 1980.

Nagel, Thomas. 'Justice and Nature,' *Oxford Journal of Legal Studies, Vol. 17* (1997), 303–21.

Nagel, Thomas. 'Personal Rights and Public Space,' *Philosophy & Public Affairs, vol. 24* (Spring 1995), 83–107.

Nagel, Thomas. 'Rawls on Justice' in Norman Daniels, editor, *Reading Rawls, new edition*. Stanford: Stanford University Press, 1989.

Nagel, Thomas. *Equality and Partiality*. New York: Oxford University Press, 1991.

Newman, Katherine S. *No Shame in My Game: The Working Poor in the Inner City*. New York: Russell Sage Foundation/Knopf, 1999.

Nozick, Robert. *Anarchy, State, and Utopia*. New York: Basic Books, 1974.

Nussbaum, Martha. *Women and Human Development: The Capabilities Approach.* Cambridge, UK: Cambridge University Press, 2000.

Nussbaum, Martha. *Sex and Social Justice*. New York: Oxford University Press, 1999.

Okin, Susan. 'Economic Equality After Divorce,' *Dissent* (Summer 1991), 383–87.

Okin, Susan Moller. 'Political Liberalism, Justice, and Gender,' *Ethics, Vol. 105* (1995).

Okin, Susan Moller. *Justice, Gender, and the Family*. New York: Basic Books, 1989.

Oldham, J. Thomas. 'The Economic Consequences of Divorce in the United States' in A. Bainham, D. Pearl, and Ros Pickford, editors, *Frontiers of Family Law*. Chichester: John Wiley, 1995.

Omni, Michael. 'Racial Identity and the State,' *Law and Inequality, Vol. 15* (1997), 7–24.

Osberg, Lars. *Economic Inequality in the United States*. Armonk, NY: M.E. Sharpe, 1984.

Padilla, Genaro. Letter to the Editor, *The New York Times*, April 12, 1998.

Parfit, Derek. 'Equality and Priority' in Andrew Mason, editor, *Ideals of Equality*. Oxford: Blackwell, 1998.

Parijs, Philippe Van. *Real Freedom for All*. Oxford: Oxford University Press, 1995.

Patterson, Orlando. 'Affirmative Action: Opening up Workplace Networks to Afro-Americans,' *The Brookings Review, Vol. 16* (Spring 1998).

Patterson, Orlando. *The Ordeal of Integration*. Washington: Civitas/Counterpoint, 1997.

Paul, Ellen Frankel. *Equity and Gender: The Comparable Worth Debate*. New Brunswick, NJ: Transaction Publishers, 1989.

Perry, Michael. 'The Disproportionate Impact Theory of Racial Discrimination,' *University of Pennsylvania Law Review, Vol. 125* (1977).

Peterson, Janice. 'The Feminization of Poverty,' *Journal of Economic Issues, Vol. 21* (1987).

Plant, R., H. Lesser, and P. Taylor-Gooby. *Political Philosophy and Social Welfare*. London: Routledge & Kegan-Paul, 1980.

Pogge, Thomas. *Realizing Rawls*. Ithaca: Cornell University Press, 1989.

Pollock, Gene E., and Atlee L. Stroup. 'Economic Consequences of Marital Dissolution for Blacks,' *Journal of Divorce & Remarriage, Vol. 26* (1996), 49–67.

Postema, Gerald J. 'The Sins of Segregation,' *Law and Philosophy, Vol. 16* (1997), 221–44.

Pulkingham, Jane. 'Investigating the Financial Circumstances of Separated and Divorced Parents: Implications for Family Law Reform,' *Canadian Public Policy, Vol. 21* (1995).

Pulkingham, Jane. 'Private Troubles, Private Solutions: Poverty Among Divorced Women and the Politics of Support Enforcement and Child Custody Determination,' *Canadian Journal of Law & Society, Vol. 9* (1994)

Radin, Margaret Jane. 'Property and Personhood,' *Stanford Law Review, vol. 34* (1982).

Rae, Douglas, Douglas Yates, Jennifer Hochschild, Joseph Morone, and Carol Fessler. *Equalities.* Cambridge, MA: Harvard University Press, 1981.

Rakowski, Eric. *Equal Justice.* Oxford: Oxford University Press, 1991.

Randall Kennedy, *Race, Crime, and the Law.* New York: Pantheon Press, 1997.

Rawls, John. *Political Liberalism.* New York: Columbia University Press, 1993.

Rawls, John. *Political Liberalism, paperback edition.* New York: Columbia University Press, 1996.

Rawls, John. 'Social Unity and Primary Goods' in Amartya Sen & Bernard Williams, editors, *Utilitarianism and Beyond.* Cambridge: Cambridge University Press, 1982.

Rawls, John. *A Theory of Justice.* Cambridge, MA: Harvard University Press, 1971.

Rawls, John. *A Theory of Justice, revised edition.* Cambridge, MA: Harvard University Press, 1999.

Rawls, John. *Justice as Fairness: A Restatement.* Cambridge, MA: Harvard University Press, 2001.

Regents of the University of California v. Bakke, 438 U.S. 265 (1978)

Rhode, Deborah L., and Martha Minow, 'Reforming the Questions, Questioning the Reforms: Feminist Perspectives on Divorce Law' in Stephen Sugarman & Herma Hill Kay, editors, *Divorce Reform at the Crossroads.* New Haven: Yale University Press, 1990.

Rhode, Deborah. *Justice and Gender.* Cambridge, MA: Harvard University Press, 1989.

Robb, Roberta Edgecombe. 'Equal Pay for Work of Equal Value: Issues and Policies,' *Canadian Public Policy, Vol. VIII* (1987).

Roberts v. Roberts, 670 N.E. 2c 72 (Ind. App. 1996).

Roemer, John E. *Egalitarian Perspectives.* Cambridge, MA: Harvard University Press, 1996.

Roemer, John E. *Equality of Opportunity.* Cambridge, MA: Harvard University Press, 1998.

Roithmayr, Daria. 'Deconstructing the Distinction between Merit and Bias,' *California Law Review, Vol. 85* (1997).

Rosenfeld, Michel. *Affirmative Action and Justice.* New Haven: Yale University Press, 1991.

Rousseau, Jean Jacques. *The Essential Rousseau.* Translated by Lowell Bair. New York: Mentor Books, 1974.

Ryan, Alan. 'Apocalypse Now?,' reprinted in Russell Jacoby and Naomi Glauberman, editors, *The Bell Curve Debate.* New York: Times Books, 1995.

Sandel, Michael. 'Morality and the Liberal Ideal,' *New Republic, 190* (May 7, 1984), 15–17.

Sandel, Michael. 'The Procedural Republic and the Unencumbered Self,' *Political Theory, Vol. 12, no. 1* (February 1984), 81–96.

Sandel, Michael. *Liberalism and the Limits of Justice.* Cambridge, UK: Cambridge University Press, 1982.

Satz, Deborah. 'Markets in Women's Sexual Labor,' *Ethics, Vol. 106* (1995), 63–85.

Satz, Deborah. 'Status Inequalities and Models of Market Socialism' in Erik Olin Wright, editor, *Equal Shares*. New York: Verso, 1996.

Scanlon, Thomas M. 'The Moral Basis of Interpersonal Comparisons' in Jon Elster and John Roemer, editors, *Interpersonal Comparisons of Well-Being*. Cambridge, UK: Cambridge University Press, 1991.

Schaar, John H. 'Equality of Opportunity and Beyond' in J. Roland Pennock and J. W. Chapman, editors, *NOMOS IX: Equality*. New York: Atherton Press, 1967.

Schneewind, J. B. *The Invention of Autonomy*. New York: Cambridge University Press, 1998.

Scott, Ian, Minister Responsible for Women's Issues. *Green Paper on Pay Equity*. Toronto: Government of Ontario, November 1985.

Selmi, Michael. 'Testing for Equality: Merit, Efficiency, and the Affirmative Action Debate,' *UCLA Law Review, Vol. 42 (1995)*, 1251–1314.

Sen, A. and B. Williams, editors. *Utilitarianism and Beyond*. Cambridge, UK: Cambridge University Press, 1982.

Sen, Amartya. *Development as Freedom*. New York: Anchor Books, 1999.

Sen, Amartya. *Inequality Reexamined*. Cambridge, MA: Harvard University Press, 1992.

Sen, Amartya. *Choice, Welfare, and Measurement*. Oxford: Basil Blackwell, 1982.

Sengupta, Somini. 'Same Subjects, More Verbs in New P.S.A.T.,' *The New York Times* (October 19, 1997).

Sher, George. 'Diversity,' *Philosophy & Public Affairs, Vol. 28* (1999), 85–104.

Shugarman, Stephen. 'Dividing Interests on Divorce' in Stephen Shugarman and Herma Hill Kay, editors, *Divorce Reform at the Crossroads*. New Haven: Yale University Press, 1990.

Silvers, Anita. '"Defective" Agents: Equality, Difference, and the Tyranny of the Normal', *Journal of Social Philosophy, vol. 25* (1994).

Singer, Jana. 'Divorce Reform and Gender Justice,' *North Carolina Law Review, Vol. 67* (1989).

Skrentny, John David. *The Ironies of Affirmative Action*. Baltimore: John Hopkins University Press, 1996.

Smart, J.J.C. 'An Outline of a System of Utilitarian Ethics' in *Utilitarianism: For and Against*. Cambridge, UK: Cambridge University Press, 1973.

Somerville, Margaret A., editor. *Do We Care? Renewing Canada's Commitment to Health*. Montreal: McGill-Queen's University Press, 1999.

Spinner, Jeff. *The Boundaries of Citizenship*. Baltimore: John Hopkins University Press, 1994.

Staples, Brent. 'The Quota Bashers Come in from the Cold,' *New York Times*, 12 April 1998.

Starr, Paul. 'Medical Care and the Pursuit of Equality in America' *in Securing Access to Health Care, Volume Two*. Washington DC: President's Commission for the Study of Ethical Problems in Medicine and Biomedical and Behavioral Research, 1983.

Statistics Canada. *Stay-at-Home Dads*. Ottawa: Government of Canada, 1998.

Steele, Claude. 'A Threat in the Air: How Stereotypes Shape Intellectual Identity and Performance,' *American Psychologist, Vol. 52* (1997), 613–29.

Steele, Claude. 'Race and the Schooling of Black Americans,' *Atlantic Monthly* (April 1992).

Steiner, Hillel. 'Choice and Circumstance' in Andrew Mason, editor, *Ideals of Equality*. Oxford: Blackwell, 1998.

Stephen, James Fitzjames. *Liberty, Equality, Fraternity*. New York: Holt & Williams, 1873.

Strange, Caroline. 'The Fine Line – Strategies for Change' in Francois Gingras, editor, *Gender and Politics in Contemporary Canada*. Toronto: Oxford University Press, 1995.

Sturm, Susan, and Lani Guinier, 'The Future of Affirmative Action: Reclaiming the Innovative Ideal, *California Law Review*, Vol. 84 (1996), 953–97.

Sullivan, Kathleen. 'Sins of Discrimination,' *Harvard Law Review, vol. 100* (1986).

Tawney, R.H. *Equality, new edition*. London: George Allen & Unwin, 1964.

Taylor, Charles. *Philosophical Arguments*. Cambridge, MA: Harvard University Press, 1995.

Taylor, Charles. 'The Politics of Recognition' in Amy Gutmann, editor, *Multiculturalism and The Politics of Recognition*. Princeton: Princeton University Press, 1992.

Thernstrom, Abigail and Stephan. 'Black Progress,' *The Brookings Review*, Vol. 16 (Spring 1998).

Thernstrom, Abigail. *Whose Votes Count?* Cambridge, MA: Harvard University Press, 1987.

Thernstrom, Stephan and Abigail. *America in Black and White: One Nation, Indivisible*. New York: Simon & Schuster, 1997.

Thernstrom, Stephan. 'Farewell to Preferences?,' *The Public Interest* (Winter 1998).

Tremain, Shelley. 'Dworkin on Disablement and Resources,' *The Canadian Journal of Law and Jurisprudence, Vol. IX* (1997), 342–60.

Trubek, David. 'Where the Action Is: Critical Legal Studies and Empiricism,' *Stanford Law Review, Vol. 34* (1984).

Turner, Brett. *Equitable Distribution of Property, 2nd edition*. Colorado Springs: Shepard's/McGraw-Hill, 1994.

Turner, Bryan. *Status*. Minneapolis: Minnesota University Press, 1988.

Unger, Roberto Mangabeira. *The Critical Legal Studies Movement*. Cambridge, MA: Harvard University Press, 1983.

United States v. Carolene Products Co., 304 U.S. 144.

United States v. Fordice, 505 U.S. 717 (1990).

Vaseleck, Jim. 'Stop Working and Put Down Your Pencils: The Use and Misuse of Standardized Admission Tests,' *Journal of College and University Law, Vol. 20* (1994).

Veatch, Robert. 'Single Payers and Multiple Lists: Must Everyone Get the Same Coverage on a Universal Health Plan?,' *Kennedy Institute of Ethics Journal*, Vol. 17, no. 2 (1997).

Vriend v. Alberta (1998) 1 S.C.R. 493.

Waldron, Jeremy. *Liberal Rights*. New York: Cambridge University Press, 1993.

Walton, Anthony. 'Technology Versus African-Americans,' *Atlantic Monthly* (January 1999), 14–18.

Walzer, Walzer. *Spheres of Justice: A Defence of Pluralism and Equality.* New York: Basic Books, 1983.

Ward's Cove Packing Company v. Atonio, 490 U.S. 642 (1989).

Weiler, Paul. 'The Wages of Sex: The Uses and Limits of Comparable Worth,' *Harvard Law Review, Vol. 100* (1986).

Weiner, Nan, and Morley Gunderson, *Pay Equity: Issues, Options, and Experiences.* Toronto: Butterworths, 1990.

Weinreb, Lloyd L. 'What Are Civil Rights?' in Ellen Paul, Fred Miller, & Jeffrey Paul, editors, *Reassessing Civil Rights.* Cambridge, MA: Blackwell, 1991.

Weitzman, Lenore. *The Divorce Revolution.* New York: Free Press, 1985.

Weitzman, Lenore. 'Marital Property: Its Transformation and Division in the United States' in Mavis Maclean and Lenore Weitzman, editors, *Economic Consequences of Divorce.* Oxford: Oxford University Press, 1992.

Weitzman, Lenore. 'Bringing the Law Back In,' *American Bar Foundation Research Journal, Vol. 4* (1986).

Westen, Peter. 'The Concept of Equal Opportunity,' Ethics, Vol. 95 (1985).

Wightman, Linda. 'The Threat to Diversity in Legal Education: An Empirical Analysis of the Consequences of Abandoning Race as a Factor in Law School Admissions Decisions,' *New York University Law Review, Vol. 72* (1997), 1–53.

Wilgoren, Jodi. ' "Texas" ' Top 10% Law Appears to Preserve College Racial Mix,' *The New York Times* (November 24, 1999).

Wilkinson, Richard. *Unhealthy Societies: The Afflictions of Inequality.* London: Routledge, 1996.

Will, Jeffrey A. *The Deserving Poor.* New York: Garland Press, 1993.

Williams, Bernard. 'The Idea of Equality' (1962), reprinted in Robert E. Goodin & Philip Pettit, editors, *Contemporary Political Philosophy: An Anthology.* Oxford: Blackwells, 1997.

Williams, Melissa. *Voice, Trust, and Memory: Marginalized Groups and the Failings of Liberal Representation.* Princeton: Princeton University Press, 1998.

Williams, Patricia J. *Seeing a Color-Blind Future: The Paradox of Race.* New York: Farrar, Straus, & Giroux, 1997.

Wilson, James Q. 'A Long Way from the Back of the Bus,' *New York Times Book Review,* (6 November 1997).

Wilson, William Julius. *The Truly Disadvantaged.* Chicago: University of Chicago Press, 1987.

Wilson, William Julius. *When Work Disappears: The World of the New Urban Poor.* New York: Vintage Books, 1996.

Wolff, Jonathan. 'Fairness, Respect, and the Egalitarian Ethos,' *Philosophy & Public Affairs, Vol. 27* (1998), 97–122.

Young, Iris Marion. *Intersecting Voices.* Princeton: Princeton University Press, 1998.

Young, Iris Marion. *Justice and the Politics of Difference.* Princeton, Princeton University Press, 1990.

Index

ability vs. effort, 45
abstract egalitarian principle, 179, 188
acculturation vs. structural integration, 134–5
achievement: across types, 45–6; circumstances and, 45; and effort, 46
adaptation: to social expectations, 98–9; to standardized testing, 98–9; in standards of living, 239; women's double disadvantage, 215–16, 218
adultery, 231
affirmative action, 9, 25, 61; background fairness and, 208, 215, 216; backward-looking rationales, 121, 124; beneficiaries of, 124–5; in Canada, 207; and civil rights, 85n7; class-based, 139–40; color-conscious, 134, 138–41; and competitions for scarce goods, 116; and competitive procedures, 138; conservative support of, 119; definition of, 116; disparate impact on whites, 113–14; diversity rationale, 121–2, 122–4, 125, 141; and equal opportunity, 138, 208; face-to-face vs. representational interactions in, 140–1; forward-looking rationales, 121, 124; in higher education, 102–3, 113, 122, 123; human capital and, 138; "innocent persons" objection to, 112; integration rationale of, 121, 124–9; middle-class African Americans and, 119–20, 123; need for, 128, 137–8; neoconservative critics of, 128–9; opinion polls regarding, 119; plus-factor, 116–17, 138; quotas and,

116, 138; race-conscious, 117, 141, 207; and racial equality, 111; racial equality and, 103; referendums regarding, 117; retrenchment of, 87–8, 102; as social choice, 113; and status equality, 111–12, 114; targetting of particular groups, 134–5; in United States, 207; and welfare state programs, 128; for women, 135n48
African Americans: access to educational institutions, 94–5; access to human capital, 136, 137–8; competitive opportunities, 132; educational achievement and, 75; in federal government programs, 137; and government-regulated apprenticeship programs, 137; housing of, 127; industrialization and, 137; integration of, 132; lack of structural integration, 135; middle class, 125; middle class, and affirmative action, 119–20, 123; moral status, 95–6; poverty amongst, 75; segregation and status equality, 132; social networks and, 135–7, 142; social status, 95; standards of living, 127; status equality, 94–5, 97–101, 101, 109; and use of test scores as cut-off points, 109, 114
African American students: enrollment at Berkeley, 99–100; enrollment in California law schools, 123; impact of standardized testing on, 93, 94–5
Aid to Families with Dependent Children (AFDC), 63n47, 128, 148
alimony, 230, 231, 240. *See also* spousal maintenance payments

Index